Percy Hetherington Fitzgerald

Kings and Queens of an Hour

Records of Love, Romance, Oddity, and Adventure

Percy Hetherington Fitzgerald

Kings and Queens of an Hour
Records of Love, Romance, Oddity, and Adventure

ISBN/EAN: 9783744692953

Printed in Europe, USA, Canada, Australia, Japan

Cover: Foto ©Thomas Meinert / pixelio.de

More available books at **www.hansebooks.com**

KINGS AND QUEENS

OF AN HOUR:

RECORDS OF LOVE, ROMANCE, ODDITY, AND ADVENTURE.

By PERCY FITZGERALD, M.A., F.S.A.,

AUTHOR OF "THE LIFE OF GEORGE THE FOURTH," "THE LIFE OF GARRICK," "A NEW HISTORY OF THE ENGLISH STAGE," ETC. ETC.

IN TWO VOLUMES.
VOL. I.

"The world's mine oyster."

LONDON:
TINSLEY BROTHERS, 8, CATHERINE STREET, STRAND, W.C.
1883.

Dedicated to

MY OLD AND VALUED FRIEND

AND SCHOOLFELLOW,

THE HONOURABLE GEORGE PLUNKET.

PREFACE.

I CANNOT but think that the following collection of curious and romantic adventures will be found interesting. They are all English, or concerned with England; and, in that view, are distinct from the collection published by my friend Mr. Becker, the heroes of which are mostly foreigners.

A great deal of what is here gathered is new, or has never been set forth with so much detail and hitherto unknown particulars. The truly romantic history of Theodore of Corsica is of course familiar, so far as its meagre outline is concerned; but here it is for the first time related at length, with details drawn from hitherto unknown sources, contemporary Italian works, MSS., etc.; and I think it may be fairly claimed that as a stirring and picturesque piece of romance it is well worth recording. So with Lady Hamilton, whose rise and fall have often been recounted; but so many curious particulars have not been brought together before. Accounts of Paul Jones and Brummel are not very accessible; though, of course, the few leading incidents in their careers are well known. The biography of Brummel is indeed marked "rarissimus" in the catalogues. In the history of the "adventurers" selected—and the word is used in its more favourable sense—a certain piquancy will be found. It will be seen that this country—usually accounted to be somewhat prosaic in character—can show forth a body of adventure and romance that compares, for interest and excitement, with any that belongs to foreign countries.

I may be pardoned for adding that the collection of the incidents that follow has been the work of many years, and has been a labour of love.

CONTENTS.

	PAGE
THE STORY OF THEODORE OF CORSICA	1
LADY HAMILTON	177
THE BEAUTIFUL GUNNINGS	271
THE ROMANTIC STORY OF SIR PHILIP FRANCIS	307
THE EARLY LOVES OF GIBBON AND PITT	339
THE STORY OF L. E. L.	363

THE STORY OF THEODORE OF CORSICA.

KINGS AND QUEENS OF AN HOUR:

RECORDS OF LOVE AND ADVENTURE.

THE

STORY OF THEODORE OF CORSICA.

CIVILISATION, which is adding so abundantly to all the comforts, and abating so many of the troubles, of social life, perhaps indemnifies itself by levying a heavy contribution from those whom it thus benefits. They have to sacrifice the picturesque and the dramatic. It is an old complaint now, that railways and steamboats are fast abolishing all local colour, and putting the world into regulation uniform, suppressing the mantilla, the sombrero, the velvet jackets and parti-coloured stockings, and enforcing the Paris bonnet and the black English hat on every head, from Dan to Beersheba, from London to the Pole. This facility of "rapid communication" has indeed swept away the dramatic business and "spoiled the trade," as it is said, of a very conspicuous class of players—THE ADVENTURERS.

The last century would seem to have been their gala-time. We can conceive the inconvenience and suffering which such a profession must have inflicted on those whom it chose to select as its victims; how for *them* it could be anything but what was poetical or romantic. To us, sitting afar off, and secure from their operations, the whole falls into the shape of innumerable dramas, on which settle clouds of mystery, to this hour never broken. The playhouses in which these scenes were enacted were the wonderful little courts which were found all over Europe —those seats of electors, princes, bishops, margraves, landgraves, grand-dukes, "free-barons," who have long since been swept away. Europe was full of intriguers, of strange men and stranger women; the post-roads were covered with chaises carrying travellers certain to be rich, as such only could travel; with soldiers of fortune and civilians of fortune. There was great gambling going on; money, station, fortune, was to be won by the players who would play skilfully, or even *cheat* skilfully. It was the splendid era for men living on their wits; and the wretched little courts, already tottering with the coming Revolution, were beginning to rock and tremble; while the scheming, half-bankrupt electors and margraves were often glad to welcome wits, which they had not, and arts and villany, at which they felt no scruple, save that of failure. Was a man growing dangerous? It was contrived that he should disappear. Was a wife in the way? There was the dungeon and a speedy and suspicious death. There were strange duels, curious "missions" when the minister sent his "instrument"—the clever unscrupulous fellow—well supplied with money and influential letters. It was the day of "*bonnes fortunes*," when one of the arts of rising in the world was through the favour of a lady. If we take up Sir Nathaniel Wraxall's curious travels, peep into his odd *chiffonnier* baskets, which he has filled in this and that court, when talking in corners to old courtiers and chamberlains, what a glimpse it gives of scenes and mysteries! He rather indicates than reveals. From little books like the *Lettres Galantes*, we see what universal junketing and intriguing went on. Watering-places like "the Spaw" seem to have been the holiday-ground where the adventurers clustered; and indeed the pastoral "hells" of Baden and Homburg have a scenery and atmosphere that give but a faint notion of what were those old times of elegant rascalship. There was no police, either in the shape of a great public opinion, working by telegraph and railway, or even of the ordinary watchman pattern. The adventurer who had been detected could get away from Venice, and begin the world again at the Hague. There he needed no introduction if his name and story were known through other adventurers; and the mist of distance and time, the long, long stretch of post-roads softened away the villany and imparted mystery. The surprising thing was that with the profession so crowded, there were yet victims enough, and profit and spoil for all. The secret lay in the seduction of their bold style of game, and in the charm of dramatic colour, which attracted even those who suspected. Liveliness, adroitness, *habileté* in manner and speech, indomitable energy, and versatility—these made the adventurer's armoury; with these he opened whatever sort of oyster he had chosen; with these he made his way to the gambling-rooms in public places and private houses, which were irresistible attractions for persons of all classes, as indeed they would be now were they tolerated, and which were kept by real or *soi-disant* countesses in their own drawing-rooms. In this rich soil the adventurer grew up luxuriantly, and in a night, like a fungus; and hither the decent part of the community were often attracted. Even now, were the decayed countesses allowed to hold tables for "E. O." and Baccarat at their houses, and furnish them round with barons mock and real, and ladies whose character was doubtful or beyond doubt, adventurers would begin to swarm again. Readers of the old memoirs and letters of the last century will recall that a favourite and recurring character at every watering-place or little capital was a mysterious "Baron" or "Chevalier," who turned up at Tunbridge Wells, say, who was received by every one, suspected, and yet who was privileged to plunder. When the great English actor, Garrick, was on his travels, he wrote home a little sketch which hints yet more than it conveys; how his two friends, Lord Ossory and Mr. Beauclerk, had met at Venice the Marquis de Prie and Don P——, and had been stripped of ten thousand pounds in a night. We turn over "The Amusements of Spa," and find him there in sumptuous state, with carriages, horses, and hotel, where there is dancing and play, and junketing from night until morning. Nor must it be supposed that these men were of the vulgar "knight-of-industry" type that is seen on the stage or in the novel—a mere swindler of our own time, whose aim is a few sovereigns. These men played for power, influence, for fortunes, and sometimes for a crown: they lived sumptuously, were clothed magnificently, were seen at courts: and their reputation was bounded, not by the place in which they lived, but was spread over the world. The glittering romances of Dumas—his dashing musketeers, who meet with such bright and stirring adventures—are scarcely overcoloured. As was said before, the materials were to their hand, and the state of society opened opportunities that were irresistible. The irresponsibility of the powerful, the corrupt and effete control of the law over these electors, barons, ministers, margraves, allowed them to carry out their schemes by the most unscrupulous means: so that others who would encounter them had to fall back on agencies of the same sort.

This may have been the secret of the employment of the adventurer, and here was his opportunity. What dramas, therefore, do we not owe to him! what stories like that of the Diamond Necklace and of Cagliostro; of Bonneval, D'Eon, Ripperda, Schrepfer, St. Germain—with a hundred such adventurers and adventures! With the agreeable and garrulous Nathaniel at our elbow, we get odd phantasmagorian glimpses, which, if not true, were at least supposed to be true. We hear him whispering with Lady Hamilton at Naples, as that heroine tells him of the Sicilian lady of rank who had made away with nearly a dozen persons by dagger or bowl, and whom her own relations were obliged to denounce and have some check imposed upon, by having her imprisoned "in a convent of a severe order." Sir Nathaniel, who was not unlike Boswell, visited this lady, and was offered chocolate by her.

Rome, too, "the Hôtel de l'Europe," was a picturesque stage for the intriguer and adventurer. Most curious was the story, told on the same authority, of the Irish doctor, who was roused up at night, at his house in the Piazza di Spagna, and carried away blindfold to a distant house, where he was forced by two masked gentlemen to bleed a lady to death. He contrived to leave the marks of his bloody fingers on the wall as he was led away, and denounced the whole to the papal authorities. "A guard of the Sbirri was appointed to accompany Ogilvie, who began by visiting the villas scattered without the walls of that metropolis. In the Villa Papa Julio they found the bloody marks left on the wall, at the same time that he recognised the apartment in which he had put the lady to death." It belonged to the Bracciano family; and it was the brothers who had put their sister to death. How strange, too, the story of the public executioner, brought from Strasburg to execute a lady in private, who was believed to be the Princess of Tour and Taxis! "I have dined," adds the baronet coolly, "with the prince at his castle."

But the most surprising picture of a schemer's life—graphic, picturesque, minute to a degree, and in the main trustworthy—is to be found in the story of Casanova, as told by himself with such liveliness and *esprit*. There we see the true *vie intime*, successful cleverness honoured and employed—now sent to the "Tombs" or "Leads;" now sent on "missions" by the Abbé Dubois; now introducing us to that dreadful society of adventurers, counts and countesses, who swarmed over old Venice, old Genoa, old La Haye, and old Paris—the "rotten" society in velvet coats and bag-wigs, and wearing swords; to that pseudo Prince Piccolomini and his wife, the Chevalier This and That, with "Sir Walpole," representative of the stray Englishman, who seemed to be drawn into such company by a fascination, and was duly made a victim; who made up the society at the Prince of Orange's, where the Sieur Casanova descended, and who after a quarrel would rise from table and go out to the wood, and settle the affair with the sword. Everywhere a Bank of Pharaoh or a game of Bassette —the bank kept by a count and his *charmante épouse*—was the favourite mode of recruiting an exhausted purse. Rome, to which all roads then led, was thought to be the adventurer's El Dorado; it was so crowded with travellers and intriguers.

"I knew," says that free-knight, "that Rome was the unique city where a man starting with nothing could arrive at everything. Such a man ought to be a sort of chameleon, who can reflect all the colours round him; he should be supple, insinuating, impenetrable; often low, pretending to know less than he does know, *having but one tone of voice*, and patient." This nice stroke shows a delicacy of observation, and he besides owns that "complaisance" was the only gift for which he was distinguished, and that otherwise he was a mere untrained steed. But it would be impossible to give an idea of this grotesque panorama, the scene of which shifts from one town to another, the rich feasts and entertainments, gorgeous dresses, sumptuous carriages, which we see in the old prints of Piranesi, and others before him—his quarrels, missions, and adventures.

But with this light we shall understand more clearly the life of a yet more remarkable adventurer, whose story has all the colours and brilliancy of a romance—that of THEODORE OF NEUHOFF, who played for a throne, won, and even kept it for some time. In the hands of Alexander Dumas the elder, most dramatic of story-tellers, it would have taken the shape of an absorbing and even chivalrous romance. Hitherto it has been only sketched. A few allusions in Walpole, a few pages in the records of adventurers and charlatans, make up all that is popularly known about this attractive hero and his story.

To the writer of these chronicles it has ever had a sort of fascination, which he cannot doubt will be extended to the reader who follows the fortune of the daring adventurer to the close; for success of a really substantial nature attended him, which itself rarely attends the adventurers who, at most, snatch only a brief and spurious enjoyment of what they seek, their fall being generally disastrous. He was in fact a *real* king, with robes, armies, coinage; his pieces are still eagerly sought by collectors; he wore his crown, and the rest. It will be a task, therefore, of genuine interest to follow his exciting career, the more particularly as it has never yet been traced.

An adventurer's eyes might well have turned to that romantic little island of Corsica, which glitters afar off in the deep molten cobalt of the Mediterranean. Its soil sparkled with the rarest and most precious of marbles—porphyry, serpentine, and alabaster—and was lavish in the more profitable blessings of olive-groves, great chestnut-trees, corn and wine. The people were a high-spirited and romantic race; full of an indomitable spirit that has hardly been done justice to, and who had maintained for a whole series of years a well-organised revolt against a powerful but fast-decaying republic. Genoa was little over a day's sail away. It had its galleys and soldiers, its captains trained in European wars; it could boast its politics, arts, wealth, and prestige; while the Corsicans were poor, rude, agrarian, and, as regards social training and advantages, almost barbarous. Yet for many, many years they carried on this war, rather than insurrection, and with results which might be called almost victorious, if we allow for the inferiority of resources. Indeed, in considering this struggle, it is impossible not to think of England and the Irish during the old days of oppression and extermination; for even during the lulls of conflict, the policy of the

Republic, when it attempted peaceful government, seemed unconsciously to shape itself on the old British principles. Thus in Corsica, as in Ireland, a government party were encouraged, who were pitted against the natives, and whose loyalty was stimulated by favours from home; an imperial system was steadily maintained of "sending over" officials and magistrates of all degrees, who became odious to the people from their airs of superior caste, and who went away enriched by spoliations and exactions. A more curious parallel still was in the practice of appointing Genoese to all the vacant Corsican bishoprics, which was long the invariable part of the English system. The Corsican gentry and leading men, if they repaired to Genoa, were treated contemptuously, or snubbed; and returning, bitterly indignant at the humiliation, were driven into the ranks of the disaffected. Some such infatuation seems often to direct the behaviour of a powerful country in its relations with a subject race. In this way the struggle went on, and the Corsicans were fairly exhausted, and remained passive rather than submissive. The grinding tyranny of the Genoese, stupid as it was oppressive, tended to render their conquest valueless and unproductive. It seemed to aim at destroying the whole social life and prosperity of the island. They levelled villages and towns, and would not let the natives gather at the coasts. The latter were not allowed to sell their produce to any but the Genoese commissioners, who arbitrarily fixed a very low price. All artizans gradually disappeared, and in the whole island they could scarcely find a single cooper to make casks for their oil and wines. They were forbidden to fish or to use nets, and were ordered to discontinue working profitable mines that had been discovered. At one period an arbitrary act forbade the making of salt on the island; now an enormous contribution was levied to reimburse the government for some advances made during a famine; while the enclosure of a common was to have the invariable result, and inflamed the popular mind to the highest degree. Now some fresh act of oppression drove them into revolt. Now the Republic, at their wits' end for resources, took the desperate step of applying to the Emperor—there was then only one emperor *par excellence*—for German troops to do their work. Some battalions then about returning home from Lombardy were graciously diverted to Corsica; and a body of some four thousand men, under General Wachtendonck, appeared in the island. The Germans, during the greater part of the century, had thus furnished mercenaries to Europe; and the innumerable electors, margraves, and dukelets hired out small armies of their subjects, or rather sold them, to needy powers, at a handsome figure per man or regiment. This humiliating traffic scattered over Europe the bones of innumerable Bavarians, Würtembergers, and Hessians—countries in which soldiers were the staple export.

Yet these new auxiliaries did not do much for their employers. They were often beaten, and had to be reinforced by a fresh body under a well-known general, Prince Louis of Würtemberg. Their heart was not in the work, or they had the old prejudice against fighting on such rude guerilla principles. Wachtendonck was often seen in London drawing-rooms—a good-natured German, who had no ill-will to "the brave Corsicans," and presently received instructions from his Emperor to act rather as intermediatory than as enemy, and strive to bring about an accommodation. This was at last done with the usual solemnities of meetings, deputies, hostages. Yet, almost as the treaty was signed, the Republic, with strange treachery, seized on the Corsican commissioners, and carried them away to a dungeon in Genoa. This insane proceeding had nearly destroyed all, when presently news came of their release, through the agency of an unknown friend who had worked unceasingly, and used secret and mysterious power to get them set free.

At last the German mercenaries were happily got rid of and sailed away; but almost before their galleys were hull-down on the horizon the bitter foes were at each other's throats again. A struggle *à outrance* commenced. The Genoese, true to their policy, thought of a general who had long before made himself odious to the people by his cruelties and exactions, and sent him over in command. The Corsicans also chose new leaders, one Giafferi and the father of Pasquale Paoli—men of a noble and Spartan character. Then set in desperate conflicts, savage surprises, and massacres, wholesale burnings of the crops, and cruel wasting of the country. Both parties were growing exhausted, but the cruel spirit of the oppressor was unabated. Famine came to their aid, and began to thin the ranks of the unfortunate people. In vain they appealed to the Emperor too, who had solemnly guaranteed for them liberty, abolition of taxes, a share in their own government, and the conventional and constitutional privileges; but he was too embarrassed with troubles of his own to think of such engagements. Their spirit never abated. They melted down their church bells into cannon. The resources of the Genoese were also beginning to be exhausted. The bill for the profitless assistance of the Germans amounted to some two millions, besides sumptuous "gratifications" for the prince and other generals. No wonder a sarcastic Frenchman applied the fable of the hare which a gentleman wished to have turned out of his pretty garden, and who with that view got the assistance of a neighbour with a hunting-party and a large pack of hounds.

The popular and more familiar character of the

Corsicans seems to have been introduced to us from the drama and the novel; and the feature most known is that of savage quarrels and the familiar vendetta. Yet looking back to this era, this rather brutal feature is hardly apparent, and we cannot sufficiently admire their more sober and heroic virtue, their indomitable and measured perseverance, their ardent piety removed from fanaticism, their virtue, and the skill with which their politics were directed.

It is scarcely wonderful that such conduct should have excited the admiration of those looking on in Europe, and that many sympathisers should have wished to aid or encourage them, or, like Boswell, have braved the discomforts of a serious journey to visit them. They had just one little weakness common to them with other excitable nations—a love for conducting their insurrections with the finery of a rather theatrical display in the shape of dresses, titles, etc.; and it provokes a smile to find them—in the midst of burning crops and levelled houses, with their oppressors gaining ground on them—busy with theatrical punctilios, meeting to construct a constitution, and carefully settling the names of their ranks, and minutely balancing the titles by which they were to be addressed. Thus Giafferi and Paoli were to be called "primates of the kingdom," and to be addressed as "royal highness." Members of the General Diet were to be styled "most serene;" and descending grades were to be addressed as "excellence," "most illustrious," with the nicely-adjusted titles according to office. These delicate arrangements might have been postponed until more tranquil and convenient times. Playing with such toys at such a moment seems inconsistent with the nature of a brave and resolute people reduced to great straits. It was rather a foretaste of a romantic mystery which was presently to envelop the island; and may have been the prompting of a yet unseen deliverer, who was soon to reveal himself with more complete and gaudy apparatus, and wished the ground to be prepared. Already there was talk and whispers of a power from the mainland who had vast influence with Eastern and European potentates, but whose time had not yet arrived. It could indeed have been noticed that the released hostages—Giafferi, Ceccaldi, and the priest Astelli—had a confident air, with a consciousness as of a secret, and were whispering and looking for despatches from the mainland. And one day, when they were reduced very low indeed, two vessels stole into the harbour of Isola Rossa and quietly landed provisions and munitions of war; it did seem as though Heaven had at last interfered and sent them this miraculous aid; though later it was discovered that this was the handsome gift of two sympathising Englishmen.

Inspirited by these succours and new hopes, they

rushed to the fray once more, attacked the little town of Aleria, one of the strongholds of the Genoese Pale, carried it, and then pushed on to attack Bastia, where, however, they received a check. Then both sides rested, a little weary. The Genoese were panic-stricken, and now thought of applying for aid to the King of Spain : for the famous Republic had become beggars to all Europe. Then there was a pause.

We can almost call up a picture of that eastern corner of Corsica one morning in the middle of March —soft, bright, and glittering, like so many mornings upon an Italian sea. It was then one of the most favoured spots of Corsica, at the edge of a vast plain, and on the distant hills could be seen rich groves of oaks and olives and chestnuts. As the Barbary corsairs, who were the terror of those seas, swept by, they could see the solemn dun-coloured Genoese watch-towers rising solitary and mournful — stone sentinels which dotted the coast all round, like the English martello towers. There were also relics of the old Roman occupation—a fragment of an amphitheatre, tablets, pillars ; and a little lagoon at the foot of the town was a perfect natural harbour, and offered the safest anchorage. Now it is all overgrown with rank ferns, and the people have to fly to the mountains to escape the pestilential malaria : the lonely dun Genoese tower still stands, the only survivor of the Corsican and Roman buildings.

We can almost see on that March morning the picture of Giafferi's encampment: the Corsican soldier, with his umber-coloured face, and his scarlet Phrygian cap of liberty, the brown jerkin, the bottle slung behind, and a rude native gun, carried by every man even to this hour as though it were a walking-stick. Now he clatters past at full speed on a shaggy mountain pony, while the women cluster round, their heads covered with the picturesque mappa. Close by, the ruins of the bishop's palace were still smoking; for that Genoese prelate had excommunicated the insurgents; and though he himself had narrowly escaped, they wreaked their vengeance on his house. Such an event threw all into a flutter of expectation. As we have seen, there had long been some faint mysterious hope of foreign rescue and assistance; and the chief had often significantly hinted that one day there might arrive a deliverer with money, arms, ships, and all resources. The conditions of such aid seemed almost too romantic to be realised; but something of the kind was looked for. It was time; for the hearts of all were sinking.

Suddenly a sail was descried upon the horizon, and a large vessel was seen slowly making for the little lagoon. Behind, two smaller craft were following. The news drew all to the beach. The soldiers clustered on shore in excitement. Now indeed the romance was going to begin, and here was the first chapter. Eager eyes discovered that the vessel carried twenty guns. It glided on into the bay, dropped anchor, and then showed the red English colours. Next was hoisted a blue flag with a white stripe—a signal to the chiefs. The crowd must have been in a flutter at this apparition; but the chiefs all had a conscious air. *They* were in the secret. Presently boats were seen putting off from the ship. There was a glitter of colours, a flash of scarlet, and a very remarkable-looking person, attended by a large retinue, stepped on shore. The heads of the chiefs were bent low. From his dress and bearing, he was a person of distinction; the crowd wondered at the tall, stately, and commanding figure, so grave and dignified, dressed in a flowing scarlet robe trimmed with rich fur, with Moorish trousers, and yellow shoes. His face was full, with a small beard and moustache; on his head was a flowing periwig and a large three-cornered cocked-hat; by his side a long Spanish rapier, and in his hand a "crowbill" cane; in his sash of yellow silk were a pair of richly-inlaid pistols. This picturesque figure, said to be dressed "*à la Franque*," or in the garb Christians wore in Turkey, was indeed likely to impress the rude natives, who saw the chiefs receive him obsequiously, and with prodigious marks of respect. Here, then, was the mysterious deliverer so long expected! But they were to be yet more confounded; for now the sailors of the English ship—it was commanded by a Captain Dick—were beginning to unload. The retinue was seen coming ashore, a complete train—officers of state, secretaries, chaplains, a steward, a lord steward, a head cook, and four lackeys; and the gaping natives must have gaped still more when they saw three coal-black Moorish slaves in Eastern dress, who were the only element yet wanting to give a hint of despotic power. The stores followed: "ten brass cannon, of which six pieces were of large bore and twelve-pounders; 14,000 muskets; 3,000 pairs of shoes; provisions of all sorts; 14,000 sacks of grain; ammunition, hats, uniforms;" and, above all, heavy chests, carried with difficulty by the English tars, and which were said to contain treasure to the amount of 100,000 golden sequins. This, for a first scene in the drama, was artistically arranged.

The chiefs, with the same obsequiousness and reverence, led the august stranger away to Campo Loro, where the bishop's palace had lately stood. The wondering crowds heard them addressing him as Excellency and Viceroy. Then it was allowed to get abroad that *this* was the powerful man who had listened to those prayers for help, which had been refused by so many kings and potentates of Europe; that he had graciously accepted the overtures of Count Rivarola, their faithful and trusty representative at Leghorn, who arranged everything in concert with the chiefs. This relief was only an earnest of what he would do. The country would yet be saved!

The whole scene of that day was indeed more romantic than any romance. We can see and hear the excited islanders, jubilant yet wondering, the gorgeous dresses, the retinue, the scarlet, the Moors, with the English vessels lying off in the harbour; a standing reminder that the whole was no dream. In a few weeks, nay, in not many days, the news was all over Europe. The story was told in the *Gazette de Hollande,* the *Courier of Leyden,* and copied into the London papers. Everybody was wondering and speculating: was it Ripperda, or the renegade Bonneval from Tunis or Constantinople; or Law, Racocksky, or the Pretender, or some other of the professional adventurers? Who was it? Who could it be? The proportions were all magnified and exaggerated. The wildest stories went about; but at Genoa, it may be well conceived, all was consternation and fury. Who this daring play-actor was, we shall now try to discover.

All sorts of minute and official accounts of his birth and career were sent abroad. Some of them are contradictory; and though we cannot accept a very high-flown portion of a little history which his own son, Baron Frederick, gave of him, and which is clearly merely adventurer's gasconade, still there is no reason for rejecting the more moderate parts, especially where they are corroborated by the inquisitive Mr. Boswell, who visited the island some five-and-twenty years after the adventure. This lively traveller and pleasant observer made acquaintance with the very Rivarola who had negotiated with the stranger, and heard from him a full account of the business; and he had besides been "at particular pains" to acquire accurate information. When this faithful Johnsonian terrier once sniffed out the true biographical trail, he never lost it.

Mr. Tilson, of the Embassy at Hanover, a month later, wrote to Sir T. Robinson, the Secretary in London, enclosing "King Theodore's letter to his kinsman," and adds: "As you think everything that tends to discover the life and actions of the Knight-Errant is to be admitted, I also send you enclosed what I met in a Paris letter in our hands;" and which is dated June 8th, 1736.

This document, which is in the British Museum, gives a very bitter and sarcastic sketch of the adventurer, who was remembered in the French capital, and had been brought up there. From this and many other accounts, which have been compared, the following may be accepted as a tolerably accurate one:

"He was the son," says his son Colonel Frederick,

"of Anthony Baron de Neuhoff, descended from one of the most noble and illustrious houses in the county of La Marck. Anthony had displeased his relations in having married the daughter of a merchant of Viseu. This marriage drew upon him the contempt of all the nobility of the country, where they pique themselves (to use their own expression) on *purity of blood*, and where the nobles never contract alliances but with persons of their own rank. This 'under-match' occasioned Anthony to quit Germany, and go to France, where he was well received by the Duchess of Orleans."

It is certain he was a youth of "great parts," as it was called, of insinuating manners and vivacity. He is described as "a very favourable young man, had an air of grandeur in his behaviour, a very captivating manner of speaking, adroit in his exercises, knowing how to accommodate himself to all tempers. At Paris he had always kept good company, though the expense of it agreed so little with his condition. His vices were those of a man of quality; and though the consequences of them obliged him to do mean things sometimes, yet these were visibly against his nature; and whenever by any lucky accident," adds the chronicler sarcastically, "he got into the possession of money, he took the first opportunity to indemnify those who had suffered by him. He had a singular passion for politics, and an unusual dexterity in discoursing on them. He recommended himself by this means to several foreign ministers, who drew from him considerable services, and rewarded them in such a manner as, if he could have concealed their favours and set any bounds to his expenses, might have enabled him to live both easily and decently."

His mother's name was Amelia, said to be the daughter of a linen merchant, who died soon after her marriage, leaving her and the baron about 11,000 florins, which, with a company of foot and the government of a small fort in Alsace, was their whole provision.

A certain Dutch envoy, who had known Theodore during some of his adventures, told Monnet, the French writer, a very minute history of this Westphalian baron, who seems to have been a sort of soldier of fortune, and was killed at the assault on Namur, when in the Brandenburg service, though only the evening before he had obtained a colonel's commission in the Spanish service. His wife, on this same authority, was the daughter of a Spanish inspector of fortifications in Flanders. He left a son and a daughter; the former of whom was born at Cologne about the year 1686, and whose sponsor at baptism was a M. de Bilderdeck, the Dutch envoy. He was then put to school at Düsseldorf. His mother, marrying again, brought him to France, and placed him in the Academy at Longpré. A Coun

Mortagne, who was about the court of the old coarse Duchess of Orleans, took care of him, and procured for Theodore the situation of page to the regent, and for his sister that of lady-in-waiting to the refined and excellent princess herself. This was not unsuitable training for a future adventurer.

He was undoubtedly a youth of parts, and, as all adventurers should, had a natural gift for learning languages. Before he was fifteen he spoke German, French, and Italian very fluently.

Count Mortagne, according to Mr. Tilson's paper, fell in love with Madame de Neuhoff, and placed her son among the pages of Madame. Afterwards the Duc de Birrenfelds gave him a lieutenancy in an Alsace regiment then quartered at Strasburg. But Baron Theodore was disinclined to quit Paris, on which the Marquis de Courcelles, who had taken a fancy to him, gave him a commission in a cavalry regiment, the Fürstenberg Horse, of which he was colonel; and as the Count was son of the Marquis d'Angeau, he had great influence. However, they soon quarrelled.

"As the qualities of the soul," says his unlucky son Frederick, "commonly manifest themselves betimes, the baron at the age of twelve years *displayed a strong passion for heroic virtue.* His favourite book was Plutarch, which was never out of his hands, and which he eventually got by heart." Thus his son:

but another account makes him at this time not nearly so usefully employed, but busy as a courtier and an inveterate gambler—which forced him to fly from Paris *criblé de dettes*. He then repaired to Sweden, "drawn thither by a passionate admiration for Charles XII.," and a wish to have some share in his exploits. But it is more likely that his genius for intrigue had begun to exhibit itself, and that he had been despatched on some of the innumerable "spying" missions which were then part of the recognised politics of every court. More earthly motives than mere "lively admiration" of a hero, or for the history of Plutarch, were at work; and, as was said at the beginning, the story of Casanova explains clearly the whole mystery of an adventurer's migrations. There, says the son, "he became perfect in the war," and also attracted the notice of Gortz, the Swedish minister, who saw in him the pliant qualities of an emissary, and used him in several intricate negotiations. One of these missions led him to Spain; and there can be little question that he was used to negotiate the strange plot between Gortz and Alberoni for placing James on the throne of England. Indeed, this scheme, in various shapes, was the other great episode of his life, and spread over many years. He left Spain loaded with favours, and returned to Sweden, where he was "graciously received" by Charles. He then attended Gortz to the Hague, where he engaged still more deeply in the Pretender's plot, and stole over to England, where he met the Jacobites, and concerted plans with them. The Swedish ambassador, Count de Gillenbourg, so far forgot his privileged character as to join the conspiracy; and diplomatic Europe was presently scandalised by learning that the sacred person of an ambassador had been profaned by the hands of London police-officers. Theodore had the very narrowest escape, and got away to Holland. This alone would make a dramatic incident in his life; and his son tantalised the public by promising a full account; but he had not the opportunity, nor indeed the encouragement, to perform his promise.

At the Hague—then a delightful and miniature Paris, and a hotbed of political intrigue—Theodore was not safe. The States General, from an obsequious complacency to England, had Gortz arrested, and Theodore only escaped the same indignity by taking sanctuary at the Spanish ambassador's. At the instance of the regent, however, both were released, and got back to Sweden, where Charles was before long killed by the Frederickshall cannon-ball, and his late minister was promptly beheaded at the foot of the town gallows at Stockholm. This rough treatment seemed ominous for those who had followed Gortz's fortunes, and scarcely suited the bloodless paths of intrigue which the true adventurer relishes. He therefore changed the scene, and next appears in Madrid, where his peculiar gifts found a suitable field; and this wretched court, still full of the French gamblers and intriguers, offered a fine pasture for our adventurer. There he worked himself into high favour, was made a colonel, and succeeded in marrying one of the queen's maids-of-honour—a Lady Sarsfield, daughter to "Lord" Kilmallock, or Kilmarnock, one of the Irish Jacobite exiles. This piece of good fortune he was said to owe to Ripperda, who had risen to the highest rank in the same profession. He enjoyed, besides, a pension of some six hundred pistoles.

A romantic incident, that reads like a passage in "Gil Blas," is connected with his acquaintance with Alberoni. "Very much out at elbows, and much to the loss of his patron, he had fallen sick. As he had scarce spirits enough to support him on his legs, so his funds were scarcely sufficient to make him eat. He had a handsome apartment, indeed, a man-servant, and a nurse, but his circumstances were so bad that she took her leave of him one morning very respectfully before he was out of bed. When his servant entered the room he started, and his master asked him what was the matter, not a little apprehensive that his nurse might have seized his watch for her six weeks' attendance. "The matter is," said the fellow, who was a Swiss, "why, here's a purse of gold upon the table as big as my head." The baron, forgetting his disorder, raised himself up, and saw on his toilet a green purse with 2000 pistoles. He ordered his servant to give it to him; and, being then helped up, put it into a drawer of his cabinet with as much coolness as if he had taken it from thence, which the poor Swiss firmly believed."

Ripperda was said to have allowed him 1000 pieces of eight a year for finding out intelligence, and writing it to his employer. He was further rewarded by a colonel's commission in a German corps, which he was given the privilege of raising, together with money; but, unfortunately, his love of expense and improvident marriage obliged him to divert a good deal of this cash to his private expenses, which obliged him to leave Spain.

It is curious to follow all the attempts he made to get his services accepted, and how he devoted himself to that *métier* of selling news or secret intelligence. He was found to be shifty, and useful.

But the adventurer can never wholly settle down; marriage does not fix him; and Theodore was unexceptionally unstable. He fell into fresh debts. No doubt, too, he had ambitious schemes and hopes of a success like that of Ripperda, but failed. His son, nothing extenuating, tells us bluntly of his next proceeding and its motive. "At first the Baron entertained great hopes from that alliance; but finding afterwards that they did not answer his expectations, he forsook his wife, who was then pregnant of a son." Others, even less delicate, add that, in addition to this desertion, he made his escape with all her jewels. The adventurer of the period always disappears with some such abruptness.

His life, having lost all appearance of official recognition, was now to become fitful, uneasy, insecure, and shifting. He again shows himself at Paris, mixed up with Law's proceedings, lotteries, gambling, with the usual finale of having to fly abruptly. Next he turns up at Amsterdam, where he contrived to swindle large sums from the merchants, whose friend and partner he became, no doubt using his hocus-pocus of high names and his pseudo-influence at courts. Next he appears in London, about the year 1727, where it was given out years later that he had stopped at The Ipswich Arms, Cullum Street, and had moved to a coffee-house, where he lay hid, and "kept his bed, pretending to be ill;" about which there is a suspicious minuteness savouring of inquiries made of the London police. Again it was said he succeeded in victimising the London merchants, and had to fly with all speed. It is but fair to say, however, that these may be some of the wild canards which the unscrupulous Genoese, who were as oddly and laboriously venomous in their tittle-tattle as old gossips, sent fluttering all over Europe. Florence was then the next scene. A fresh story says he appeared at Rome, where he gave out later that they had three times attempted to poison him. But at Florence we begin to get out of the vapours and uncertain bogs in which the adventurer walks, to tread firmer ground, and see distances and dates more accurately. His son says he was made "minister resident" to the Emperor—a transparent fiction, unless indeed he was one of the usual unrecognised schemers which every court then made use of, and coolly disavowed or sacrificed if discovery followed. The Genoese spies must have had their suspicions of him. On his successful attempt they issued a sort of hue and cry with a *précis* of his life, which has certainly an air of great truth. They said that in London he had passed as a German, and in Genoa for a Swede; in other places for an Englishman; that it could be proved from passports and other papers that he had always been changing his name—passing as Baron von Naxaer, Von Schimer, and even as Smith. One of his Spanish proceedings, they said, was getting money to hire some German mercenaries, which he embezzled; and considering that his son pursued the same sort of agency, this has an air of probability. He had borrowed some five hundred pieces from Jaback, the Leghorn banker, and was arrested on a charge of defrauding. He contrived then to get a shipowner to become his security. He next had to go into the common hospital of the city to be cured of illness; and on his recovery set off to Tunis, where he represented himself to be a physician, and finally arranged his plot. All this is in keeping with the adventurer; even dates and names are given; and this dealing with shipowners and merchants and bankers was the adventurer's routine in the days when merchants were very daring and speculative in their enterprises.

While he was at Tunis news arrived of the outrage of the Genoese in seizing on the Corsican deputies. It may be remembered that Prince Louis of Würtemberg was in command of some of the German troops in the island, while another prince of the same house had served with Charles the Twelfth in Sweden, where Theodore had known him. Here was a link for the adventurer, who was not slow to remind Prince Louis of this connection. The adventurer, as again we see in Casanova, would find old acquaintances turning up in every city and court, sometimes at intervals of long years, and sometimes awkwardly enough. "His attachment to the interests of Prince Maximilian in Sweden," says Theodore's son, addressing the reigning Duke of Würtemberg and Teck in a dedication. It is really not improbable that he may have had some influence over Corsican affairs through this channel; and the rather remarkable change in the feeling of the Germans, who, after coming to subjugate the island for the Genoese, then became its advocates, while the Emperor was its patron and guarantor, may have been owing to the skilful or crafty interference of Theodore, who was actually in the city with the prince. As I have said, there was no official accrediting of agents from the charmed circle of diplomacy—anyone with wits or cleverness could be *ipso facto* a diplomatist. A versatile schemer was a minister at five minutes' notice. In fact, as we learn from Casanova, it was in a sort of routine for "the clever" to get an introduction to a minister, who, as a probation, tried them as humble instruments, and, according to the dexterity exhibited, sent them away on more important business.

From the Italian coast he was looking wistfully over at the little island where the game was going on. As he thought of some other games played with success, of the men he had known who had played them, a scheme occurred to him that was not so far-fetched. He had already plotted for a throne with Gortz and the Pretender; he had seen Ripperda and Law rise to seats on only the second step lower than a throne. Now here was a throw for him.

The deputies detained were Giafferi, Ceccaldi, Aitelli, and Rafaelli. Giafferi was a man of a noble and gallant nature, bold, brave, temperate, and of the same temper as Paoli. Rafaelli was a priest, and with him, or more probably with the canon Orticoni, an agent of the Corsicans on the mainland, and who was applying to all foreign courts in turn to take up "the cause of the Corsicans," he established very close relations. When he learned his interest and close associations with the Würtemberg family, it was natural that they should turn to a man of such influence.

The dedication by Colonel Frederick of his little book to a prince of this house seems to prove satisfactorily that these intimate relations existed.

"To his most Serene Highness the reigning Duke of Würtemberg and De Teck, Count Montbelliard, Lord of Haydenheim,' Justingen, etc., Knight of the Order of the Golden Fleece, and Field Marshal of the Empire, etc., etc., etc.

"SIR,—The book I take the liberty to present to your Highness is yours of right, as it contains the materials for a history of a people, among whom a Prince of *your illustrious* House,[*] already celebrated for his military exploits, no less distinguished himself by his political knowledge and his humanity. My father owed to it also the celebrity which brought on him his misfortunes. His attachment, when he was in Sweden, to the interests of Prince Maximilian,[†] who, then young, was so highly honoured by Charles XII., procured him the favour of Prince

---

[*] Prince Louis of Würtemberg.
[†] Prince Maximilian of Würtemberg.

Louis. This was the first cause of his connection with the Corsicans, and of his future exaltation to the throne. The protection of the illustrious house of Würtemberg having thus, Sir, been long conferred on us, my attachment to its interests is natural and hereditary. I venture to flatter myself, therefore, that your most Serene Highness, looking upon it as such, will do me the honour to afford me still the opportunity of proving my admiration of your great qualities, my zeal for your glory, my gratitude for those distinguished obligations you have conferred on me, and the most profound respect with which I am your most Serene Highness's most humble and most obedient servant—FREDERICK."

He accordingly had many interviews with these envoys, in which he played the *rôle* of patron, affecting a certain coyness and hesitation and startling difficulties." He was not rich, but he was very liberal; and would often make use of that saying of Alexander, that his treasure was deposited among his friends. Therefore the deputies conjured him to grant them his protection, which he did the more willingly as he foresaw as well as they that the Genoese would return to the charge with more violence than ever.

He made them sensible that the peace between them and the Republic of Genoa was not a peace, but a deceitful shadow of one; that the ill-will of the Genoese towards them could not be abated in the least, for one always bears a mortal hatred to those one has grievously offended; that in running over the history of those Republicans they would find that they had rendered themselves famous only by their evil deeds; that their glory had no other foundation than ruin, robberies, treacheries, and execrable murders. He added that, as they had always fallen a prey to so many different nations, who seemed to have conquered that fine kingdom for no other end but to destroy it, they could hope for no end nor mitigation of their miseries but from a total change in the state; that they ought to form to themselves, therefore, a plan of government suitable to their inclinations— either set up a republic or elect a king; that this was the only means he could suggest in order to procure them a solid and lasting tranquillity.

"To this discourse the deputies answered with grief that they were but too sensible of the truth of what he had said; that the state of their affairs was really melancholy and deplorable, their lives and fortunes being entirely at the mercy of these tyrants, who were more formidable to good men than to the vilest wretches; that their proceedings were unprecedented; that they took informations without denouncing them to the parties accused, whom they judged and condemned without so much as hearing them; that the least surmise passed with them for a crime, and the smallest appearance of guilt was always punished with death. They concluded that, not being able to bear any longer so many scourges and devastations, they were resolved to break their chains at any rate; but that it was necessary they should be headed by a man whose birth might inspire them with respect, and whose talents might guide their efforts, for want of which all their revolutions had proved unsuccessful. That for this purpose they had pitched upon him, and begged he would take upon himself so glorious an enterprise, which would furnish ample matter to posterity to immortalise his fame; therefore, that he would vouchsafe to be their deliverer, and give them leave to offer him the crown as a recompense.

"The baron, as one may easily imagine, was agreeably surprised at so great an offer, which he did not in the least expect. He, however, declined their offer; but being afterwards pressed to give them an answer, he said to them: 'Gentlemen, the affair which you mention is of the highest consequence. I can as yet see nothing in it but danger and obstacles; let us then take time to weigh the whole maturely, and seek means to prevent the inconveniences that surround so intricate an affair, and at the same time secure to ourselves a happy issue.'

"The deputies renewed their instances a few days after with more vehemence than ever; upon this the baron asked them whether the offer they had made him was by order of the body of the nation, or whether they had done it of themselves? The deputies answered they had done it of their own accord; but that they were very sure the nation would desire no better. 'Well then,' returned the baron, 'if it is so, I am willing to run all the risks that so dangerous an enterprise is liable to, to free so brave a people from slavery; and if I fail therein, I shall at least have the glory of leaving a noble example to posterity.' He then enjoined them to return to Corsica, to inform their countrymen of his goodwill towards them; to exhort them to be firm and unanimous in their resolutions; to hold themselves in readiness, without, however, discovering their designs, whilst he should make the necessary preparations for the accomplishment of their wishes."

According to one account his claim to his elevation was founded upon services less romantic than intercession for prisoners. He is described as acting as commercial agent for the Corsicans; freighting vessels for them; disposing of their merchandise; acting, in fact, as commission agent. Yet he contrived to invest himself with a suitable air of mystery, and the Genoese spies could never make out who he was, but reported him sometimes an English lord, an Italian priest, or even a German prince.

It should be mentioned that in their extremity the Corsicans had been, as it were, hawking about their island, offering it to various influential potentates.

As was to be expected, there was "a national party" who did not approve of this proceeding, headed by one Astoldi, who said "that they did not fight to change masters." The Canon Orticoni, who seems to have been one of the "fighting priests" of the pattern that Ruffo was later in Italy, actually repaired to Spain, and made a formal offer of his island to the king, who in courteous terms declined the embarrassing present; but was willing, he said, to accept of a couple of regiments of sturdy Corsicans, to be raised in the island; on which the Canon declared heroically that "he came to offer their hearts, not to sell their bodies." All this was going on apart from the negotiations with Theodore, which was the work of another faction; for, as is invariably the case, the island was rent by parties. Theodore took occasion to sound Astoldi on the phrase "they did not fight to change masters," and he entertained the plan favourably, being for "a free state," with a chief of their own.

Another agent of the Corsicans, Count Rivarola, was living at Leghorn—also watching the interests of his countrymen—a gentleman of moderate opinions, well-affected to the republic, but whose moderation had only exasperated that insane government. Many years later, he furnished young Mr. Boswell, who was then going over to the island, with letters, and encouraged him. Theodore, passing from Genoa to

Leghorn, saw much of this Corsican, and had the art to persuade him to come into his plans. No doubt the bait he hung out before Rivarola and the other deputies' eyes was the influence he possessed at the Emperor's court; and he was not long in persuading them that the sole chance for the islanders was to consolidate themselves into a monarchy, and that this step would be a safeguard against those wretched internal quarrels which helped to make them the prey of a foreign power. The result of these discussions was, that Theodore agreed to their proposals, and it was arranged that they should get the consent of their countrymen to make him king, in return for which he engaged to procure them the protection of a great power, to furnish them with stores, arms, and all sorts of supplies. He would not ask them to fulfil their part of the contract until he had given earnest, as it were, of his, and had arrived with ships and stores. This singular arrangement was duly concluded; and the daring adventurer had then to think how he was to set about his scheme.

At this time there were two other adventurers on the boards, who were known to Theodore, and whom he thought of at this stage of his programme. One was the famous Bonneval, then at Constantinople, later to be a distinguished renegade, who donned the turban and became Osman Pasha; the other was Racocksky, once Prince of Transylvania, but who had been deprived of his kingdom, and had gone to Turkey, to the Grand-Seignior, waiting for something to turn up. Theodore did not long hesitate. After trying the ministers of Spain and other courts, he at last took the energetic step of sailing for Constantinople. The voyage was then a perilous one; but the adventurer did not want for courage. Even thirty years later, the waters between Leghorn and the African coast were swept by pirates, and the name of Barbary corsairs made the Laird of Auchinleck pause before he could bring himself to embark. It was said that Theodore was captured, and carried to Algiers, where he was imprisoned, and only released on payment of a thousand sequins. He, however, got successfully to Pera, where he saw Racocksky, whom he dazzled with a plan for the recovery of his lost throne. He mapped out a scheme, in which the Turks were to cross over and make a new invasion of the empire, and so excited his hopes, that Theodore was introduced to Bonneval. That was not to be the last embassy made to the renegade. A few years later, Casanova, who, as it were, holds up a torch by which we can read the history of his brethren, came on a mission from an important cardinal at Rome to this clever adventurer, and gives a graphic account of the portly European Pasha and a "library," as he called it, where he kept his European wines. We can hardly accept the glittering programme which this company of adventurers are said to have mapped out; but we may conceive that the adroit and persevering Theodore could have so far prevailed as to have received letters and promises of patronage, and perhaps substantial assistance, in the scheme he was meditating.

His scheme was this: "He proposed," his son tells us, "to render the Turk master of all Italy, to make the Island of Corsica serve for a kind of warehouse to the Moors of Tunis and Algiers, from whence they might easily and without any risk make descents on the coasts of Genoa and Tuscany, whilst the Moors of Tripoli disembarked on those of Calabria, and the Turks in the Marche of Ancona. He showed the facility of that enterprise almost to a demonstration. He added that this conquest would open a way into Germany, that one might penetrate into Styria through Frioul, and then set up the Ottoman standard before the gates of Vienna with more ease and success than it was done by the Vizier Kara Mustapha. That they might there be joined by another Turkish army by the way of Hungary; and thus the house of Austria would be irrecoverably lost. Racocksky, charmed with Neuhoff's plan, referred him to Osman Pasha, Count de Bonneval, to whose counsels and conduct the Grand-Seignior afterwards owed all the advantages gained by his arms over those of the Imperialists. Bonneval, naturally inclined to great enterprises, and irritated also against the Emperor, was immediately sensible of the extent of this plan, and made the best of it at the Porte. It was agreed that succour should be granted to the baron, but on condition that he should hold Corsica as a fief of the Porte; that in the meantime proper measures would be taken for the conquest of Italy under the direction of the Count de Bonneval and Prince Racocksky."

Theodore next appeared at Tunis, worked on the merchants, contrived to draw in the English consul, who, like his nation, favoured the " brave Corsicans ;" and at last this indefatigable man succeeded in so far discounting his future chances as to obtain, either from the Dey or from the merchants, sufficient to equip his theatrical little expedition. There was a wise policy in his starting from that African coast; for he brought with him a dim and Eastern sense of grandeur and support. All these operations, this journeying about, these applications to the various courts, took two or three years.

He was certainly a gallant adventurer, and his perseverance deserved to be rewarded. He had now succeeded. His little flotilla was lying in the Bay of Aleria; this theatrical chevalier was sleeping on the first night of his arrival, having cast off his scarlet caftan; and the impulsive Corsicans believed they had now among them a saviour who would raise up their nation. The likeness to the Irish still continues, who, during the old Rebellion, were always looking out for strangers to make a descent on the coast "dressed in green and gold."

But that was to be about the most romantic scene of the whole piece. With the next morning the more serious business was to commence. As was mentioned, the news spread far and wide, and at once reached Genoa, which was only a day's sail away. They were half frantic with rage, but were more affected with spite. They sent abroad almost absurd little biographies, depicting him in the most infamous colours. But both the islanders and Theodore himself behaved with moderation, not advancing hastily, but making sure of their ground. He spoke to the leaders with great candour, and told them that the ships they saw were only a portion of the succour that was to arrive; that more was on its way—a declaration which proved to be correct within a few weeks. But he declared to them, with great plainness, that what he wished for was the crown; that it would be for their interests as well as for his; and that his relations with the various courts, powerful as they were now, would be on quite a different footing when he should be able to address them as an elected king.

This ingenious argument had its effect. Giafferi and Paoli, with Costa, the leading lawyer of the country, were no hot-headed patriots, but wise and thoughtful men. They weighed the matter, and agreed in the meantime that he should take the title of viceroy, until a formal appeal should have been made to the people. Meanwhile he assumed all the trappings of state. Cannon and sentries were placed at the door of the palace. He was served off silver; he went to the cathedral in state, and attended by guards. Then Giafferi and the deputies gave out to the people what they had kept secret—that it was to him they owed their liberation from the Genoese dungeons. A wonderful being! Even his titles rang out sonorously: the Lord Theodore, Grandee of Spain, a Lord of England, a Peer of France, a Count of the Holy Roman Empire, and a Prince of the Holy See!

In this elation he could not resist writing the glorious news to a relation in his native town, a Baron Drost, to whom he wrote affectionately after an interval of many years. This letter is given in the little French "Mémoires Secrets;" but Gregorovius, the delightful Corsican traveller, says he saw the original in MS. in the island. This curious corroboration of what one would at first be inclined to treat as a bit of romance, induces us to accept other details as founded on fact. This person had been a sort of guardian of Theodore's childhood at Brandenburg and in the regions about Rouschenberg, where various cousins were staying; and after an interval of long years, Theodore recalls himself to his recollection. He glosses over with some odd apologies his own wild career and disappearance, laying it all to the account of "the disorder and disarrangement occasioned by some evil-minded persons, and perhaps *also through my natural desire to travel incognito.*" His sole aim all this time was to return triumphantly home, and provide for these relatives, and "annihilate the calumnies" that had been sown abroad about him. In fact, this would seem to mean that he had been cast off by his family, who were scandalised by his irregular escapades. Now, however, he had the pleasure to announce to them—and a most piquant announcement it must have been—that he had attained to his present glittering elevation; and all he was anxious for was, that his friends and relations should come out and gather round him, and share in his great good fortune.

There is a strain of exalted piety all through this curious production, in which he speaks a good deal of the "divine assistance," and of his aim to make the whole enterprise "redound more to the honour of God and the good of his neighbour," attributing all his success "to the grace of God." This was, no doubt, chosen to suit the naturally fervent tempers of the Corsicans, who mingled with their patriotism a very high strain of devotion. This document was dated only a few days after his arrival; and in due time the Baron Drost accepted the invitation, and set out to join his royal relative.

There is a curious link between this adventurer and a remarkable man of our own day, who also won a kingdom, not for himself, but for another. It is strange to think that Theodore's blood ran in the veins of Joseph Garibaldi, and may be accountable for those daring freaks which have made that name famous. Among those who had joined him was a certain Giovanni Battista Sinabaldi; and this Corsican he despatched home to Westphalia with the letter to Baron Drost, or as some say to his mother, still alive. The envoy arrived in safety, and was greatly struck by the charms of Catherine, Theodore's sister. He wrote for Theodore's consent to their union, which was graciously accorded. The pair settled later at Nice, where the husband became a doctor, and his son is said to have been the grandfather of Joseph Garibaldi. If this be so—and it is attested by the registry lately discovered at Ruggeberg—the bold captain at Marsala is the nearest claimant to that kingdom of Yvetot.* No doubt the same messenger brought back Theodore's son, a lad of about ten years old, and dignified with the name of the "Prince of Caprera." He too was to have a dismal history of his own, and was old enough then to

* See *Athenæum*, 1860.

be able later to recall the curious and romantic scenes of his early boyhood.

It was often repeated, that European powers were working behind the scenes. This was the belief of the Marquis d'Argens. There could be no doubt that vague assurances were given to him of some support in the future; but they were afraid to interfere, as it was known that the Emperor and the French court, while hesitating themselves, would resent and not tolerate the appearance of any great power on the stage. These great supporters of the divine-right theory were known to be looking with jealousy on this mushroom monarchy, which yet seemed to have a greater vitality than might be expected from a mushroom origin.

Mr. Boswell, who met all degrees of persons, and who would not have scrupled to question leading diplomatists as to the reports spread abroad concerning Theodore, applied himself to finding out the truth of the matter. "Theodore," he says, "was a most singular man, and had been so beaten about by change of fortune, that he had lost the common sentiments of mankind, and viewed most things as one who is mad, or drunk, or in a fever. His scheme was to amuse the Corsicans with hopes of foreign aid, and by the force of hope to carry them forward. This might have succeeded; in which case he could very easily have said, that the foreign aid would have come, had there been occasion for it; but they had behaved with such spirit as to require no help." This seems a fair and rational view.

Theodore at once saw the fatal effect of divisions and jealousies among these hot spirits, which had hitherto paralysed all his efforts; and he straightway assembled the tribes in a great plain, and made them solemnly swear an eternal peace among themselves; making them, besides, invoke the penalty of death upon their own heads, if they should prove false to their vow. This politic stroke had the happiest effect; and one of the "Neri" and one of the "Rossi"—two factions of the island—having renewed the old quarrel, he had them both summarily hanged, in pursuance of their own compact. This severity, it was said, completely extinguished these old vendettas—again so like the Irish faction-fighting—and he then prepared for a solemn act.

Sunday, April 15th, must have been another glorious day for the adventurer to look back to, years after. At Allesani, a little village beyond the Tavignano, there was a convent, and only thirty miles from Bastia, where the Genoese were encamped, all the Corsicans assembled. Deputies from every commune or *pieve*, from the clergy and monasteries, formed a congress, while thousands of the people remained outside, and waited in anxious expectancy. Everything was done admirably, decorously, and with wisdom by this surprising nation, who were kept straight, as it were, by some clever counsellors and lawyers, for which Corsica even then had a reputation. The scene must have been a picturesque one. The conditions were drawn up; a regular constitution, better than many a one framed under more favourable auspices, was adopted; and the crown offered to "the Baron de Neuhoff," with these conditions. It was to be settled on him and on his line, and, in default of heirs, on any successor he was to appoint. All were to be of the Catholic religion. In all acts he was to be controlled by a Diet of twenty-four members—at least, in such acts as related to taxes, war and peace, and commerce. All export-taxes were to be abolished. A fixed sum should be charged for salt; and above all, the Genoese were to be chased from the country. No foreign troops were to be tolerated, save such as his majesty should please to introduce into the country. (The poor Corsicans believed they were presently to see the horizon covered with white sails, sent by a great foreign power to help their king.) The annual "family-tax" should not be higher than three livres each; and widows were to be exempt from all taxes—a rather touching provision, which showed how the cruel necessities of the war had called for such an exemption. It was provided too—which showed a calm forethought

—that a public university should be forthwith established and endowed; all offices were to be conferred on natives alone. Giafferi solemnly read these conditions to the people, who accepted them. Then the Baron Theodore signed them, and was sworn upon the Gospels to observe them. Next all proceeded to the church of the village, where high mass was sung; and, the high mass over, a pastoral coronation took place, when a crown of simple laurel and oak-leaves was placed on his head by the generals, and in the old classical fashion he was carried out on the shoulders of the chiefs and shown to the people, who were shouting frantically, "Long live Theodore our king!" "Liberty for ever!" From the gloomy yard of the London King's Bench prison how his eyes must have looked back wistfully to that fair Sunday morning—to the high mass in the village church where he sat enthroned, and to the music of those shouts!

It must be said that the adventurer, now that the scenic business was over, showed a most practical spirit. The man who had known and perhaps served under the great captain of Sweden, at once turned his experience to profit. He formed the straggling guerilla corps into twenty-four regiments, and introduced strict discipline and drill. Four of the chiefs he made colonels, with regular appointments, reaching to the modest sum of 400 livres. The muskets and shoes were distributed among the soldiery; and the first exercise of his prerogative was to dub a leading citizen of Aleria a knight. He lived in what was called a palace; had a special guard of 300 men, who were seen with drawn sabres; and two cannons opened their brazen jaws at his gate. Then he set himself to the distribution of offices. Costa the lawyer became Garde des Sceaux and Chancellor of the kingdom. Another doctor, Cafforio, was Secretary of State, with the title of Count; Arrighi was Secretary of War, Taglio Minister of Finance; Castagnetti and Fabiani were appointed military commanders of provinces; while Luis Giafferi and Paoli were appointed generalissimos and governors of the kingdom, with the title of Excellency. Countships and marquisates were distributed with a lavish hand.

All these things, magnified by travel, intrigued the world and disquieted the Genoese; and it was presently given out that three more vessels had arrived with succour and stores. The Republic seemed utterly scared; their soldiers, cooped up in Bastia, had to look on at these strange proceedings. At Genoa all they could do was to search the police-registers, and with such materials as they could find there, compose a spiteful, fretful proclamation, in which, with a sad loss of dignity, "we, the Doge and procurators of the Republic," describe the adventurer as "the *soi-disant* Baron Theodore." It reads like the scolding of an angry woman. They described him contemptuously as some mountebank, "dressed up in Eastern fashion, who had come with some cannon and powder," and "who had given away a few little gold pieces." As it was their duty to look after the welfare of their Corsican subjects, it was only right to let them know the quality of this impostor. They artfully said that he was given to magic and the cabala, hoping with this insinuation to turn the clergy against him. They gave the little police description of him that has been already quoted. "Everywhere he has swindled someone; having cunning enough to keep his schemes secret until he has got away, when everything is discovered. A letter from a German gentleman in Lisbon, and dated the February of the current year, proves all this convincingly." Then they quote the deed of his discharge from jail at Leghorn, dated the 6th September, 1735, and sworn before the notary Jean Baptiste Gumano, and that he was there received into the public hospital as a common pauper. They had ascertained, they said, the history and characters of those who made up the retinue. The "chaplain" was a degraded priest, who had been dismissed from a convent at Tunis; there were two runaway youths from Leghorn, called Attiman and Bondelli; a certain Christoforo, brother to Bongiurno, a doctor at Tunis; and one of the blacks was Mahomet, a notorious galley-slave. No doubt there were some grains of truth in these sketches; for the adventurer cannot be very nice in the choice of his followers, and can only pick up the irregulars of society and those in a lower grade than himself. The Doge was "anxiously solicitous" lest a man of such "depraved manners" should have an evil influence over his dear subjects in Corsica; and pronounced him guilty of treason and *lèse-majesté*, as also those who favoured him, and "would disturb the repose of our people." This complacent document was signed at the palace on the 9th of May, and duly published and scattered over Corsica.

For the moment it had no effect. Even at Bastia the common people, as they read it on the walls, wrote under it: "Long live King Theodore!" But in due time it began to make an impression, as his son owns. When the excitement had worn off, the stories were repeated; and the son also thought it was not a judicious step, the taking up the challenge, and replying to them in the same tone. Theodore said publicly: "Since the Genoese say I am a mountebank, I'll come and play on their stage at Bastia!" This document was headed grandly: "Theodore the First, primarily through the grace of God and the most holy and undivided Trinity, and secondly by the choice of the *true* and ever-glorious liberators and fathers of the country, King of Corsica." It is in a tone of banter, of scoffing, scarcely dignified.

He never thought it necessary to give them notice of his attempt. He would now, therefore, tell them that he had changed his abode, being quite tired of wandering, and that he thought, as they were so near to him, it was only polite to give them notice. Their representative at Bastia should also hear of his having a new neighbour, but in another shape. They said he was a disturber of the peace. How, pray? Who had disturbed the peace in Corsica all these years back? They talked of *lèse-majesté;* whence did they derive *majesté* at all, if not from their cupidity and trading, and that greed of money which invites over Turks and unbelievers, and was the subject of laughter in England?—a merchant there directing a letter to " Mr. ——, Doge and general dealer!" This was an answer to the charge of his bringing Mahometans with him. He went back to history, to the years A.D. 1272, 1317, and 1373, when he showed that the Genoese joined the Turks for pillage. This was all childish enough; but he wound up with a bold defiance in a better tone, saying he would have 10,000 men at his back, and money to pay them. As for their charges, they were simply lies. He hoped, sarcastically, that in the future combats at least *one* Genoese would be seen leading on their troops. But he doubted it, as they were too much engrossed with their traffic and bills of exchange. This curious document was "given at the Camp"—

he had already begun to move—"in July," and countersigned by his chancellor.

Having thus met their gasconade with something like gasconade, he turned to serious business. Under his unwearied exertions, things actually began to take shape. Some trained officers had arrived—possibly in the three new ships—and were placed in command. Over 20,000 men were collected and disciplined. There was an air of organisation abroad. The Genoese, now scared, kept close within their fastnesses. The king even exercised a most tangible and satisfactory proof of royal prerogative, namely, that of coining money, and struck, or caused to be struck, on the Continent, a number of silver and copper pieces. They were rather clumsy performances, and the silver specimens were very scanty indeed—they were of the class known to the French as *pièces de nécessité*, and a pendant to King James's Irish gun-money. But the greed of collectors all over the world was greatly excited; they were eagerly bought up at four zechins apiece for cabinets; and when the supply failed, a spurious mint was set to work at Naples.* Mr. Boswell succeeded in picking up a five-sous piece.

* An engraving of a copper coin is given in the works of Lord Orford, vol. i. p. 155. The obverse consists of a royal crown, underneath which are the letters T. R., surrounded by two branches of laurel, with the date, 1736, below. In the centre of the reverse the sum is indicated, viz., "*Soldi cinqui;*" the legend, which is nearly defaced, appears to have been "*Re per il bono publico.*"

He contrived to find leisure to arrange a simple code of law, criminal and civil, which he himself administered; sitting, inquiring, examining witnesses with great pains and impartiality. This, however, may have occurred at a later stage; for the present moment his hands were full; and within a month from his arrival, he was in the field and advancing to the attack. He unfurled the Corsican colours, green and gold, with the motto "*In te, Domine, speravi,*" fell upon Porto Vecchio and Sartene, and carried both by a *coup de main*. Flushed with this success he arrived before Bastia; in front of which he dated his replies to the Doge, and haughtily summoned the garrison to surrender, giving the commander six days to leave the island, and telling him that in case of refusal he would force him. Here again was gasconade; and the commander replied in the same tone, fortifying his answer with a broadside which disordered the assailants. He then formed a new plan: to divide his forces into bands, and attack the various forts simultaneously. Arrighi, the "minister at war,"

There was another piece, the half of this, of the same metal; and also a third coin, value unknown, with the effigy of the Blessed Virgin Mary impressed on one side of it, accompanied by the following motto: "*Monstra te esse matrem*"—show thyself a mother.

There is a print of this last in a curious French work on coins, published at Paris, entitled "Recueil général des Pièces obsidionales et de nécessité," par M. Pierre Duby. 3 vols. 4to.

was sent to San Fiorenzo; others were detached to Ajaccio, San Pellegrino, and various places. They had some successes; and made a prize of large stores of arms, which the Genoese had sent out to arm the natives of a district. Thence Theodore rallied again round Bastia, the siege of which he turned into a blockade, cutting off the water and provisions; and as the people of that quarter were known to be favourable to the Genoese, he levied a war contribution which was estimated at about 700,000 livres. Two wealthy seigneurs called Angeli were punished by a fine of 4000 livres each. Another district, called Calenzala, having shown signs of hesitation, and not unnaturally considering that they were completely at the mercy of the Genoese, he sent them a stern notice that they must prepare to have their lands ravaged with fire and sword, which speedily caused them to make up their minds. The country was thus swept; then the Genoese took the characteristic step of enlarging the galley-slaves, together with the scum, or cream, of the dungeons of the superb city, and formed them into a band of 1500 men. These wretches were turned loose upon the country, did all kinds of excesses, and acquired the nickname of Oriendi or Vittoli, after an infamous murderer who was held in execration. The great Republic itself had descended very low indeed.

Meanwhile, it was only in the usual course of things that some reaction should set in, and that an enthusiastic and impetuous people should have its moments of discontent. One act of severity caused deep murmurs. A certain Count Casacolli, who had once before gone over to the Genoese, was now discovered in a plot. The council of Theodore, as it was supposed, had him shot summarily. On the other hand, a certain Marquis de Silva Bastia was discovered in a plot with the rebels, was put on board a galley of the Republic, and carried off to a dungeon.

The gazetteers and chroniclers now all at once changed their tone. The indefatigable Genoese sent abroad rumours that the people were tired of him, and discontented at his cruelties and severity; that a third party was forming in the island; and that the relations of the executed Casacolli, having lured one of Theodore's generals into a deserted part of the country, had there "arquebussed" him. There were most likely grains of truths in these reports; for the people were impulsive and changeable. But they were soon refuted by some really brilliant achievements. The skirmish at Ziglia, on the 20th of July, when the Genoese were routed—a repulse three days later at Isola Rossa, when their boats were scattered, and they were driven back with the loss of four hundred men and of their commander Marcelli—was a significant refutation. Eight hundred muskets, fifty barrels of powder, and five months' pay for the soldiers were the spoils of this little victory.

Later, at Turiano, close to Bastia, forty Corsicans held a body of 1000 Genoese at bay for nearly six hours. Theodore himself led an attack on Leuto, where the inhabitants had gone over to the Republic, summoned them to surrender, routed the Genoese who opposed him, and hanged some prisoners by way of reprisals for similar barbarity on the side of the Genoese. At the same time he sent word to their commander that, if the system was continued, he could give no quarter. Indeed, the general of the Republic was in sore straits. His soldiers were deserting in bands, and the whole garrison of San Ildefonso disappeared one morning, each soldier carrying off two muskets. Inside Bastia there was confusion; and he was preparing to try by court-martial the Colonel Marcelli, who was thought to have behaved badly at "Red Island," but who obtained sanctuary in the church of the Jesuits. Gradually the places they held were growing smaller in number every day, and could be counted on the fingers. Yet all this time the Republic kept up its game of "brag;" was never wearied of sending out its scandal and gossip. "I remember," wrote one from Paris, "this man's wife very well; she died here a few years ago in great destitution. She was an Irish young lady; sister, I think, to Lord Kilmallock. He pretended after their marriage to raise a regiment, and through her interest obtained the money in advance, which he spent on himself." This was not the only story. Meanwhile the Genoese were being hard pressed, and now could only get their supplies—even water—from the sea.

Theodore, while playing the part of captain, found time to think of civil reforms. He began by according liberty of conscience to all, on the model adopted in Holland—perhaps an injudicious step among such a people—and encouraged everyone of every religion and country to come to the island by the bounties of free worship and grants of land, and a promise of churches built at his own expense. The invitation was at once accepted, and a whole crowd of Greeks and Jews poured in from the Morea and Tunis, who immediately established themselves in a quarter of their own, and began to build. A more questionable toleration was the reception of escaped galley-slaves, which, however, may have been meant as a counter-stroke to the Genoese. In Bastia the privations were growing so severe that there were wholesale desertions, and he was able to form a whole regiment of fugitives, who were chiefly Germans. Many French, Turks, and Spaniards — for such was the mongrel character of the Genoese host—found their way to him; and to the Moors he generously gave the means of returning to their own country, dismissing them with the rather theatrical condition, that they should release an equal number of Christians. He re-established trade, opened salt-works and factories of firearms and fabrics, and actually commissioned privateers to prey on the Genoese commerce. This wonderful man really performed prodigies. Knowing how precarious was his condition, he was no less unwearied in striving to get support from abroad; and the most characteristic and daring of his schemes was his making an attempt to get the imperial court to receive an ambassador from him. It was ill-naturedly given out that he had descended to use the influence of the wife of a *maître d'hôtel* to the Grand Duchess to carry on the intrigue; but it is more probable that he would have used his old Würtemberg influence. A more practicable scheme was a negotiation for the use of a large band of Albanian mercenaries under Count Carafa, who were to arrive in the island; but obstacles came in the way, and he presently found that the Grand-Seignior was so engaged with the prospects of a Russian war, that it would be impossible for him to think of "the conquest of Italy."

But worse was to come; for presently news reached him that Carafa and his Albanians had hired themselves out to a more profitable employer, the King of the two Sicilies. This news could not be long concealed. Already the fickle islanders were beginning to murmur, and to ask why the succour that was on its way from the foreign king, emperor, or sultan, did not appear. It required all his shifts to keep them quiet. They seized on some acts of very necessary severity as grounds for dissatisfaction. The execution of Casacolli was talked of angrily and with flashing eyes. That Colonel Arrighi, whom Theodore had made commander of a district, had left a little fort in charge of only twenty men—the news of which came to the ears of the Genoese, who attacked and, after a desperate resistance, took it. He had fully five hundred men whom he might have employed in its defence. Theodore came hurrying up to punish; but the culprit fled to Reno, whither the king pursued him, and was reported to have fired his house; and the mother and sister of the colonel are said to have been burnt. It is unlikely that Theodore would have wittingly committed such a blunder; but the story went abroad, distorted, exaggerated, and the dissatisfaction swelled every day. The "third party" were gathering, and actually defeated the Genoese themselves. The king kept up his pretence bravely and laboriously; going up hills and searching the horizon with his telescope, to see if the coming fleet was in sight. Crowds of sham couriers would arrive with sham packets.

But all this would not do. Fresh difficulties

began to arise. Rumours were whispered about that the intriguing Genoese had prevailed, now on the French Court, now on the Spanish Court, to interfere. To the clergy, too, Theodore had become odious: first, on account of its being supposed that his religion was but an adventurer's religion; and, secondly, because of his toleration and encouragement of the Turks and Jews. This was enough to taint his character with the fervent islanders, who had placed their cause under the tutelary aid of the Blessed Virgin, whose image was on their coins, and who prayed like Joshua before they rushed to battle. There were stories, too, of frailties and complaints from his subjects; and on an injury of that kind, the Corsican brother or husband takes down his double-barrelled gun. "Theodore," says his son, "who loved his subjects as much as if they had been his own children, reprimanded them like a father."

But such treatment had little effect. A plot formed against his life was discovered, and three of the conspirators executed. This step filled up the measure of his unpopularity. These men, too, were related to some of the noble families. Something like a mutinous feeling began to show itself; and Theodore presently found that the only people on whom he could rely were those whose future fortunes were dependent on him, through office, or the hope of still greater advancement. The party who called

THE STORY OF THEODORE OF CORSICA.

themselves "the Indifferents" was growing formidable; and it was said that it had been joined by Hyacinth Paoli, the father of Pasquale. He was a brave warrior, and could write poetry after a battle. Happily this rumour was not true. It actually came to a battle between the rival parties, in which the royalists were defeated. But he had a whole host in Giafferi, who kept with him to the last. These were alarming signs and tokens, and Theodore was too shrewd to neglect them.

He took a bold step: summoned his parliament to meet him, on the 2nd of September, at Casacoconi, where a most curious scene took place. It was infinitely creditable to the moderation of both parties. He was strongly dissuaded from this dangerous step; as, if he had nothing new to tell the people, they would be certain to wreak their resentment upon him, they were so inflamed against him. All the *pieves* sent their deputies, more, it was believed, from curiosity than otherwise. "Theodore," says his son, "came and placed himself in the midst of them with that air of grandeur and boldness that makes vice tremble, and causes a just terror to succeed a foolish audacity." He made them an harangue, referring to what he had done already, and retold the old story of the mysterious and unknown powers, and of fleets already upon the sea. But one of the chiefs stood up, and said that he had told them this very often, that he had given the same assurance again and again. The matter was fairly and honourably discussed; and in the end his eloquence prevailed: it was agreed that they should wait two months more, say to the end of October. The Genoese version was, that after this date he should abdicate if the succour did not arrive; a version proved false by the event.

Alas! the little romance was already fading out, having lasted some four months—long enough for a romance. The son gives a highly-coloured account, and says the whole ended in repentance and renewed loyalty. "Astonished at the confidence with which he put himself into their hands, the Corsicans changed their murmurs into protestations of attachment; they confessed their faults, calling him their benefactor, their saviour, their king; they promised to obey him in everything he should command, and to shed for him the very last drop of their blood." However, the engagement was to last up to the fatal October. The result showed his tact and boldness. With this prospect before him, he was not in the least dispirited, but set to work on fresh attempts. Again he took the field, encountered various bands of the Genoese, and routed them with his old success. In due time moneys arrived, with which he fitted out galleys, and pursued those of the Republic with equal success; then determined to make a bold *coup*, and try what a theatrical stroke would do for him.

He put himself at the head of fifty horsemen and three hundred *fantassins;* and bearing in mind that the old loyal nobles and seigniors lived in the districts on the other side of the mountains, he set off to Sartena, down at the southerly end of the island. There the Count Ornano, the Istrias, and other families met him at the head of a band of gentlemen, and received him in state. Theodore then proceeded to play a little piece for them, which was sure to touch their aristocratic sympathies. He proceeded solemnly to establish an order of knighthood—a step that had indeed been provided for by an article in the Constitution. It was a politic scheme at that moment; and the dim and shadowy rumours of new-made knights, and of costly robes, of the king himself giving away these honours, would drift over the mountains, and awe and attract the wavering. It is some testimony to Theodore's instinct, that the pageantry of an installation should have been recently used for the same end.

This order was called "The Order of Deliverance," and the edict was "given at our chamber in Sartena," on the 16th September. He said it was intended to "render respectable before Europe the nobility of this country;" and he promised to use his best influence to obtain a solemn confirmation of the order from his holiness the Pope. Meanwhile, he would declare the privileges and honours, so that the members should be received with great distinction, not only in their own country, but in all other countries; "in spite," adds the grand-master, "of the malice of the Genoese, who have evoked heaven and earth to make the people here appear contemptible." The qualifications were magnificent. Every knight was to be of noble birth, and his family must have followed no trade for two generations back. They were to be treated as nobles of the highest degree, and to be styled "most illustrious" and "excellence." They were to be exempted from all taxes and contributions. Their house was to be privileged against the officers of the law; and they were to have access to the palace—*at least to the ante-chamber*. They alone were to have all offices of command. They were to accompany the king to battle, and each was to maintain two soldiers. The business view of the whole transaction was, that each knight was to *lend*, in return for his patent, the sum of 250*l.* sterling, for which he was to receive 10 per cent. from the state. The theatrical side was a splendid installation, by the king himself, with gorgeous dress. They were to wear a rich sky-blue mantle—resembling in this the Knights of St. Patrick—with a cross and star of fourteen points. The star was to show on one side a naked figure of Justice, carrying in one hand a sword; in the other, a balance, in one scale of which was a drop of blood, and in the other a leaden ball; underneath the balance was a triangle, containing the letter T, which seems to have a masonic air; on the other side of the star were Theodore's own royal arms —a Moor's head and a broken chain—an allusion to his escape from the Algerines. Everything about these decorations was minutely laid down; and an alternative was naïvely but wisely permitted as to the material; for the statutes mentioned "gold, or yellow-coloured;" "silver, or white-coloured." In *petite tenue* they were to wear the ribbon and cross; the "grand prior and grand commander" a great double ribbon. All religions were eligible; and they were to repeat every day a little office of two psalms: "*In te, Domine, speravi,*" and "*Deus noster refugium et virtus.*" Theodore, recalling one of the most striking ceremonies at St. Peter's during holy week, required the knights to stand round the altar and draw their swords during the reading of the Gospel. The knight was placed on his knees before the king, who received him, and thus spoke to him: "I dub you knight of the most noble Order of Deliverance. From us alone must you bear to be touched three times with this naked sword, and to us shall you be obedient in all things, even unto death." Then he touched his shoulders with the sword, the new-made knight rose up, swore "faith and lealty" upon the Gospels, and the knights present received and embraced him as their brother.

Poor Theodore! One more bright day for him:

a grand ritual, when he was still playing at being king. Only two or three weeks were now left. Yet, again, it was something to look back to; for the nobles and gentlemen of that southern district crowded to him, and were eager to be enrolled. He made counts and barons of many of them at their own request, and the Order actually enrolled some four hundred knights. About a hundred of these were said to be foreigners, who, from sympathy, or from curiosity and the "fun of the thing," as the malignant Genoese gave out, were eager to join. He thus showed himself a skilful and worthy adventurer; for the *coup* succeeded, and this stroke attracted others.

A short time passed over in idle expectancy, during which time it was rumoured on the Continent that his brother-in-law, the Count Trévoux, had come from France with stores and some 30,000 louis d'or. This, if true, could not have helped him much. But he was beginning to hear the murmurs once more; and he now prepared for the last act. It was as skilfully arranged as the first.

He assembled the estates once more at Sartena on the 14th of November. All the deputies assembled. He entered the hall, seated himself on the throne, then rose and addressed them.

He then exhorted them " to remain faithful and loyal to their sovereign, and no longer to disgrace themselves by seditions; as, in that case, he would forsake them for ever, and cease to recognise them as his subjects." He added, "that in accepting the crown he entertained no other ambition than that of enfranchising them, at the expense of his repose, and even of his life, from the tyranny of the Genoese, under which they had so long groaned; and it was painful for him to remark, that they themselves formed the chief obstacle to the completion of his wishes. Royalty, considered by itself, had no charms in his eyes; he was ready to resume his former rank without regret; and, although his finances were exhausted, he still possessed an intrepid mind, that could scorn the rigours of poverty, and glory in resembling the Fabricii of antiquity, who considered honour and virtue as their sole treasure."

This short oration, added to the misfortunes of their prince—misfortunes which they now accused themselves of having created, or at least augmented—produced a sudden effect on the assembly, the members of which instantly arose, as if by unanimous consent, offered to renew the oath of fidelity, and promised to spill the last drop of their blood in his defence.

He added that he thought it not fair to keep them any longer in a state of suspense, and that their fidelity and confidence were entitled to special exertion and recognition on his side; and that therefore he had come to the resolution of going himself in person to see after the assistance which had been promised to him, and which was so mysteriously delayed. The honest people then told him that he had still all their confidence and loyalty; that they believed in him; and that they did not wish him to leave them; but that he could act as he pleased. He then selected a number of his leading followers, who were to be governors of districts, appointing the Marquis Hyacinth de Paoli and the Marquis don Louis Giafferi to be administrators of the kingdom.

The roll of these nobles reads gallantly enough— the Marquis Hyacinth de Paoli and the Marquis Don Louis Giafferi, who were termed marshals-general of the kingdom; the Marquis Lucas Ornano, the Count John Felix Ponzoni, the Count Durazzi, the Chevalier Antonio Suzini d'Aulle, the Count Mari, the Chevalier Fernandi, the Count Puillicio, the Count Casabianca, Colonel Sampieri, the Chevalier Leravalle, the Count Sucini, the Marquis Matra, &c. &c.

Ornano, Sampieri (one of the gallant Casabiancas), with a crowd of counts, generals, and "sieurs," he made governors of districts; and then, on the same day, issued a farewell proclamation to his subjects, "from Theodore I., King of Corsica," for the proper government of his kingdom during his absence. "Having resolved," he said, "to cross over to the

THE STORY OF THEODORE OF CORSICA. 73

Continent, fearing that we have been deceived by those who were entrusted with the negotiations; seeing, moreover, the months roll by without any sign of the succour that has been promised to us; and being at a loss to know what can be the cause of the delay, we have thought it only our duty to comfort our people before our departure by explaining to them the real reason of this expedition, and by appointing faithful commanders to all the sure posts of the kingdom, so *that all the supplies and munitions of war we shall send over shall be duly received and taken care of.* We enjoin everyone to assist them and obey them, under pain of our royal displeasure; and at our return we shall show our royal favour and goodwill to those who have so behaved, and punish severely all who disobey them."

Before his departure he had also issued the following edict :

"November 1st, 1737.

"THEODORE, by the Grace of God, King of Corsica, etc.

"Whereas our enemies, the Genoese, have represented us as a usurper, intruder, and disturber of the Island of Corsica; and whereas many evil-disposed persons in the said island, moved by private and personal interests, have endeavoured to lessen the glory of our administration, and to bring our government into contempt: Be it known, therefore, unto all Christian people, that Theodore de Neuhoff never interfered with the affairs of Corsica till, by the breach of the treaty with the inhabitants of that island, under the guarantee of his Imperial Majesty, the Republic had deprived itself of all just title to this kingdom:

"Theodore de Neuhoff, at their earnest request, and in a special capitulation for the saving of their just rights and liberties, has taken possession, and has compelled the Genoese, not only to abandon the whole country, but to surrender some of the fortresses, so that they possess nothing now save Bastia and six other fortified places."

After enumerating the advantages his coming had brought to the natives, he goes on:

"As they were restored to the free use of the soil, so they are encouraged to cultivate it by enjoying its produce without domination; for whereas the Genoese would not suffer them to dispose either of grain or fruit to any other than their own community, who seldom gave them half as much as it was worth, they are now at liberty to sell where they can. The rivers, lakes, and sea-coasts are farmed out by the Republic to the Catalonians, while the poor Corsicans were deprived of nets, boats, and salt.

"In consequence of these changes they are repairing all their villages near the sea-coasts, which the Genoese forced them to abandon and demolish, to prevent them having any intercourse with foreigners. This permission of building, planting, and vending the profit of their labours has already produced artisans in Corsica. It is now no strange thing to see tables and joint-stools made there; nay, some have had the ingenuity to frame bedsteads; whereas, under the government of the Republic, a Corsican scarce knew the intent of a saw, and they were forced to make use of earthen pots to keep their wine in, for want of coopers to make casks.

"Proper encouragement is now given for discovering and working the iron, copper, and silver mines, and of which the Genoese forbade the inhabitants so much as to speak, at the same time that they deprived them of the finest salt in the world."

He then mentions as a proof of their prosperity that the very foreigners have preferred his service to that of the Genoese; and " His Majesty has a regiment of Life Guards, composed of eight hundred German deserters, well armed, clothed, and disciplined."

He had also proclaimed liberty of conscience, with many other emoluments, and had thus drawn over a multitude of Greeks and Jews, and allowed each nation to build a town in which they are actively employed; and above eight hundred foreign Protestants are likewise settled in Corsica, where they are setting up several advantageous manufactures.

The king had also made it his principal care, not only to draw thither large quantities of foreign coins, but has also, since his accession, taken care, for the honour of his government and the encouragement of his subjects, to coin about 500,000 crowns.

In conclusion he says :

"Let, then, the candid and the ingenuous, whether natives or strangers, reflect on the past and present situation of this island and its inhabitants, and to them let it be left to determine which has the best title to the government of both—the Republic of Genoa or Theodore de Neuhoff.

"THEODORE.

"Done at Corte, November 1st."

The day for his departure arrived. He travelled across to the north, to the little port of Aleria, where he had landed on that morning some eight months before. Immense crowds attended him down to the beach; all the nobles clustered round, and remained with him to the last. The people, by a mournful silence, showed how they were affected; even those who had been opposed to him could hardly restrain their tears. He then gave them his last injunctions, conjuring them to be united and recollect his instructions. There was a certain wisdom in this departure. Had he been of the common pattern of adventurer, he would have stayed on, contriving all sorts of mean shifts and pretences, until his prestige had utterly gone, and he had been ejected with contempt and humiliation, never to rise again. Theodore went away as he came, with a very promising future to discount.

It was a French vessel, and carried the French flag. With him he took a small suite—his faithful chancellor Costa, a secretary and chamberlain, and two young Leghorn esquires. He also brought some thirty Genoese prisoners. Almost as soon as they got out to sea, a Genoese galley was seen in pursuit, and, it was said, with Rivarola himself on board, who would have boarded the little craft but for the earnest remonstrances of a Spanish officer, who pointed out the danger of insulting the French flag. Thus he was to have the luck of another Corsican adventurer upon the high seas.

The next day the little bark reached Leghorn, and a simple abbé, with some other passengers, came ashore. The Genoese prisoners he "made a present of" to an officer in one of the King of Naples' regiments, and his own immediate retainers entered the same service. No doubt this gift was meant to propitiate that monarch. Not until he had taken post for north Italy with his faithful chancellor, and Costa's son, and his secretary, a son of Ceccaldi, was it known that the abbé was the King of Corsica. Immediately the French captain was thrown into prison by his own consul for violating the neutrality laws; but, added the accounts naïvely enough, he did not pistol himself as the English sailor had done. He was, in fact, released after some explanations.

The gazettes and chronicles were now wild in their speculations; they all had the news. It was reported by one from Leghorn, that "a French vessel had put in here, having on board the Lord Theodore and his prime minister. They went ashore, and immediately took post-horses, it is believed, for Bologna." He remained just one night with an old friend, the captain of the port, and was away in the morning. Where had he gone to? This was indeed but the beginning of much "posting" from court to court; for he dared not let the grass grow under his feet. The gendarmes would have it that his journey to Rome—then a perfect Hôtel de l'Europe for all intriguers who swarmed thither—was for the purpose of arranging a bargain with the Pretender. Then he was away to Pisa, Ravenna, and, above all, tried hard to get to Naples, but could not succeed; next he found his way to Constantinople, to try to get aid from the Grand-Seignior; but the latter was too much taken up with other quarrels. These were the stories; and there can be no doubt that he thus went round to all the potentates, striving not unskilfully to discount his crown, as it were. He was in a good position to do so; for he could tempt the ambitious with this fair prospect—that he was in possession; that his subjects were well-disposed; that he was willing, in return for substantial aid, to hold the island as deputy, and in the interests of those who so assisted him. It was a pity indeed to let so reasonable and promising a chance pass away; and it is surprising that no adventurous power was willing to take up Theodore's security. The truth was, it was too jealous a business for the great powers; and it was too dangerous for the smaller ones, who were warned by a menacing growl from the grander kennels. The pursuit of this will-o'-the-wisp hope led him a weary dance for several years all over Europe.

Now the hopes of the Genoese might well revive. Their jubilation, however, was to take the usual undignified shape. No sooner had their galley returned from its unsuccessful pursuit, than the spies at Leghorn and other places were sent to collect the usual *chiffonnier's* bushelful of gossip; and the Republic presently sent out one of its gossiping proclamations. It was a tissue of falsehoods. It set forth, in a sort of preamble, that the baron, finding that he was becoming odious to his subjects, had determined to make his escape; that he had to do so suddenly *in the night*, taking Costa and two under-secretaries, named Fozzari and Loggi, with him; also his *valet-de-chambre* Agata, a Florentine, together with two pages, "whom an *esprit de libertinage* had forced to run away from their father's house." This affected accuracy shows the policeman's hand. "*With this worthy company,*" goes on the manifesto, "he contrived to get across the mountains to Aleria," where he found a French vessel ready to sail, commanded by Captain Délugée, of St. Tarpé, who was just weighing anchor for Leghorn, with a number of Spanish deserters, whom some officers of that nation had come over to reclaim. It must be confessed that this is a more probable explanation than Theodore encumbering himself with a number of soldiers to offer as a present to the King of the Sicilies. This captain made difficulties at first; but "was persuaded by the entreaties of Theodore, and the curiosity which the Sieur Délugée had to know more intimately the author of so notorious an attempt." The passengers on board observed that he was dressed as an abbé, and noticed that he was most uneasy and disturbed until the vessel put to sea. The reason, they said, he escaped in the galley, was the presence of these Spanish soldiers, which the Genoese captain wished to respect. "They then tracked him to a house in the port of Leghorn, and saw him into a chaise the next morning. He had with him three chests filled with dresses and papers;" a fact, we may suppose, they ascertained from the customs. It was also ascertained at Bastia, "that a few days before his departure he had secretly sold all his plate to raise a little money." The nation that could issue such tittle-tattle as a solemn state paper richly deserved Theodore's taunt as being a nation of hucksters and traders.

But the faithful Corsicans did not let this pass. Within a week or two, on December 1st, they had issued a reply warmly refuting these calumnies, and defending the absent adventurer. They declared that they were full of love and gratitude to their lord, " King Theodore the First," who, from the moment of his landing, had done nothing but labour for their good. They denied solemnly the stories of his being obliged to escape: that he left with the sole view of promoting their interests, and that " they continued bound to him by the most tender affection and the truest fidelity." To give a sure proof of this, the leaders had all signed this declaration at Corte; and, as a farther proof, it should be signed by every person in authority all over the kingdom, in every department, town, or even village, by every one on this side of or beyond the mountains. There is something almost touching in this honest declaration of fidelity, which is infinitely creditable to their hearts, and as rare as it is creditable; for with the multitude the absent " are always wrong," and are soon forgotten or lost sight of. The withdrawal of substantial assistance is the signal for the crowd to turn its eyes away, and look out for another idol : hope is usually too impalpable a food to live on.

About ten days later the first-fruits of Theodore's exertions were exhibited in the arrival from Leghorn of his old friend and original sponsor, the Canon Orticoni, who brought letters from him, and who came sheltered under the title of almoner to his majesty the King of the Two Sicilies. A Spanish galiot brought with him a party of missionaries, who spread themselves over the island, and succeeded in stirring up fresh enthusiasm. All the tribes assembled once more at Corte, to hear the letters read. "All received with satisfaction the commands of his majesty." Then they renewed their oaths of allegiance, and confirmed once more to him and to his descendants his title and throne. "To this end we make known to all whom it may concern, that we shall always observe an inviolable fidelity towards the royal person of Theodore the First ; and that we are resolved to live and die for him as his subjects, and never to acknowledge another sovereign than him. Once more we swear upon the holy Gospels in all points to keep the oath of fidelity in the name of the here-assembled people." This was all embodied in a manifesto, and was duly registered "in the grand chancery, and signed with the great seal of the kingdom."

Thus stimulated, these faithful Corsicans proceeded to take the field once more, and advanced with such spirit, that they quite drove Rivarola back, and shut him up closely in Bastia. The garrison, trying a sortie, only fell into an ambuscade, where they suffered more miserably still. Rivarola now ordered his advanced guards to inform the natives that the Republic was willing to ratify a treaty with them; that Theodore was "a mere vagabond now in gaol, from whom they could expect nothing." Upon this the whole army assembled threw themselves into a great circle, and, after keeping up for some time a deep silence, at last set up a general shout: "Long live our prince! Long live our parent! Long live Theodore I., King of Corsica!" They then made a general discharge, and, advancing close under the walls, cried out: "We will have no king but Theodore! We will never return under the government of the Genoese!" The winter was very severe —the ground covered with snow and ice, and provisions very scarce. Camping was therefore accompanied with sore privations, and the governors of the Corsicans thought this a fair opportunity for striving at some temporary accommodation. They made some proposals, which were received indeed, but only on the haughty condition of "the rebels" laying down their arms. This was as scornfully rejected, and both prepared for a new struggle. But the Corsicans were to know presently the reason of this confidence on the Genoese side. That Republic had determined on one last and desperate effort. They borrowed from the bank of St. George a sum of 500,000 crowns, and concluded negotiations with one of the great marts of Europe where fighting-men were to be hired —the congenial Swiss. They secured three regiments and twelve Grison companies, and got together a perfect fleet of ships and galleys. Thus prepared, as a preliminary *coup* they issued one of their characteristic proclamations, scandalous almost in its terms. It is evident that they had found out that to deal with Theodore required something more than contempt or ridicule. They degraded him now, calling him simply "the said Theodore," not acknowledging his baronship. The proclamation was full of fury and spite. It set out their "just indignation" against him, Costa, and Fozzari, "our subjects," who by the most "execrable" means have disturbed the whole country. "We therefore fix and offer a reward of 2000 golden genuines to anyone who will deliver up to us, *or kill*, any of the above-named men. This sum will be paid down by a tribunal of our state inquisition. We promise never to divulge the name of anyone who will have delivered up or killed any of the party."

This proclamation—which, it will be observed, was an invitation to anyone to pursue the unfortunate king over Europe and murder him, with an implied indemnity and certain reward, should he escape to their territories—was sure to have results; and the "sub-secretary," it was said, soon made an attempt on his life. His son also tells us that an attempt was made to poison him no less than three times. We may accept this statement; for Europe was overrun with bravoes and schemers ready for any attempt; and the state which could issue such a paper would not be slow to find direct agents to carry out its wishes. Theodore, of course, heard of their plans, and not unnaturally was said to have been a little scared. At all events, he kept himself concealed with great care, and for some months was quite lost sight of. But a letter from him soon arrived in the island, full of mysterious allusions. He knew all that was going on, he wrote, far off as he was. He heard the rumours of an attempt at accommodation; but he *was sure* they would not dream of *that*, with enemies who had " carried their insolence so far as to treat our faithful ministers as though they were common criminals, and to let their fury extend *even to our royal person.*" This last stroke is admirable. At the end he reminded them of his promise to stand by them and deliver them. From this skilful letter it was believed that he was still on the Italian coast; but he had got to Turin, where the Marquis d'Ormea discovered him, and he had to leave. From Turin he reached Paris, which he had to leave promptly, according to one account, because assassins, hired by the Genoese, had fired three shots at his carriage, which passed right through without touching him. According to another —possibly his own—he had interviews with Cardinal Fleury and Count de Polignac; according to a third, and a not improbable one, he received orders to quit the city in forty-eight hours. He gave out that he was going down to Marseilles to embark, but secretly went in the contrary direction, and took the road to Normandy. He went on board at Rouen, and reached the Hague—a suitable neutral spot, and a good *pied-à-terre* for intrigue—where he remained about three weeks. He stayed fifteen days with a Jew, Tellano; and then wrote to a Dutch friend, to hire a house for him outside Amsterdam. This was done; but when he arrived, it was found that the owner of the villa was absent with the key; so he had to put up for the night at a low inn outside the town called The Red Stag. While waiting, the news got wind. Perhaps the owner of the house betrayed him. The police came and arrested him for an old debt of 5000 florins. There were great curiosity and excitement in the town to see him; for at Amsterdam and the Hague adventurers were respected. He would have discharged this debt, and had a bill on a banker there for 30,000 florins, but who, on this, took the alarm, and said he must hear from the drawer of the bill first. On the news spreading, other creditors, even from England, poured in detainers. There were the old debts for arms and supplies. But so skilful and seductive a man was not to be thus checked. There were numbers of the merchants and traders whom he spoke with, and for whom he painted his great prospects with such skill and colouring, that he persuaded them to come forward and help, and be his security for the rest. There was a curious scene when he was summoned before the burgomaster and magistrates at the great town-hall to complete this arrangement. He declined to appear, unless with his sword and cane—privileges which were conceded. An immense crowd gathered round the building, and filled up the Kalver-straat while the stately Theodore pleaded his cause within. He put everything with such art, that he was allowed the security of friends being accepted for part, and his own for the rest. The excitement was so great, that he slipped away privately by the back of the building. Then he disappears for a time.

The French or Genoese police discovered a good deal about him and his connection, and the people with whom he kept up a correspondence. At Rome— where his son, "the Prince of Caprera," was being brought up by the Jesuits, and hearing lectures on astronomy from Lobkowitz—it was found he used the address of a nun at St. Dominico's; sometimes that of a count living by the Porto del Popolo, and a tourist whose house was near St. John Fiorentini.

It was found that these correspondents used great arts in sending off their despatches, having peculiar folds, and putting them into no less than four envelopes—one directed Signor Valentini; the second for a pretended Baron Stoss (or perhaps Stosch, Walpole's *commissionnaire*); the third for the English consul at Venice; and the last, containing the letter itself, for a Baron Stephen Romburg. Baron Romburg was Theodore himself. In various parts of the world he had secret allies and friends—a Capuchin who was busy with the philosopher's stone; at Naples, the Dutch consul, a princess, and an Irish officer; at Leghorn, the captain of the galleys.

All this is reliable; for Taussin, "the apothecary-major," received and used Theodore's intercepted letters, and despatched them to head-quarters. The Genoese obtained letters of his to a Parisian lady, who lived at a grocer's near the Grève, in the Rue de la Poterie; one was dated Nov. 2nd, 1737. He complained of not having heard from her in reply to his plans about the grand project, and bade her write under cover to Baron Drost, "Grand Commander of the Teutonic Order," at Cologne. He wished for news about the rumoured occupation of the French, which would only lead to blood, as "my people" would not break their oath. "Give me news of my dear nephew, and preserve yourself for your lover and king, Theodore." He spoke of his creating some four hundred new knights, whom he hoped to get over into the island. He was writing to the Dey, and had received 60,000 florins from Amsterdam. There was of course a good deal of vaunting here; and from his protestations of devotion it is not improbable that this lady made part of the expedition which later set out. The Genoese too were on the look-out for him; and a person was arrested at Savona who they thought was he.

The tide of successes of the brave islanders began to produce its effect. The Genoese party about Bastia and Ajaccio, who exactly corresponded to the "British party" in English colonies, began to waver. The population at various seaports which were awkwardly exposed to summary treatment began openly to join the safer, because the winning cause. Everything was prospering. The Genoese were at their wits' end. Their bands of assassins and enlarged galley-slaves had not profited them. A little more, and they felt their island would be lost to them. They again thought of applying for foreign aid. The former assistance of the Germans had been of a costly and unsatisfactory sort. They now cast about for a more powerful, and perhaps more unscrupulous, ally, and their eyes rested on the court of France, where Fleury the cardinal was reigning. The Marquis de Brignole was despatched to negotiate this unworthy bargain. Their proposals were listened to for many reasons.

For a long time the French had been watching with uneasiness and suspicion the strange little drama going on in Corsica, and they were not inclined to accept the story that Theodore was a puppet; they were, in fact, waiting to see the slightest symptom of interference from Spain, or any other quarter. But it may be suspected their real distrust was of England, whose fleets were cruising about, and who, for commercial purposes, was supposed to be greedily seeking an *entrepôt* in the Mediterranean, and thus destroy the flourishing trade of Marseilles and Toulon. Application was accordingly made to France, who listened eagerly. Soon the dockyards at Toulon rang with preparations, and soon—by the beginning of 1738—a French fleet of transports was getting ready to sail for Corsica.

This international jealousy might have much to do with it, as it was well known that there were many private patrons of the Corsicans in England, who were assisting them with a support that went beyond sympathy. It was said, too, that the Genoese were making great efforts to dispose of the island; and as France could not have tolerated such a transfer, she might have been constrained to compensate them for this opposition to the plain but substantial aid. On whatever grounds, the interference was monstrous and unjustifiable. It almost seemed as though the uprising of any country was a common danger for all despots, who, like neighbours at a fire, hurried from all sides to extinguish it. On the 12th of July the treaty was signed, and for the rest of the year troops and ships were being collected at Antibes.

News of this arrangement soon drifted over to the island, and, though misty and uncertain, filled the Corsicans with consternation. Indeed, the artful Genoese had proclamations printed, which they scattered over the island, announcing that the Emperor of Germany and the King of France were going to force them to submit. Consternation and doubt reigned everywhere, until news came over of the hum and note of military preparations at Antibes.

Nothing is more remarkable in this struggle than the moderation and propriety of every act of those who directed the unfortunate patriots. Paoli and Giafferi drew up a humble and touching petition to "the great king," in which was set out the whole case of the Corsicans—the old story of their oppression, and the still older story of the protection and assistance they had received from a whole series of kings of France. They added that they only took arms to preserve their property, honour, liberty, and life, no one of which the Genoese would allow them to keep. This was presented through Boerio, a native Corsican, who represented the Spanish court at Venice. No attention was paid to it, and the preparations went on slowly. The Genoese, meanwhile, either alarmed at the delay, or shrinking from the enormous expense of this new assistance—compared with which the hire of a few Swiss and German regiments seemed a trifle—began to think of accommodation; or the new commissary, Mari, who had replaced Rivarola, thought he might turn his *début* to some profit, and inaugurate his rule with a show of conciliation. They sent proposals of submission and accommodation, offering amnesty and indemnity, and the handsomest terms, and inviting a deputation. Such splendid yet suspicious offers made the Corsicans pause. One reason was said to have prompted this unusual fit of indulgence: their spies had reported that Theodore was on his way, and that his indefatigable agent, the Canon Orticoni, was at Nice, preparing to cross over. But very soon they received their answer.

A messenger now arrived, bearing letters from the king. These were from Amsterdam, where he still was, and bore date the 21st of October. They were full of spirit, hope, and encouragement. This wonderful being told his "dear ministers and loved subjects" that he heard of this report of the interference of the French king. He was confident that this was a mere *lying* story, and could console himself accordingly; but should it turn out so, he conjured them to consider carefully the course they should take. He could hardly think they would dream of tamely submitting to the old yoke; but if they were still inclined to maintain the struggle, he would stand by them, shed the last drop of his blood, and work night and day in their interest, and send them succour. This was no boasting; for at that moment he was wearing out the patience of the too speculative Amsterdam merchants. Presently arrived some officers who had seen Theodore, and they confirmed what he wrote. He would be there presently, and had all but made his arrangements. They hesitated, and not unnaturally. Two days after Christmas, a great assembly of all the tribes was gathered. These hopes and prospects were fairly canvassed, and it was gallantly resolved to have faith in their coming, and reject the recent advances.

The Genoese learned the rejection of the offer by the shouts and acclamations in the camp—the cries of " Long live Theodore, our king !"—and the discharge of muskets. They were infuriated. Threats and menaces were exchanged; and, one of their little Corsican privateers being captured, Mari, the commissary-general, had the commander hanged on the spot. This ferocity led to a savage and almost dramatic reprisal; for the Corsicans, accepting the challenge, selected forty out of two hundred prisoners in their possession, and hung them close under the walls of Bastia, with a very legible inscription over them, " *to avenge the death of Columbani.*" Notice was also given to the Genoese commissary that if he dared do the least violence to any of the sailors in his power, each death should be paid for by the sacrifice of fifteen Genoese lives. This wholesome menace had a salutary effect upon Mari, who became more temperate and merciful.

Inspired with a new enthusiasm, they rushed under the very walls of Bastia, and, in spite of the cannon and musketry, raised the same unwelcome cry at the very ears of the besieged; further assuring them they would have no other king or ruler, and that if he died, they would cling to his family. Thus fortune seemed again to favour the persevering Theodore, far away as he was.

It was now known for certain that the French were to come; nay, might be expected in a couple of weeks. Many a tartan and felucca, fluttering from one coast to the other, had reported how the transports were collecting at Antibes, and the soldiers were gathering, and nearly ready to go on board. Comte de Boissieux and the Marquis de Contades, experienced generals, were to command. This was, indeed, alarming; but the islanders were not daunted; and though there was a small and prudent party who thought it hopeless, with their raw levies, to oppose the disciplined troops of the most Christian king, they got ready for the struggle with an energy that surpassed everything they had done before. The whole country flew to arms. A levy of "a third" had been asked; but the enthusiasm was such, it took the proportion of "a half." Every man came with his eight days' provision; they fell naturally into cohorts and regiments; and all these forces were directed on Bastia, where it was expected the French were about to land. There were about forty thousand men under arms; and as it was calculated the French force would not exceed three or four thousand, their hopes of immediate success were reasonable. But some of the leaders knew well, that behind these few regiments was the whole army of France, and they encouraged this show of resistance in the hope of obtaining better terms.

In some alarm at finding these menacing preparations going on, the gallant people drew up an appeal to the public, in a very spirited strain. It ran:

"DECLARATION OF THE PEOPLE OF CORSICA.

"We confess, declare, and make known to the whole world our will and positive intention that by reason of the intolerable oppression which we have suffered for a long while, under the tyranny of the Genoese, we did some years ago choose Lord Theodore, Baron de Neuhoff, king of the island of Corsica; that to him we now submit, and do intend for ever hereafter to submit to his person—*whom God preserve!*—as also to his descendants; and moreover, that when we gave hostages and appointed certain deputies with full powers, we never had it in our mind or thought to retract the inviolate election of his said majesty, but only to demonstrate to all the crowned heads, particularly the King of France, the oppressions which we have suffered from the Genoese, and the validity of the election of our King Theodore; the most Christian king not having perhaps been informed of the misery of the people of Corsica; and to this end, that the said monarch, if he ever formed a design to seduce the kingdom of Corsica under the Genoese tyranny, might know that all the inhabitants had rather, with a salvo to their religion, deliver themselves into the hands of the Turks than the Genoese; the massacre of seven hundred of the principal Corsicans, which happened three years after the zealous resentment of Sampieso the Corsican, and this, too, after having obtained a guarantee of France, being still in their memory. For this reason we declare that the hostages and deputies have made an ill use of their commissions, contrary to their former election and submission, and that, by this solemn act, the nation does now and for ever confirm the election of the said Baron de Neuhoff, for King of Corsica, on the Isle of Caprera, with the annexes and dependencies, and that we do cheerfully and unanimously declare the said baron to be our lawful king and sovereign, and, in consequence, submit our persons, lives, and fortunes to the disposal of our King Theodore, whom God preserve!

"Done in the Great Square of the Convent of Tavegna, where we were all assembled, Friday, January 16th, in the year of grace 1739.

"Ratified, in the name of all the people, by us, who are appointed generals and commanders,

"HIACINTHO DE PAOLI.
"DASHEWIS GIAFFERI."

There was a busy scene at the little port of Antibes. The Nivernois, Auvergne, Sarre, Bassigni, and Du Roi regiments were huddled into the small town. The weather became violent, and they were kept some weeks before they could embark. The officers had no amusement but in waiting on their general or in dining together. Presently the *Flora*, a frigate that was to convey them, came round from Toulon. On the twenty-fifth they were all on board; but the winds were so unfavourable, that it was impossible to get out for a week more. Such was the embarking of an expedition in those remote days; and it offers a curious contrast to the vigour and promptitude of recent French expeditions, yet the object of which it so curiously resembled. But French thoughtfulness and management in points which they could control have always been the same; and the details seem to have been excellently planned. There were separate vessels for the oxen, there were chaplains and surgeons and workmen, and a staff of "post-office officials."

An "apothecary-major" of the army has told the whole story very graphically. For the first two or three days the sea was calm; then a dreadful storm arose, in which they were tossed about. The transport, like the true pattern of transport, was old and leaky; and it was not until the morning of the 6th of February that they began to make out the Corsican coasts, and were puzzled by the strange Genoese towers which dotted the shore. As the wind went down, and they coasted along, they noticed from the deck the lines of little villages all deserted, and charming country houses exquisitely situated. At eight o'clock on the morning of the 7th they were drifting on to the coast, and by evening were crowding into the narrow little port of Bastia. The supplies and *matériel* were disembarked here; but the commander and the soldiers had landed at San Fiorenzo, a little port on the west. Already the news was fluttering over the island, on the mainland, at Leghorn, and the intrigues were beginning. Salvini, a patriot priest at Leghorn, offered, under secrecy, to the French consul there, his services and influence with Orticoni, to bring over the Corsicans to submission; offers which were forwarded to the French general. To Orticoni he wrote also, and the letter was forwarded by the consul, and was put into the French commander's hands almost the very day of his arrival.

The canon's answer was most touching. He could hardly read that letter, he said, without weeping; the dreadful news that they were to be forced once more under the Genoese yoke had spread despair and consternation—the greater because they had been led to hope that France was about to take them to herself, and make them her subjects, as they had been centuries before. He had read Salvini's news to Paoli and Giafferi, and to a few more; but they had thought it better to keep this fatal news a secret. "In fact," said the canon, "the people think that the arrival of the French is to be the signal for our liberties; and they can scarcely contain the joy and the confidence they have in the French." He engaged to do all that he possibly could to bring round the assembly to everything that the French king could wish. "I will do this, and," he added, "not so much for the reason that we have nothing now to expect from King Theodore—in whom, as far as I was concerned, I never had any confidence—as for the veneration we have always entertained for the adorable and sacred name of the King of France." They had, besides, not strength enough to resist his power. As for the suggestion, that all the leaders should quit their country and retire to a foreign land, it was a suggestion of the wicked Genoese, for whose advantage it would be to have the people defenceless and deserted by their chiefs. He then proposed that they should put up their prayers at the foot of the altar, and pray for divine guidance.

Hyacinth Paoli was on his road to the assembly, when news of the French landing reached him. He wrote at once to the French consul at Bastia in the most humble strain, affecting also a warm love of the French nation, and saying that every man in the assembly was inclined towards them, and was certain that they had only come to deliver them. But he was much disquieted; he begged humbly that the commander would restrain his soldiers from any excesses, and would receive a deputation, and let them know what *were* the intentions of his majesty.

This Salvini appears to have been playing a double game. He had engaged himself to the French; yet as his means of support depended on such scanty allowances as came to him from the island—" the shipping of some oil" from a little *pied-à-terre*— he had to move cautiously. The popular voice was against the French. His letters were always being intercepted; once they fell into the hands of Rivarola, who had put the worst construction on them, and whose base motive he knew: jealousy lest Orticoni should have all the credit of the arrangement. A worse misfortune was, other letters being stopped by the French, in which the general read some uncomplimentary things of his nation. The excuses Salvini wrote were almost grovelling. He deprecated the wrath of his excellency—his sole aim was the advantage of France—and seems to have succeeded in dissipating these suspicions. This restless man was always in communication with his countrymen, still cautioning them against Rivarola, "who calumniates me everywhere he can, inventing the most monstrous impostures." Then he had to invent a cipher to guard against his letters being read; in short, the arrival of the French seemed to give notice of a beginning of the end; and many of the "patriots" were eager to be the first to make terms.

Bastia meanwhile exhibited a new and busy scene —its little harbour crowded with vessels, the mole covered with figures, and the French troops scattered through the narrow streets of the town, where they were billeted about. The general was made welcome by Mari at the château, who asked him to dine; but the officers had to submit to inconveniences. Food was scarce and dear; the townspeople were hostile. When a ball was given, the Corsicans stayed away, and only a few wives of the Genoese officials appeared. Everyone seemed to be *ennuyé*. The great convent of the Lazarists, noble and spacious, looking down on the sea, was given up to a battalion. The soldiers and officers found it very dull indeed; they were disgusted with everything. There were no squares, as in France. The *pavé* was rough even to Frenchmen's feet. They saw some things, too, that surprised them—the heads of the unfortunate rebels stuck on the wall, and an extraordinary picture at the gate, representing the execution of a rebel whom they had tried to hang, and whom they cut into pieces over a fire. They were amused at some very *bizarre* things—the ugly men; the women, who would not receive their addresses; the singular custom of gathering round the body of a deceased friend, and asking it, "Why did you die?" Some of the young drummer-boys of this date might long after have found themselves veterans landing in the Irish bay of Killala, on another hostile expedition, and have heard with wonder the wild natives keening over their dead, and putting exactly the same question. In a short time hatred and contempt mingled with *ennui*. They deemed the natives about them as half savages. By-and-by, a company of tenth-rate French comedians arrived, and a little theatre was opened, the officers subscribing for the season, and the men being admitted free. The whole, indeed, might be read as happening a few years ago in Algiers or Mexico; for French routine and manners seem to be always the same.

The French looked out wistfully across the cobalt Mediterranean. Now a great Genoese galley, carrying cannon, and worked by slaves and criminals, would come sweeping into the harbour, salute the fort with four guns, and be saluted with two. This boat brought pay for the Genoese soldiers. The criminals were bound to their oars, but the slaves were allowed to go on shore under guard; and the French saw with wonder these unhappy Turks and Algerines walking about, and offering their trifling wares—handkerchiefs, etc.—for sale.

The French general was a man of singular tact and firmness, and almost from the first day of his arrival had those useful qualities put to constant test. The Marquis Mari—the Genoese commissary, a man of address and good birth, but wedded to the old "ascendency"—at once began to press for severe measures. He, indeed, imagined, and not unnaturally, that the assistance which they had secured on such costly terms was to be bestowed in carrying out their policy, and that the French were to act as their deputies. Almost at their first interview the general undeceived him. He was courteous, but immovable. He had come as the friend of both parties, not to make war, but to bring about an accommodation. "Nothing," said the soldier to his friends, "could be more affable or noble than the bearing of the marquis. I am sure his sentiments are quite in harmony with, but certainly those of the Republic are quite opposed to, the object of our expedition." When asked how they ought to make a commencement, Mari eagerly proposed that they should make a raid, and carry off some of their cattle and crops, and that this would strike terror; that then a proclamation should be issued, ordering them to submit, surrender their chiefs, and give up their arms. He protested loudly against recognising the chiefs, or receiving any deputation, which would only be an encouragement. The discussion was warm; the general wrote home for instructions. Immediately, he was "served," in legal phrase, with a solemn protest against receiving these rebel leaders. Every step of this business does, indeed, suggest the blind and dull principles of the "ascendency" party, who seem to behave much the same in all countries.

Meanwhile, there were not wanting signs and tokens to encourage the natives. From various intercepted letters which were being secretly passed backwards and forwards, we can see what a network of intrigue was spread over the island. These all alluded to mysterious vessels seen off Naples or on the coast, to secret agents, of whose faith suspicion was entertained, but for whose honour the letter-writer could answer; and they showed the petty jealousies and rivalries of the Corsican leaders. The refugees or agents at Leghorn could pursue the safe *rôle* of exciting doubts and jealousies among their countrymen, hinting that Rivarola was engaged in the unworthy task of seducing over Corsicans, to sell them as troops to the King of Spain.

As Theodore's cause now seemed hopeless, these spies were loud in disparaging all that concerned him. Should the mysterious vessels ever appear, he had nothing to do with them. It was simply a freight of stores and merchandise which some speculative Dutch merchants had been induced by Theodore to consign to Leghorn, whence it had been reshipped by another agent, Bon Giorno, was to touch at Corsica, and be exchanged for oils, leather, and other products of the island. This was the artful view of the agents, who may have been gained over by the French or Genoese consuls at Leghorn; but the arrival of the ships themselves on the 5th of February, only a day or two before the French, was a dramatic refutation; and the ships cast anchor at Aleria, with Captain Sinabaldi, Theodore's brother-in-law, and young Costa on board. There were also some experienced officers of various nations, with 100 barrels of powder, arms, lead, and 500 pairs of shoes. They brought news of Theodore, whom they had left in Germany making preparations, and who was to arrive himself very soon. This assistance was indeed opportune; and though the crowd did not perceive the commercial nature of the arrangement, and that oil and other products were being taken in, a grand *Te Deum* was chanted, and hopes in the absent king revived. Nothing, indeed, could have been more skilfully arranged than these attempts to keep up and titillate, as it were, the flagging loyalty of popular favour; for, a few days later, came Colonna, a famous name in the island, known to be deep in Theodore's confidence, and a skilful captain. Another week, and no less than fourteen German officers, who had seen service, made their appearance from Leghorn in a small vessel, with some stores and munitions of war. They, too, brought news of Theodore, who was soon to be on his road. These strangers were received with delight; such instalments conveyed the idea of power and of something doing. They were of course no more than adventurers or soldiers of fortune looking for employment. One of them, Captain Drevitz, an officer of some reputation, placed at the head of a small band, very soon justified his good name by a brilliant little affair at Isola Rossa, which was taken by assault. The commander of the fort was recognised as a traitor and deserter, and was believed to have attempted Theodore's life. He was punished with barbarity—his tongue cut out, his hand chopped off—Colonna sternly telling the other prisoners, who were required to look on, that it was because he was a traitor that he was thus dealt with. But this was not all. A Genoese brig, laden with stores, and driven by the storm into Porto Vecchio, was immediately attacked, and the crew overpowered. She was speedily refitted, manned, and turned into a privateer.

By the middle of March the people had solemnly selected three deputies—Dr. Giafferi, Orticoni, and

Cugiuni, another priest—to whom was to be entrusted the delicate office of treating with the French general, and of being detained in an honourable captivity in his camp. Giafferi was away at Corte when he heard of the duty intended for him; but he set off at once, though the road was fraught with peril, and the people of that district not well affected to him. His letter is very simple and touching. He said he knew he ran the risk of assassination, that even already God had permitted him to be exposed to the risk of falling into no less than two ambuscades directed against his life. "Still I shall go. All my regret would be to die without glory or profit, or rather with the reputation of having been a traitor to one's country, to whose vengeance I had nearly fallen a victim. Reports, too, reach me of an intention to burn my house." This simple patriot had another little anxiety: he wished to lay aside his free and picturesque mountain dress, and have a suit of the regular French pattern made, in which to present himself, which had to be ordered for him in Bastia, the only convenient place in the island where such things could be made. This, with some other matters, prevented them setting out, and they had to apologise humbly to the haughty French. Heavy rains, which came down for days, detained them still more, so that it was not until the last week in March that they reached the camp. They arrived mounted, attended by a party of grenadiers who had been sent to meet them. Everyone came out to stare at them, and the *gandins* of the army could not contain their amusement or wit when they saw the palpable awkwardness of Giafferi in his new clothing. Still there was a haughty and composed air about him which tended to restrain their mirth. He did not seem more than eight-and-thirty. Orticoni, they remarked, was a man of about fifty, with a very *spirituelle* manner. They were lodged at the convent of the missionaries, at the expense of the general; were treated at first as guests, but soon found that they were in a sort of honourable captivity.

There is something touching in the picture of these brave and single-minded men—full of honour, good sense, and piety—thus passing through the ranks of the frivolous and scoffing French, who were not able to restrain their merriment at their simple and old-world air.

Then they began to have interviews with the general in his cabinet, which set in with neutral courtesies, but gradually grew warmer in tone as the deputies showed they were not prepared to accept an unconditional submission to Genoa. Soon growing impatient, the general addressed a blunt and somewhat haughty despatch to Paoli and the Corsican chiefs, in which he told them plainly they must dismiss every notion of arrangement save that of returning under the yoke of their old masters, and that they must trust to the king to make this settlement as favourable to them as possible; and he bade them, as it were, impress this cruel fact on the deputies who were with him, arguing with whom seemed to fatigue him. Almost the same day a letter reached him from the Leghorn abbé, proposing afresh that France should take the country to herself, or hand it over to the Holy See; or he was willing to get the chiefs to make a secret agreement to submit to the king's arrangements in everything, even to going back under the Genoese power, he of course assuring them that this was only to save appearances; whereas, publicly, they were to protest they would never submit to this last humiliation. He enclosed a despatch for the unsuspecting chiefs, strongly pressing on them the advisability of this course.

The Republic and her agents looked on with great uneasiness at these coquettings, and could scarcely dissemble their impatience. But the French general was master of the situation, and met this pressure with imperturbable phlegm, though he was presently to find himself no match for their secret and skilful artifices. The aim was to discompose the rather precarious relation between the natives and the French, already so delicately balanced that a very slight influence would convert it into hostility. It was an infinite tribute to the moderation and patience of the Corsicans that they could have restrained themselves so long. Very soon agents were busy in the more distant districts, scattering rumours of a general and enforced disarmament, sending abroad whispers that the leaders had settled all in their own interest. There were distracted counsels and much agitation; and finally, several mountaineers having carried off some cattle which belonged to the consul, an overt act was committed, which inflamed the French. The general affected to suppose that he had been played with all this time, and seemed to make the whole nation responsible for the disorderly act of a few.

Almost at the same time news came that a heavily-armed galley, carrying no less than eighteen guns and a hundred-and-twenty men, had put into Aleria. She brought powder, muskets, and general stores, and six more German officers. Again fresh news of the wonderful Theodore! This was *his* ship and armament; more aid was on its way! In a few days two vessels were scouring the coast—a tiny fleet of privateers, with the Corsican flag flying—green and yellow, and the inscription: "*In te, Domine, speravi.*"

Far away, and perhaps unconscious of what was going on, Theodore pursued his unwearying efforts. Now, on the 8th April, arrived another lieutenant of reputation—Frediani—with fresh supplies, and a letter of encouragement and promise to his "illustrious ministers of state and marshals-general." He bade them assure the faithful people that he had not abandoned them. His absence was solely owing to a visit to his own friends and relations, whom his many letters had never reached. For the love of Heaven let them not be dismayed by the menaces of the Genoese or the cunning of the French—all would be well. Let them only continue this devotion "to our royal person," and let them bind the people by a solemn oath never to submit themselves to the domination of the Genoese. His marriage was about to take place, and that alliance would strengthen the power he had to help them. In a few weeks he would be on his way; they would see him, "their king and father," who was determined to conquer or die. This spirit-stirring document came from Eybach, and was dated the 19th February; so that he could hardly have received certain news of the arrival of the French. Frediani brought more powder and munitions of war.

The chiefs were sorely embarrassed. They saw the danger of any trifling with the French. They had themselves lost faith in Theodore, or at least saw that it was fatal to encourage him in presence of a French army; and after much anxious thought, determined to suppress this proclamation. But his envoy refused to be a party to this concealment, and openly published its contents. Again the people were excited, the spirit of the old romance became alive, and an agitation that bade defiance to all moderate counsels began to spread; the cry now was, to break off all negotiation, and expect the coming of their king. Rumour, too, was heard of another Dutch vessel seen off Gaeta; and a few weeks later another strange barque succeeded in putting into the lucky port of Aleria, having successfully eluded the vigilance of the French galleys which were cruising round the coast. The people crowded to the beach, and found that she brought no less than thirty-two bronze cannon, three hundred barrels of powder, with lead, and other munitions of war, in charge of Baron Drost, Theodore's nephew, a brave and spirited young man. He addressed them, and told them that Theodore was at last on his way, with vast succour—"frigates of war, arms, supplies of every kind," he told them. The *éclat* of this arrival was so brilliant, that the crowd did not consider that the strange vessel was taking on board a return cargo of oil, coral, wool, honey, and such things. The two-and-thirty bronze cannon overpowered all reflection; and it was said that the French general was so alarmed at this substantial shape of aid, that he had word privately sent to Theodore that the French were really thinking of acknowledging him, but that the presence of the Baron would destroy all chance of accommodation. The truth is found in a very humble letter which Paoli and his friends sent at once to Bastia, assuring his excellency that they adopted his idea of getting this "pretended baron" out of the kingdom, and that they had sent people to manage the affair skilfully. In any case, they did not think the stranger had power to cause any trouble, for they had carefully warned the people against him. These poor chiefs were indeed trembling under the responsibility that had been cast upon them, held accountable, as they were, both by their own followers and the imperious strangers. They seemed to have succeeded, probably by holding out to Drost some hope that his uncle would be considered; and he retired to Leghorn to wait events. He had not to wait very long.

The Amsterdam merchants were then known as among the most speculative in Europe—insuring vessels, and curiously mingling the mysteries of the cabala with their commercial dealings. It was the richest town in Europe; everyone—in the words of a writer of the last century—"tormenting" body and soul, not to enjoy money, but in the hope of dying rich. Ships clustered here, and their magazines were bursting with all the stores and treasures of the world. Their *spécialité*, too, was the *matériel* of war, "many nations sending to them to buy arms, buff coats, belts, etc.; and there are even shopkeepers here who are said to be able to deliver arms for four or five thousand men, at a cheaper rate than they can be purchased anywhere else." Casanova gives a picture of these wealthy traders, who lived luxuriously, and not after the manner of the conventional type of the burly burgomaster. The Hague, close by, supplied a crowd of adventurers, to whom this abundance of wealth was a temptation.

Here, in this congenial atmosphere, appeared the ardent Theodore. His persuasive tongue was never weary of describing to the merchants his golden prospects; it never rested in painting the certainty of success, if he was only properly supported. These seductive pictures at last had their effect; and he induced the three great houses of Boom, Trouchain, and Neuville to consider his project. These enterprising traders actually formed themselves into a great company, on the model of the large Indian societies. They obtained either the connivance or actual support of the Government, and bound Theodore down, in case of success, to special advantages to be accorded to Dutch trade. These surprising speculators proceeded to fit out a regular squadron, heavily armed, and furnished it with supplies of every conceivable kind. The merchandise was their own venture, but the warlike stores they risked with Theodore: 6000 muskets and bayonets, 2000 pairs of pistols, 24,000 pounds of powder for cannon, 100,000 pounds of finer powder, 200,000 pounds of lead, 2000 grenades, 1000 bombs, 50 drums, 50 standards; musical instruments;

6000 pairs of shoes; canvas for 1000 tents, and 1000 beds; stores of all kinds. There were, besides, twelve 24-pounders, three culverins, and twelve 12-pounders; with 8000*l*. or 9000*l*. Twenty-four chests were put on board, containing the private effects of the king, and a perfect treasury of 500,000 livres, to pay the troops, and help in founding commercial establishments. Such was the miscellany poured forth by the rich magazines of Amsterdam for this splendid adventure. We may admire this wonderful Theodore —the magician who conjured up this show—as he sailed away triumphantly out of the Amstel with this royal squadron.

They did not seem to have dreamed of this at Bastia. The negotiations were dragging on. As a French galley would come in, commanded by Captain Villeneuve, the general would go on board and dine, and be recreated with cheerful music. But the soldiers were growing more disgusted with the place, and more savage against the people. The officers wrote home, complaining that "the ladies were kept secluded, and the men were jealous." The chiefs had sent in their famous and admirably-drawn appeal to Cardinal Fleury, who replied with plain but merciful logic, telling them that they must resign themselves; that they had belonged to the Genoese, and must go back to them. De Boissieux, growing impatient, and perhaps pressed from home, was in no temporising mood, and at last demanded hostages for the good behaviour of the people, and who were to be sent to Paris. They submitted cheerfully even to this degradation, were put on board the galleys, and taken to France.

But now, at the end of August, a courier arrived at Bastia with a despatch from the Marquis Mari, the Genoese consul at Cagliari in Sardinia, containing some startling news. At noon, on the 14th of August, a large Dutch vessel of war, carrying sixty guns, with two Dutch merchant vessels, came into the harbour, and saluted the town with fifteen guns. They said they had come from Algiers and Malaga, and were now bound for Leghorn. Some of the crew having gone ashore, a sailor was heard to say carelessly that they had cannon and stores on board which they were to leave at Corsica; that they wanted provisions, and that they wished to avoid the French galleys which were on the coast. The consul was speculating over these rumours, when, on the following morning, another Dutch vessel came in, carrying fifty guns, crowded with men, and, having saluted the other vessels, sent off a boat to them. On this the consul sent to the viceroy, who despatched a German major, who could speak Dutch, to offer his compliments. This was a mere pretext; but he ascertained nothing. Other officers, who wished to see the ships, were refused admission. Some of the sailors who were wandering about were then arrested by the police, and questioned;

but nothing could be got out of them. The next day the officers came on shore, and paid a visit of compliment to the viceroy. With all this information the courier was at once despatched. It was picturesque enough, but alarming too.

Other couriers followed on his heels, with fresh details from the French consul Paget, and the viceroy himself. The new features were, that the two merchant-vessels had sailed out, but still kept in the offing; and that, while one of the war-vessels held communication with the shore, the other jealously refused admission to everyone, and allowed no one to leave it. The captain was said to be sick below, and no one could see him. On the deck of this secluded frigate soldiers could be made out, and the glitter of trumpets and horns could be seen; farther, the smaller vessels were found not to be so much merchantmen as small galiots, carrying from ten to twelve guns each. The whole was most suspicious: they had taken down their sails, and seemed to have no intention of moving; more suspicious still was the saluting of the first vessel by the second, as though there was someone of distinction on board; their stories to the officers of health and of the port seemed to be all false; in short, the general conviction was that King Theodore was on board; and they appeared to be waiting for despatches. This is one of the many dramatic pictures in the adventurer's life: the little capital all on the *qui vive;* the great vessels reposing tranquilly, after the long voyage, in the pretty Sardinian bay; the mystery; the glimpses of the soldiers on the deck; the inquisitive boats gliding round; and Theodore himself on board, keeping close, and waiting for news with anxiety at his heart.

It had been a long voyage. The wary Dutch merchants, whose capital of "five millions" was thus embarked, had placed it all in the hands of a sort of supercargo, or chief captain, with strict instructions that he was to deliver nothing without payment, which was to be made at Alicante and Malaga. This was the Genoese story; which seemed highly improbable, unless they put faith in the dim vision of support from Spain. One vessel was called the *Frakel,* and was commanded by one Railman; another was under Captain Wiemanbaum, who proved to be a thorough scoundrel. In due course they touched at the two places; but the persuasive Theodore beguiled the captain with excuses, and induced him to continue the voyage. Another story ran, that Theodore's vessel had stopped at Algiers to try what could be done to tempt the Bey again; and his arrival at Cagliari seems to support this. They were about two months on the voyage. A young Dutch lad, who had been on board the *Frakel,* fell into the hands of the French. He was dull, or difficult to understand because of his language; but his account has an air of dramatic mystery too. His name was Kelmor, and he was servant to a passenger, who, though a sailor by profession, was of good family, very rich, and whose name was Sniden Terxel. They made the island of Sardinia, where he had seen a large and beautiful town the name of which he could not recall, and where they had been saluted with cannon. While they were lying there, Theodore had come from the other vessel, accompanied by a colonel, four or five officers, and four servants; there were two small craft filled with those in his retinue, which was said to reach fifty—the old list of a secretary, a commissary, a *maître d'hôtel*, two surgeons, two cooks, two squires, four chasseurs, and the rest. There was a magnificence in all this; but the true adventurer does everything with this sumptuous show. And his brother adventurer, Casanova, when he set up his establishment at Paris, had his hotel, and lackeys, and secretaries, and cooks, and carriages. All these, the Genoese said, were the very scum of the earth, composed of Italians, French, Germans, of all degrees.

Theodore had to wait a long time while despatches were passing and repassing. The King of Sicily was induced to send orders to the viceroy to seize Theodore; but the viceroy judged this too imprudent a step, and so the Dutch lay there tranquilly waiting. One morning the three larger vessels made sail out of the port; the others, "the four Pinquas," followed later. On this occasion he determined to land in the south, passed by the Straits of Bonifaccio, when he encountered a storm, or gave out that he had. He passed by the bay of Porto Vecchio, and finally, on the 13th September, dropped anchor off Soraco, a little higher up. To his disappointment, he found that they would not receive him at Porto Vecchio, and he had to go on; this was a shock. The people crowded to the shore; but they showed more curiosity than loyalty. The worst was, the chiefs held aloof, and tried to make the people follow their exmple. They watched and wondered, but Theodore did not appear; he, however, sent a letter to them. He told them that the storm had scattered his fleet, and that he had only three ships; but that the rest would arrive presently. "You know my love for you," he went on; "see what I have done. Do you now keep your pledges, as I have done mine. But my fixed resolution is not to disembark from the deck of this vessel until you let me know whether you still recognise me as your king. If you are not in the same mind—which I cannot bring myself to believe—then I must abandon you to your enemies; and you will repent your want of faith, while I shall go and end my days happily in some new shape of life." This adroit address had good effect. The crowds increased; curiosity and impatience, and indeed their old impulsive loyalty stimulated them, and very soon rose up the old cry, "Long live Theodore our king!"

He wrote in quite another tone to a village priest, and the letter shows his natural anger and disappointment. He found, he said, that the inhabitants of Porto Vecchio still persisted in favouring the enemy, and refused to give him up the fort at the entrance of the harbour. He wished them to be persuaded to be loyal; he would forgive them all that had passed, and would treat them as faithful subjects; but they must submit at once, or he would take prompt measures to punish and chastise them; they must send him four hostages.

To his old friend Matras, whom he had created a marquis on his first landing, he wrote five or six days later. But things had mended then, and looked brighter. "Thanks unto God, *my dear marquis*, I am arrived safe, in spite of all persecutions and treacheries. Come speedily to join me, with all our faithful friends. I wait for you, and will welcome you with open arms. Be sure to bring horses with you for me and for my suite; besides about two hundred beasts of burden for us and for our baggage. Be of good heart. In a few days we shall see the other vessels which the storm has scattered. Remember me to madam the marchioness. Bring all you can with you, *well armed*, and about two hundred who have no arms. I will supply them gratis, and with powder, ball, etc.; but as for stuffs, iron, leather, linen, etc., everyone must buy or exchange what he wants." This was significant. Poor Theodore! of all the rich stores of 24-pounders, the thousands of muskets, &c., he could dispose of only a pitiful two hundred. He then adds: "As the people seem all divided and distracted, you must order them, in my name, to bring in here plenty of wine, grain, and cattle."

The Genoese about there were in mortal terror. A Captain Ettori spurred away from Porto Vecchio to the commissary at Bonifaccio with the news, and with Theodore's letter, which the village priest had given up. The commissary was going to send on the letter to Bastia, but the captain and another (Captain Doria) fell into a tremor, and said they would kill themselves if it was not given back to them, as, if the fort was taken by assault by Theodore, they would be asked for it. The commissary had to yield to these cravens, and sent off a galley with the news to Bastia. The unlucky Theodore had chosen for landing-place an awkward district which was in the power of his enemies; and the people were afraid.

At last the eventful day of his long-expected coming arrived. He landed. It was another triumph. They received him with transport, and with frequent discharges of musketry—the usual rustic shape of congratulation. Then he began to disembark the stores. He engaged local craft in his service, and one of the "patrons" subsequently gave him an agreement which has a ludicrous pomp about it.*

But almost at once came a check. After six barrels of powder and a few cases of muskets had been landed, the unloading was suspended. We learn that the supercargo, faithful to his trust, declined to furnish any more, save on the terms of the directions he had received. There was no money to buy them, and no produce to exchange for them. This official must have been that sailor who was rich and of good birth. Everything was at a standstill; but an unexpected event was to show the poor adventurer that the tenure of his life was nearly as precarious as that of his fortunes, and that a double series of dangers menaced him. While these matters were in train he used to sleep on board one of his vessels. One night he awoke with a curious presentiment that he was about to be burnt alive. He went to sleep again, and was awoke by the same vivid impression. He roused his servants, and taking three of them with him, went to look for the captain, Wiemanbaum, whom he found

* The name of the boat was the *Jesus Maria Joseph and the Souls in Purgatory;* and the agreement was signed: "In the kingdom of Corsica; for the service of his majesty King Theodore the First, for such time as shall be agreeable to his majesty." It was signed by his majesty on the one part, "Theodore."

actually busy in preparing to fire the powder-magazine. The man fell at his feet and confessed it all; and on the next day he told the people of this marvellous escape; and it was then discovered that it had been the night of the feast of St. Julia, the patroness of the island. With so devout and excitable a race this had a prodigious effect. Theodore sentenced the guilty conspirator—who was said to have been bribed by the Genoese—to be burned alive, but graciously commuted the sentence into hanging at the yardarm of his own vessel, which example was duly made. But there is another version of this business scarcely so romantic. This captain was said to have been supercargo, and was showing himself impracticable, declining to disobey his instructions and allow the stores to be landed. Mr. Boswell heard in the island that Theodore had put him to death; and it did seem probable that he had invented this plot as an excuse for getting rid of a troublesome impediment. His situation was indeed hopeless, and might tempt a desperate man to such an expedient. But subsequent proceedings show that he had the real supercargo arrested at Naples; and such violence is quite out of keeping with Theodore's character and policy, for it could scarcely have helped him. The captain would have been supported by his other captains. The story is indeed exceedingly doubtful; for when we think of the class of persons who surrounded him, and that there was at that moment the splendid and tempting reward offered by the Genoese to anyone who should destroy him, nothing is more likely than that a fresh attempt should have been made on his life. Nothing, too, is more likely than that such a colour should have been given to the story by his enemies. We shall see presently that he took a less severe mode of punishing the uncomplying captain.

At Bastia, meanwhile, the French general became seriously alarmed, and wrote over to France for reinforcements. At once he assumed an insolent and haughty tone, and seemed inclined to hold the deputies in his power, and the absent chiefs accountable. He specially accused Paoli of being faithless; a charge that wounded that brave patriot, and who wrote to justify himself. Ten days after Theodore's arrival, Paoli flew to Corte, to try and stop the growing excitement, and to show the chiefs "the certain peril and terrible precipices" at the edge of which they were standing. He called a little assembly, and set the danger before them; but the crowd gathered round, and told him roughly that the French had treated them dishonourably and faithlessly, and that they would avail themselves of this welcome assistance. He frankly told them at Bastia that he could not make head against this movement without danger to his life; at the same time he would not lose sight of them, but do all he could to moderate and keep them within bounds. He was indeed, he said, between Scylla and Charybdis. "I know not on which of these two rocks my shipwreck is to take place, but am ready to submit to whatever lot Heaven sends me." Another might have been reasonably suspected; but this man was truly noble and single-hearted, and he had all through been consistent. He only cared for what he considered the real interest of his countrymen, and would save them from the cruel perils into which this fatal and dazzling temptation would hurry them.

On the 22nd the general sent out his proclamation in the sternest terms, warning the people "to take care what they were going to do." The clemency of the king, his master, had been very great; but his indignation would be no less if he heard of their giving any countenance to "this adventurer." Some had dared to encourage him; let them beware. And it was a fresh proof of his majesty's indulgence to give them all this notice. Later he issued another, in still stronger and hostile terms, telling them they would forfeit all advantages of the treaty. Any house receiving "the person calling himself Theodore" would be razed to the ground, and the owners treated as traitors. This was plain-speaking; it was followed up by action as prompt. The Marquis de Sabran, in command of the frigate *Flora* and another vessel, was sent to cruise on the western coast, coming down towards Ajaccio. Meantime the Genoese galleys had been scouring the coast, and at five one morning made out four vessels at anchor in the bay of Sagona. These were overhauled; and the account they gave was that they had no cargo, that their commanders were away with King Theodore, and that they had his orders to wait until their captains returned. An armed pinnace was placed to watch them, and cut off communication with the shore. The vessels were seized and sent off to Bastia, and the captain of the galleys reported minutely to his Genoese principal how the Frenchman had saluted him with five guns, and how he had saluted the Frenchman. They had heard from the peasants about Sagona that some thirty persons had landed there, among whom were two or three women, and had applied for shelter at a convent, but had been refused admittance. They had eventually got in through the church, and the next day had been taken by a friendly canon to Guagno, his own village. These men, it was noticed, were dressed up in a strange blue uniform, and, it was discovered later, were in the service of the Elector of Cologne.

Soon the *Flora* and her consort came into the bay; and at this apparition, one of the Italian barques slipped its cable and proceeded to steal out to sea. The frigate fired three cannon-shot, which at once stopped its flight and brought it to, when it was boarded by the king's officers, and searched. It was found to be laden with arms and ammunition of all kinds ; chests carefully sealed up, with others containing a quantity of green uniforms braided with yellow, intended for the unlucky Theodore's soldiers ; also a quantity of papers in French, German, and Dutch, and some patents, made out in the latter language. Theodore was now at his wits' end. The other captains stood firm. Perhaps the attitude of the chiefs was too hostile for him to trust himself among them ; or news had come that the negotiations had been concluded, and that an arrangement had at last been settled by the King of France with the Genoese, which the French general now announced was already in his hands, and of a most favourable sort, but which he threatened to withdraw. The uncertainty as to its terms would have had a powerful effect. Some thought Theodore would not have wished to play this rather costly stake, and would have preferred to wait until the game took a more favourable turn. A false step now, and he could never hope for so splendid an equipment again. But the adventurer can never reckon on the chance of being allowed to sit down to another game ; and a later step of his shows that he was still eager to stake all there and then.

Seeing no issue, and finding his hopes every day growing fainter and fainter, at last Theodore had to yield, to endure the humiliation of going on board and sailing away. He had influence enough to persuade the captains to make for Naples, where the three mysterious Dutch vessels dropped anchor in the bay; and where Theodore, as soon as he touched the shore, went to have an interview with the Dutch consul. The clever adventurer was not defeated yet; he had one more card to play; and the astonished captain presently found himself in an Italian gaol, having been arrested at the instance of his consul. The ground of this detention was that he had refused to fulfil his contract with Theodore, in not landing the stores and remaining off Corsica. He protested the reason was the certain danger of his ships being captured. It actually turned out that this Dutch consul was an old and eager partisan of Theodore's, and he had determined to detain the captain in prison until he had consented to return to Corsica, and give security for the performance of his duty. The adventurer of the last century had friends and acquaintances all over the world. He made them in every town; and useful auxiliaries thus often turned up in the most unexpected manner, even after long years of interval. Thus at *tables d'hôte*, and hotels in the Exchange at Amsterdam, or in the Place of Saint Mark, the versatile Casanova was often "intrigued" by a face that seemed familiar, and which proved to be that of some old friend, now destined to be of service.

The French ambassador picked up all he could, which was not much; for Theodore, or "the person who was given out as such," kept himself concealed, and no one could get to see him. The marquis hinted at some other proceedings of his own, but would not be more explicit, "as they had no cipher" arranged. Everyone seemed to think Theodore was waiting to appear in Corsica again, and it was supposed would contrive to get the stores and merchandise into Italian vessels, and have done with the Dutch ships. The next news was that he had disappeared from Naples; and the French ambassador was alarmed by an express from the Leghorn consul, that Theodore was believed to be on his way to Corsica again, but that the Dutch captain would not yield. So powerful a person as the Marquis de Pussieux, ambassador of his most Christian king at the court of Naples, was not to be opposed by a mere Dutch consul; and after a few weeks' intriguing and "protesting," the tables were turned, and Theodore was arrested and imprisoned at Gaeta. Then he disappears for a season. How long he stayed there, or how he was enlarged, we know not. To such a man it would have been no difficult task to set himself free. There, however, this act ends.

It was a pity he had not come a few weeks later, when the gallant people, now at last in possession of the terms offered to them, had boldly challenged both

French and Genoese, and in their first battle had inflicted a humiliating defeat on the soldiers of the most Christian king, cut them to pieces, and forced them to carry on a humiliating guerilla war. The French general, worn out with a disease which he had brought with him to the island, and with mortifications and vexations, sent for the deputies to his deathbed, and there unreasonably accused them of treachery and dishonour. This was not the irritation of a dying man; for a decree banished them from their native land. A new commander, the Marquis de Maillebois, arrived from France; and then the struggle went on again.

Notwithstanding failure and absence, the feeling of the people was with the absent Theodore; and when they came to choose their chiefs, they selected only those who were favourable to him. He still sent them his despatches, full of encouragement and promises, fixing a time when he would certainly arrive—"*by the twentieth of May* at furthest."

There were other signs of him. A gay stranger presently arrived, and proved to be Theodore's nephew Frederick. He was received rather roughly at first, and stripped of everything he had, even to his shirt, the people threatening to hold him responsible for the due arrival of his uncle: this, at least, was written home by a French officer. But now came proof of Theodore's intentions—a ship with stores and supplies. There was a complete reaction. The nephew was associated with the other chiefs, was made "a field-marshal," and proved himself a valuable ally, a spirited and dashing leader, who gave the French a world of trouble. When the other chiefs were obliged to make terms, he kept on the struggle, and was the last to submit. A regular assembly was called. It was solemnly resolved to continue their allegiance to the man who was so constant to them.

Still, the contest at last became hopeless. More French troops were poured in; and Paoli and the other chiefs, despairing of success, came to terms, and were forced to leave their country. Theodore's nephew obtained honourable terms on capitulating, and was also allowed to withdraw. The island was thus composed to a temporary tranquillity; and all seemed at last over for Theodore.

He had gone straight to London, and there must have found some sympathisers to help him substantially. He seems to have got into high society; not very difficult for a man of such address and so remarkable. It was reported in gossip that he showed a great admiration for Lady Stanhope. It was said also that he had made a connection with Lord Carteret.

A class of persons, always ready to help in such a cause, enabled him to make some sign on the Corsican coast, and to keep himself in the mind of those he might call his people. But he could not do much.

Three or four years passed away, and a grand European war was drawing on. Spain, France, the "Empress-Queen," were all being drawn in; a sort of "free fight" was imminent, and the petrels of blood and confusion were fluttering in the air. Here was an opportunity. England would be against France; and there were many in rich England as interested in Corsica, and as disinclined "to empty their heads of the subject," as Mr. Boswell was. England had a fleet, and where could that fleet harass and destroy the French so effectually as in Corsica? As a matter of course, then, Theodore again appears in London, where he goes about beseeching and appealing to political and private people. Again he prevailed. Funds were found; he bought arms and stores, and obtained even a passage on board a king's man-of-war, commanded by Captain Barclay, to Leghorn. They touched at Lisbon, and at Villafranca; and at last he was at Leghorn once more, on the 7th of January, 1743. There he found a crowd of Corsicans whom he knew, either exiles or reduced in purse. There, too, and at Florence, he met Walpole's Sir Horace Mann, whom he knew well, but on whom he could make no impression.

Walpole heartily commended his friend for his caution; but Theodore was not daunted. General

Breitewitz was then administering Florence in the name of Maria Theresa; and Theodore applied to him; painted in brilliant colours the prospects of the situation—which, indeed, seemed certain enough—the trade, the alliance, and not improbably the ultimate possession of Corsica. No one, it was admitted, had so persuasive a tongue as that "comely, middle-sized man, very reserved, and affecting much dignity." And he quite persuaded the governor-general, who promised to consult his court. He did all he could, but was not warmly received; and Theodore was put off with evasive answers. This was disheartening; but who so full of fresh chances as the adventurer? In a few days the British squadron, under Admiral Matthews, comes into Leghorn. Nothing could have been more apropos. Theodore is presently with the admiral—a true specimen of the British captain of those times—and was pressing his schemes upon him. He explained his plans in the old gorgeous colours; and the admiral, who was known to have a thorough contempt for all foreign and "Romish" things, and whose sailors had pillaged a church and hung a crucifix round a monkey's neck, no doubt was willing to annoy a Republic which still boasted an Inquisition. He seems to have listened to the seductive Theodore; took him and his stores on board the *Vengeance*, and with the other vessels, the

Salisbury and the *Princess*, made sail for Corsica. Again it must be repeated: "Wonderful Theodore, whom nothing could dispirit!"

The squadron arrived off Isola Rossa on the 30th of January, 1743. Theodore went on shore as of old. Down flocked the people; once more were heard the cries of "Long live our king!" The arms and stores were distributed, and there were universal joy and enthusiasm. Theodore, carried away by his reception, was betrayed into an injudicious step, the issuing of a proclamation—one of his weaknesses—conceived in a most injudicious spirit. "Thanks be to God," he said, "he was once more able to meet his faithful subjects, after all the sufferings and persecution he had undergone, and all the efforts made to hinder his return." He conceded a general pardon, with exceptions. He pointed the moral of the past. "The weakness of some, the treachery of others, the want of union among the chiefs—these were the real causes of all our disasters, at the very moment that I brought you the means of driving out the Genoese. But let it be a lesson. Let experience warn you. Rally round me, and I will devote my life to your happiness."

This curious document seems to belong to the reign of an *opera-bouffe* monarch, and it is worth while setting it out at greater length. It gives fatal evidence of the precariousness of his position.

"MANIFESTO.

"THEODORUS THE FIRST, by the grace of God, King of Corsica, and Grand Master of the Military Order of Redemption.

"Having, thanks to Providence, the consolation, so ardently desired, of finding ourselves in the midst of our faithful subjects in our kingdom, *malgré* the many losses, treasons, persecutions, we have suffered, and in spite of the methods everywhere pursued to dissuade, interrupt, or even totally prevent our return with the necessary succour; infamous and monstrous methods, into which entered not only our enemy and their instruments, but also the perjured and perfidious chiefs, who, from particular views, for diabolical ends, and betrayed by chimerical ideas, have most unworthily deserted us, and abandoned our kingdom and faithful subjects to the lawless tyranny of the Genoese, and had, further, the execrable temerity to employ all sorts of frauds in order to seduce a great number of their simple and imprudent countrymen, and engage them shamefully to turn their backs on their unhappy country in her greatest distress, and to serve as allies of the Genoese:

"Having, on the other hand, full confidence, and even infallible certainty, that all our subjects, convinced by the mischief they have suffered, and the excessive grievances they have felt during our absence, have thoroughly apprehended the methods used to impose on them; that they have called to mind the solemn and inviolable oath of obedience and fidelity which they have sworn to us, and in consequence thereof must know themselves obliged by God and man to submit themselves to our royal will, and to labour, with a sincere zeal and incorruptible fidelity, to procure the welfare of us, and that of our kingdom:

"In testimony, therefore, of our royal and national clemency, we grant to all our subjects, by these presents, a general pardon for whatever they have done, contrary to their oath of allegiance, injurious to our royal right, or against the welfare of our kingdom; excluding, however, after mature deliberation, and declaring for ever excluded from this, our most gracious pardon, the infamous assassins of our late most dear General Count Fabiani, of happy memory, *as also the perjured felons and traitors, Hyacinth de Paoli; the Canon Erasmus Orticoni; the Priest Gregory Salvini;* declaring them not only banished for ever out of our kingdom, but commanding also that all their effects, of whatever kind, be confiscated, in order to their being divided, by way of recompense, among the widows and children of our faithful subjects who have sacrificed their lives with so much zeal, for the defence of our sovereign rights, and of their dear country.

"It being further our will and pleasure that this

our declaration and commandment should serve as a definitive sentence, and have all the force and vigour necessary against the said perfidious enemies of the commonwealth, to cover them with shame, and to stamp eternal infamy on their names, we this day, once for all, and definitely, declare them guilty of high treason, and as traitors condemn them to the most ignominious death, in case they have the temerity to set foot again in our kingdom; and, to strengthen further our most just sentence, we forbid, under pain of death, without remission, and confiscation of all their estates, all and every of our subjects of what sex, rank, or condition soever they be, to have any correspondence whatsoever, direct or indirect, with the said felons, Hyacinth de Paoli, Erasmus Orticoni, and Gregory Salvini, or with any other their adherents, by whose artifices they have been induced to abandon our royal service and their country in its greatest distress, and this to the no small benefit of our enemies, the Genoese; to receive the pay of France, Spain, and Naples; to all there, however, as persons subpœnaed and betrayed, we of special grace grant our pardon, but upon this precise condition, and not otherwise, that they return to our obedience and into our kingdom, and this within the time and space peremptorily of six weeks for such as are in Italy, in either Spanish or Neapolitan services; and in the space of three months for such as are entirely in France or Spain; and in case they shall not return within that time, we will and ordain definitely, and once for all, that they be and remain perpetually banished out of our kingdom, and their goods confiscated."

He then proceeds in grandiloquent terms to declare that it was "our unalterable resolution" to support the just rights of Her Majesty the Queen of Hungary and Bohemia; also to allow any of her subjects in the service of the Grand-Dukes of Tuscany to continue in that service; and engages to aid those sovereigns to the best of his ability. As for such of his subjects as were in the service of the Pope, or the State of Venice, he allowed the former one month, the latter three months' grace before returning. As for those who were in the Genoese service, if they did not instantly return, they would be treated as banished persons, and their goods confiscated.

"In consequence of our gracious condescension, and of our general pardon, we steadfastly hope that all our faithful subjects will concur with us in the general enterprise of uniting and reassembling all such as are disposed to live exiled from our country; and we direct this document to be published in all the *pieves;* for such is our royal pleasure. To this end we have affixed it with our hand and sealed it with our broad seal.

"Given at Bologna, in Santa Reparata, January 30th, 1743, and in the seventh year of our reign, which God render happy and exalted."

Having seen the chiefs and told them his plans, and how he would soon return, having debarked a considerable number of arms, with ammunition, shoes, hats, watch-coats, and other stores, he retired on board his ship, but continued some time on the coast to see how his orders were obeyed. He had the satisfaction to hear of the surrender of Corte, and then sailed for Tuscany.

As he was on board, some of the more influential deputies came to wait on him, and quietly put some questions to him as to what his hopes were from other powers, especially the very direct and awkward one: *was the English squadron going to support him*, and to act against the Genoese? He could only answer in generalities, and talk of the Empress-Queen. There were mysterious powers in the distance, who would arrive by-and-by with ships, and money, and soldiers. The deputies answered very coldly indeed, that the people wished to be sure, and have earnest of these promises; they did not wish to be deceived again. And yet it was suspected, and reasonably, that this was the old jealousy or malice; for here was the English squadron off Corsica, and England was on good terms with Genoa.

This repulse was a fatal blow. The deputies, returning, reported unfavourably—that he had no power, no resources, no support; and the crowd, easily led, turned away. The rough Matthews, who

Walpole supposed would have addressed the Pope in good coarse terms, would no doubt have sworn at Theodore as an impostor, have seen how things were, and would have allowed but a short delay. And so the sails were spread; and it must have been with a sorrowful and heavy heart that the poor adventurer saw the pretty shore he so hungered for, and had made such gallant efforts to win, fade on the horizon. This was the last *coup*—the fourth act. He was never to see that island or the blue Mediterranean again.

A little barque was wrecked on the Genoese part of the coast, and a sham Capuchin was taken with a great deal of money about him, and no less than thirty-two letters, written for the purpose of exciting an insurrection in Caprera. But the heaviest blow was to come from England. The Genoese ambassadors were working in all directions; and their envoy at London—no doubt thinking of the English aid already sent, and of the shelter which Theodore was reported to have received at the English consul's at Tunis—addressed a formal memorial, full of complaints, to the King of England.

"MEMORIAL OF THE GENOESE MINISTER IN LONDON, PRESENTED TO HIS BRITANNIC MAJESTY.

"SIRE,
"The sentiments with which my Republic has all along endeavoured to preserve a solid corre-

spondence with the Crown of Great Britain, and studied always to deserve the goodwill of your Majesty and the Kings your predecessors, are well known to your Majesty and the whole British nation. Upon all occasions the Republic has had the happiness to be informed by her envoys and ministers at your Court of your kindness to her, and that her behaviour was agreeable to your Majesty when stating that the Emperor Charles VI. had assisted them, and after his withdrawal that the French King had come to their aid.

"The Republic communicated that treaty to your Majesty, and beseeched you to enter into engagements so just by guaranteeing her Corsica in the same manner as had been done by the Emperor and the French King.

"Though your Majesty did not think fit to accede to that treaty, yet you were so good as to make answer to the Republic's minister that you were pleased with this mark of her regard and attention; that you looked upon the succour offered by France as the best and only means to put an end to the rebellions; that the Republic might be assured of the favourable attentions of your Majesty, who had given her proof thereof before any other prince did, in expressly forbidding all officers of ships under English colours to transport to Corsica arms and warlike stores, or to hold any manner of correspondence with the rebels.

"After such signal proofs of your Majesty's regard for the Republic and the recent assurances which she has received on account of what was lately done by Admiral Matthews' squadron, we have advices from divers parts that Theodore de Neuhoff, known in the world to be the author of the troubles of the kingdom of Corsica, was in the British seas, and intended to set sail for the Mediterranean. We have since learned that he appeared on the coast of Portugal, on board an English man-of-war, commanded by Captain George Barclay; that it was currently reported at Lisbon that he was going to Corsica with arms and ammunition. Afterwards we had advice that he landed at Villafranca in the said ship, and at last that he put into Leghorn about the middle of February. That he received then on board his ship several of the principal of the exiled and seditious chiefs of the Corsicans, who had been dispersed in several towns in Tuscany; that he had a private conference of several hours with General Breitarty, who came from Florence to Leghorn, and went on board an English ship with the British consul. In fine, we heard that the said Theodore departed from thence with those chiefs of the rebels, all embarked in the same ship, in the night of January 30 last (N.S.), steering towards Corsica, in company with another English man-of-war called the *Salisbury*, commanded by Captain Peter Osborn; that a few days before, the said Theodore had despatched an emissary to Corsica, one Vinceso by name, in another English man-of-war, and had caused a seditious edict to be dispersed, dated in the seventh year of his reign, in which edict he discovers his views and intentions against the tranquillity of Corsica.

"The Republic has received fresher intelligence from her commissary-general and commandants of forces in Corsica, viz., that the above-named emissary of Theodore had landed in the island; that he was spiriting up the people to a new rebellion; that he promised them the arrival of Theodore, with several English men-of-war, land forces, and a great quantity of arms and ammunition. The said commissary-general and commandants also write that the *Revenge* and the *Salisbury* had appeared on the coast and landed gunpowder and other warlike stores, at a place called Isola Rossa; that these ships cruised in that sea in order to intercept, as it is said, the succour that might be sent from Genoa to the places in the island, and that in the meantime they actually stopped with their long-boats all the coasting small craft under Genoese colours, taking out their cargoes, and detaining the vessels some time; that Theodore, being still in the *Revenge*, had summoned the commanding officers of some little forts to surrender, otherwise they would be treated with the utmost severity.

THE STORY OF THEODORE OF CORSICA. 145

"On which the Republic makes a warm remonstrance to his Majesty, 'and cannot,' it says, 'express the surprise and confusion which so positive and circumstantial accounts have caused here. She cannot form any conjecture well enough grounded about the cause of so unforeseen an event. She cannot imagine that the admirals and captains of the English ships can, in their own names and through personal views, be guilty of such attempts.' He begs therefore that 'the necessary *éclaircissements* be given to the Republic.'"

Being pressed thus warmly, the English minister was complaisant, and on the 26th of July a proclamation was issued in the *London Gazette*, forbidding any English subject to furnish supplies or assistance of any sort to those who were rather offensively described in the *Gazette* as "the Corsican rebels." Here was something to appeal to, by way of precedent, in reference to recent doctrines about the recognition of belligerents. It was a most cruel stroke, and had much the same effect that the refusal to recognise the Southern States had upon their fortunes.

Theodore was put on shore at Leghorn, then went to Sienna, and obtaining an English passport, set off to London. He had sent on complaints and "despatches" to his English friends. He arrived himself, and was now to become one of the luckless band of outcasts, a current of whom have so long oozed through the obscurer quarters of the great city by Soho and Leicester Squares, having a refuge indeed and shelter, but treated with the harmless contempt which always alights on those who have fallen, or who have failed. For about twelve years he was to live here, waiting and watching, hoping for something to "turn up;" but it never did, and the game was over for ever.

In London we have a few glimpses of the fallen adventurer. He lived in lodgings in Mount Street, Grosvenor Square—not a bad situation, and close to the Mount Coffee-house. There was some curiosity about so strange a man, who had seen so much, and had so much to tell. Men of that class who had seen adventure, like Paoli, and Poniatowski later, often have success in the *salons;* and we have glimpses accordingly of Theodore as he flits across the checkered scenes of London society. In 1749, Walpole was to meet him at Lady Schaub's, to drink coffee, owning he was curious to see him. He told Boswell later of his disappointment, and that the king never spoke a word. "Dulness or pride was the motive," as he good-naturedly imputed it. But Boswell explained it more charitably. "I suppose he had been so dejected, and so hurt with his misfortunes, that he was become sullen and indifferent."

Indeed, all through, the wit was very pleasant and smart on the poor adventurer and his kingship, scrupulously styling him "his majesty," just as he would sneer at one of the pasteboard kings of Drury Lane.

This was only in the true key of the time; for Lord March and Sir Hanbury Williams were merry on all kindred topics, though there was nothing so ludicrous in the spectacle of one who *had* been a real crowned king, and who had fought in the field for his crown, and had made really spirited and gallant efforts to recover it. How he lived was a mystery; but he was still looking wistfully to his island. Debt and pressure were sure to come; and the following year, 1750, Walpole wrote out, as an exquisite jest, that the poor adventurer had been arrested and lodged in the King's Bench. Theodore's son tried to give a sort of dignity to this misfortune by saying it was a plot on the part of Gastaldi, the Genoese minister, who had £450 lent to Theodore by some merchants, and then had him arrested. Theodore, suspecting some such attempt, had influence enough to obtain a residence in some privileged place, possibly in an ambassador's house, out of which the bailiffs drew him by a pretended message from Lord Granville, to whom Theodore repaired, full of hope and joy. Mr. Walpole was immensely amused, and talked of sending Hogarth to paint him in jail.

Now began a new shape of life—the squalor and degradation of a debtors' prison. A few friends thought of him, and occasionally sent him a little aid. Lady Yarmouth and Lord Granville were among these Samaritans. Some used to go and see him from mere curiosity, and to hear him tell his story. The rusting and fatal process of confinement for debt had the usual curious effect, degrading and affecting him precisely as it did the Mr. Dorrit of fiction, giving him a spurious importance in that wretched place, and making him take a sort of pride in his old dignity. He maintained this burlesque state, received visitors, sitting on his poor pallet, under " the top of a half-tester bed." There he would tell his tale, and receive any little " testimonial." There he was visited by Dr. Nugent, of Literary Club celebrity, who, when on his travels, interested a German court for a whole evening with the curious account. There came Monnet, the lively French actor and manager, who was very intimate with him. He was persuaded at times to knight some of his visitors, and add them to the ranks of his " Order of Deliverance." And in the year 1800 there was alive an old gentleman who had received this honour, and who, among his friends, was styled facetiously " Sir Michael." " Doctor Miller of Maidstone," whoever he was, used to show the sword with which these honours had been conferred, and had been presented with it in acknowledgment of some kindness to the fallen adventurer. His son, Count Frederick, "the Prince of Caprera," Lady Sarsfield's son, was now also in London, struggling to earn a pittance by the usual conventional means, teaching a little French and Italian—the first shabby-genteel resource, being of course employed out of charity, and his teaching but of small profit. He used to repair to the King's Bench, and share the crust he earned with the prisoner.

Some two years thus rolled away. The state of the debtors' prisons was then attracting attention, and a committee of the House of Commons was taking evidence on the treatment of debtors. Theodore, as being the lion of the place, and perhaps to gratify the curiosity of the senators, was duly examined. No doubt the fine gentlemen thought it was a rare piece of sport, and called him "his majesty." Whether from this publicity, or from other reasons, it was determined to make an effort to set him free; and Dodsley, the bookseller, and some other friends, determined to try if a subscription could be raised. A new journal, the *World*, had just been started, in which Lord Bath, Mr. Horace Walpole, and other persons of wit and fashion, were writing; and Mr. Walpole volunteered to make a diverting appeal for this sham king in distress. Accordingly, on Thursday, February 22nd, 1753, a bantering essay made its appearance; a few days before, Theodore had obtained "a day-rule," or leave of absence, which was, no doubt, in connection with this business. This little curiosity, which was preserved, ran :

"BANC R. The bearer, Theodore, Baron de Neuhoff and de Stein, hath this day a rule of Court to go out of the prison of the King's Bench granted to him, to transact his affairs.

"(Signed)   L. COTTAM.

"Dated this 12th day of February, 1753."*

Mr. Walpole, in his appeal, moralised over the fall of earthly monarchs, and alluded to the hard fate of Edward II., Richard II., and Charles I. He then described Theodore's career. "When he had discharged his duty to his subjects and himself, he chose this country for his retirement, not to indulge a voluptuous, inglorious ease, but to enjoy the participation of those blessings which he had so vainly endeavoured to fix on his Corsicans. . . . Theodore, though resigned to his fortunes, had none of that contemptible apathy which lifted our James II. to the supreme honour, etc. The veracity of an historian obliges me not to disguise the situation of his *Corsican majesty's revenues*, which has reduced him to be a prisoner for debt in the King's Bench. . . .

* This was in the possession of his granddaughter.

The debts on his civil list were owing to no misapplication. . . . His diet was philosophic, his palace humble, his robes decent; yet his butcher, his landlady, his tailor, would not continue to supply an establishment which had no demesnes to support it," etc. He then proposed that a benefit-night should be taken in the playhouses, and he was sure that Mr. Garrick would play "the self-dethroned Lear" —"a piece which, from some similitude of circumstances, I should *recommend for the benefit*,—and be a competitor with Louis le Grand for the fame which results from the protection of exiled kings." Thus the King's Bench would "become as renowned for Garrick's generosity to King Theodore as the Savoy is for Edward III.'s treatment of King John of France."

He then announced that Dodsley, the bookseller, was appointed "high treasurer and grand librarian of the island of Corsica for life," and would receive subscriptions. These, he affected to believe, would not be large, owing to the scruples of the champions of hereditary right. There were two pieces of King Theodore's coinage announced as being in "the hands of the high treasurer aforesaid, and will be shown by the proper officers of the exchequer of Corsica."

The whole of this seems in the worst taste, but is exactly the fashionable tone of the time. We need only recall Lord Chesterfield's letters to the

Dublin printer, George Faulkener, in the same spirit of ungentlemanly irony. It is not surprising to learn that the whole was considered "a good hum," and that even the charitable could not tell whether it was meant for jest or earnest. A note had to be added to the next number, explaining that the whole was serious. The generous Garrick at once gave a night, but the subscription was a failure, producing only £50; and it is not wonderful, after being thus introduced, that the ex-king had some dignity left, and seemed to have been deeply hurt at the liberty taken with him. He even sent a lawyer to Dodsley, threatening him with an action. "This, too," says Mr. Walpole, greatly shocked, "after taking the money; . . . that does not lessen the dirty knavery. . . . But I have done with countenancing kings." Had he said, "with *persiflage* of kings," it had been more appropriate. It might seem ungrateful on the poor debtor's part to treat Dodsley, who had taken trouble about him, in such a way. But the beggarly pittance, he felt, might have been far larger had it not been for Mr. Dodsley and his friends. A debtor's gaol dulls many more refinements than these. No wonder his son wrote of him that " he sometimes found assistance in the compassion of the humane; but oftentimes they made a barbarous sport by insulting his fortunes, *and accompanying their benefits with abusive jests.*" Could there be a more piteous complaint? A couple of years before he died we find him addressing letters to various patrons. Their tone provokes a smile.

"ILLME. SEIGNEUR ET HONORÉ COUSIN,

"Although I had not the comfort of receiving an answer from your Excellency, I still venture to flatter myself that you have my interests at heart. Full of this confidence, I have recourse to you, begging all your good offices in my behalf with your friends and relatives to find me the means, by the aid of a subscription, to rescue me from my difficulties, being reduced to the last state of wretchedness. Through want of cash I don't know where to turn to, having to put up with the insult of being dragged by my enemies from one jail to another, on habeas corpus, for a debt of twenty guineas, *formé par un Bussher*, to crush me. I ventured to write to the Duke of Portland, begging him to assist me; but I had the mortification to learn from my messenger that he was surprised to find that I should think of writing to him, as he knew nothing of me. Unless something is done and you kindly interfere, I can only look forward to see myself perish, actually wanting the common necessaries.

"8 juillet, '54.

"Under cover to Mr. Da Costa, in Devonshire Square.

"Deign to send me an answer, and console me."

"Having recovered somewhat from my wretched sickness, I venture to have recourse to your Excellency, asking your good offices in finding me the necessary assistance to secure my release from this terrible imprisonment. My credit is all gone, and I have been obliged by my sickness to sell everything I had, so that I now find myself on the eve of destruction (*crevé*). In this state of things I implore you to find for me the assistance of a loan of £1000 sterling, with which I can settle everything here and set off for your part of the world. Have pity on my deplorable condition, for which I am not in the least responsible, recommending my case to your friends. I am still confined to my bed.

"To Count Bentinck, May 12, '54."

A couple more years went by; and an Act of Parliament being passed for the relief of a batch of insolvents, as was then the custom, Theodore filed his schedule, and was included. There is not a more curious paper on the files of insolvency.

Surrey } "A schedule or inventory, containing a
to wit. } full and true account of all debts, effects,
and estates, both real and personal (of what kind or nature soever) of Theodore-Stephen de Neuhoff, a German from Westphalia, and late of Mount Street, Grosvenor Square, now a prisoner in

the King's Bench prison, and a list of the names of all and every person and persons that are anywise or how much indebted unto him, the said Theodore-Stephen, Baron de Neuhoff, and the witnesses that can prove the same, pursuant to an Act of Parliament made in the twenty-eighth year of the reign of his present majesty, King George the Second, entitled an Act for the Relief of Insolvent Debtors.

Debtors' names and places of abode.	Sums due.	How due, and for what.	Witnesses and vouchers thereof.
That he is entitled to the kingdom of Corsica, and hath no other estate or effects but in right of that kingdom.			

"The above-written is a full and true schedule, as aforesaid, of all my estates and effects whatsoever, except wearing apparel, bedding for myself and family, working tools and necessary implements for my occupation and calling, and those in the whole not exceeding the value of £10. Witness my hand this 24th day of June, 1755.

"THEODORE, BARON DE NEUHOFF."

"A German from Westphalia!" The law knew nothing of his royalty; and with a grim humour set down his airy claim in "a schedule!" It is worth a whole volume of essays and morals.

Walpole, however, came forward again, but in quite a different spirit. The sight of this broken, discharged debtor wandering about may have affected him. In a grave and serious tone he appealed once more to the public. This was a true *amende*, and he seems to have been kind and charitable to the outcast, who made him a present of perhaps the last relic left of his old throne, "the great seal of the kingdom of Corsica." Here is the appeal, from the *Public Advertiser:*

"AN ADDRESS TO THE NOBILITY AND GENTRY OF GREAT BRITAIN IN THE BEHALF OF THEODORE, BARON DE NEUHOFF.

"The Baron, through a long imprisonment, being reduced to very great extremities, his case is earnestly recommended for a contribution to be raised to enable him to return to his own country, having obtained his liberty by the late Act of Parliament. In the late war in Italy the Baron gave manifest proofs of his affection for England; and as the motives of his coming here are so well known, it is hoped all true friends to freedom will be excited to assist a brave though unfortunate man, who wishes to have an opportunity of testifying his gratitude to the British nation.

"Those who are pleased to contribute on this occasion are desired to deposit their benefactions in the hands of Sir Charles Arsgyll, Alderman, and Company, bankers, in Lombard Street; or with Messrs. Campbell and Coutts, bankers, in the Strand."

The poor baron's eyes were at last turning to his own country—to that corner of Westphalia where he had been born—"here to return, and die at home at last." But this attempt was to be as unsuccessful as the former. For some months more he was to be seen wandering about London, and at last would seem to have wandered back to the old prison, where, in December, 1756, the end of that exciting and weary life drew on. It was not a royal ending. With his last sickness on him, he one day called a chair for a ride, and having no money to pay the chairmen, he bade them take him to the Portuguese ambassador's, in South Audley Street. That minister was not at home; perhaps was not at home for the troublesome applicant whose visits had usually the one aim and object. He then had himself taken to an obscure tailor, living at No. 5, Little Chapel Street, Soho, who had known him in days perhaps a trifle "better." This man humanely took him in. A mortal sickness was upon him. He lingered only two or three days; and on the 11th December he died.

As we pass through that retired street, or alley rather, and look up at the old houses, we always think of the dying moments of that poor wayfarer: how the alternate glitter and squalor of his eventful career must have fluttered before his glazing eyes; the bright days of glory; the blue Mediterranean; the squadrons of vessels; the roars of the crowd, and the shouts of "Long live Theodore our king!" and how all this faded out and gave place to the dull walls of the tailor's lodging in Soho.

We are not surprised to learn "that there were difficulties about his burial"—a significant phrase. But Mr. Wright, "an opulent oilman of Compton Street, came forward, declaring that for once in his life he should like to have the honour of burying a king." Thus, even to the grave, this unbecoming burlesque was to follow him. It must be said, too, that it was only in England that this unworthy ridicule was played off on fallen dignity; elsewhere he was always spoken of with compassion and respect. There was something, however, that peculiarly "arrided" Cockney sensibility: a Mr. Charron, an artist, whose parents lived in Soho, perfectly remembered the *corpse lying in state!* Even the undertaker's bill was kept and shown as a jest. Here is a copy:

"Joseph Hubbard, coffin-maker, undertaker, and

sworn appraiser, at the Four Coffins and Crown, in New Street, near Bread Street, Carnaby Market, St. James's, Westminster, performs funerals, both public and private, at reasonable rates, and as cheap as anywhere in London.—N.B. Buys and sells all manner of household furniture.

"*For the Funeral of Baron Neuhoff, King of Corsica, interred in St. Ann's Ground, December* 15, 1756:

	£	s.	d.
"To a large elm coffin, covered with superfine black cloth, finished with double rows of brass nails, a large plate of inscription, two cup coronets gilt, four pair of Chinese contrast handles gilt, with coronets over ditto, the inside lined and ruffled with fine crape and inseared	6	6	0
A fine double shroud, pillow, and nutts	0	16	6
Four men in black to move the body down	0	4	0
Paid the parish dues of St. Ann's	1	2	8
Paid the gravedigger's fee	0	1	0
Best velvet pall	0	10	0
Use of three gentlemen's cloaks and crapes	0	4	6
A coach and hearse with pairs	0	16	0
Cloaks, hatbands, and gloves for the coachmen	0	7	0
Beer for the men	0	1	0
Attendance at the funeral	0	2	6
	£10	11	2
Received in part	8	8	0
Balance due	£2	3	2"

Had Charles Lamb seen this, he would surely have used it as a pendant for his famous bill with its item of "wrought gripes;" and in fact some of the items, such as "ruffled with fine crape," are the same.

He was laid in a mean corner in the burying-ground of St. Ann's, Soho, "among the paupers." What a grave for an adventurer! yet not out of the game of chances which the adventurer plays.

Mr. Walpole set up a monument to him in St. Ann's, Soho, "surmounted by a crown, taken from one of his Majesty's coins," and with the following inscription :

> NEAR THIS PLACE IS INTERRED
> THEODORE, KING OF CORSICA,
> WHO DIED IN THIS PARISH, DECEMBER 11, 1756,
> IMMEDIATELY AFTER LEAVING THE KING'S-BENCH PRISON
> BY THE BENEFIT OF THE ACT OF INSOLVENCY;
> IN CONSEQUENCE OF WHICH HE REGISTERED
> HIS KINGDOM OF CORSICA
> FOR THE USE OF HIS CREDITORS.
>
> The Grave, great teacher, to a level brings
> Heroes and beggars, galley-slaves and kings.
> But THEODORE his moral learn'd ere dead;
> Fate pour'd its lessons on his *living* head,
> Bestow'd a kingdom, and deny'd him bread.

Almost the same sort of melancholy yet dramatic attraction is offered by the fate and career of the so-called Colonel Frederick, the son of Theodore, a poor adventurer, well known in London towards the end of the last century, and who "hung loose," and very loose, upon society. This hapless being might have also figured in Casanova. He lived forty years in London; "his figure," we are told, "was familiar to thousands; his company was courted by many; and his misfortunes, during the latter portion of his existence, were but too well known to the world; for it would be vain to deny that the early part of his life is involved in inexplicable mystery.

"He was with his father during his brief reign in Corsica. A friend who knew him, relates how they took refuge in England; and Frederick remained with his father during the whole of his residence in this country, and principally contributed to support him while the Corsican king was confined for debt in an English prison.

"He was afterwards patronised by the late Duke of Würtemberg, to whom he was distantly related; and he was allowed a pension from the court of Würtemberg till the duke's death. Before he threw himself wholly on the patronage of the Duke of Würtemberg, he lived at the court of Berlin as a kind of reading secretary to the late King of Prussia; but not being treated with the kindness he had reason to expect, he attached himself to the duke. When he asked his majesty's permission to enter into the service of the Duke of Würtemberg the King made a faint attempt to retain him; but, finding that he was resolved, he haughtily said: 'Well, it is right that one beggar should live with another.'

"The colonel, if we are right in our recollection

of his story, married a maid of honour to the great Maria Theresa, Empress of Germany. Frederick had made application to the court of Vienna for some employment through the medium of a recommendation to this lady, who was so struck by his person, manners, and good sense, that, as she afterwards acknowledged, she had purposely delayed to urge his application, in order to prolong his attendance, and have more frequent interviews with him. At length they married; but the union did not tend to advance his interest; on the contrary, it seemed likely to overwhelm him with the cares of a family. The lady did not long partake of his misfortunes, but died soon after having produced a son and a daughter. The son was killed in America as he was gallantly fighting in the service of this country. He was a very handsome and intelligent youth. The daughter is still alive; and is the heiress of nothing but the misfortunes of her family. She has been married many years, and is now in very untoward circumstances, with three daughters to support. The daughters are very fine and accomplished young women; and one of them is said to possess literary talents of no inferior order."

There is a short account of Colonel Frederick, drawn up by himself, in the "Mémoires pour servir à l'Histoire de Corse":

"Genoa prevailed. Theodore lost his own liberty

because he had endeavoured to defend that of the Corsicans. He was confined for a long time in a disgraceful prison, where he suffered a thousand humiliations without a single murmur. He knew how useless it was to complain, and was conscious of the necessity of submitting to his fate. Deprived of his sceptre, fortune, and friends, his sole resource was in Providence and the tender pity of his son, who repaired to England on purpose to accompany him to Corsica, whither Theodore flattered himself to be able to return once more, and that, too, through the assistance of Great Britain.

"This son, like himself, was entirely destitute of the gifts of fortune, and he was but ill adapted for the acquisition of wealth, as his temper was little suited to the frivolity of an age avaricious of pleasure, and anxious for the attainment of riches and honours, even on the most dishonourable terms. Avoiding festivals and public entertainments of all kinds, he was modest in his manners, simple in his dress, tenacious of his words, reserved and close in his mode of life; in short, he retired, as it were, within himself, in order to live with that virtue of which he scorned to make a parade. He was accustomed to say, 'That it was proper to know, but not expedient to tell, everything.' *Omnia scire, non omnia exequi*, was his favourite maxim.

"He even became an author, and endeavoured

to gain a livelihood by his pen during his distress; he also taught the Latin, Italian, and Spanish languages, that he might be enabled to maintain his own children, and succour his unfortunate father.

"His family, with better opportunities of information, say he was born in 1725, which makes him seventy-two years of age at the time of his death; and this is not at all unlikely, as he lived a temperate life, and avoided every excess. Indeed he himself seems expressly to assert this in his "Mémoires":

"Ensuite il (le Baron de Neuhoff) épousa lady Sarsfield, fille de Lord Kilmalock, et demoiselle d'honneur de la reine. Le baron conçut d'abord de grandes espérances de cette alliance; mais voyant dans la suite qu'elles ne répondoient pas à son attente, il abandonna sa femme, *étant enceinte d'un fils, qu'elle mit au monde l'an* 1725."

In another of his own publications he tells us "he was bred a soldier, and had made several campaigns under the most experienced generals of the age." He adds that, when the Corsicans made so gallant a stand in defence of their liberties, "he himself, with Buttafuoco and Colonna, two Corsican gentlemen who had served with distinction in the regiment composed of their countrymen, in the service of France, offered to join Paoli in so glorious a cause; but he rejected the offer.

"He spoke French, German, Italian, and Spanish with great fluency; and he acquired a considerable degree of perfection even in English. On his first arrival from the Continent, about the year 1754, he betook himself to the teaching of Italian, and subsisted for several years by that means. At this period of his life he got acquainted with many men of considerable celebrity, and Macklin and Garrick are said to have been his scholars. By the latter he was promised great things; the former he introduced to Mr. Wedderburn, the lord chancellor, who at that time wished to get rid of his northern accent, in which he has most effectually succeeded. He himself was also his lordship's instructor.

"During the confinement of his father he visited him frequently, and is said to have shared his scanty pittance with that unfortunate monarch in a manner that would have done credit to the most affectionate son.

"By a German lady, whom he married abroad, he had two children; the one a son, the other a daughter. The first perished at the battle of Germantown;*

---

* We are told that Frederick, "a handsome youth, was introduced by the late Sir John Dryden, Bart., then an officer in the Guards, to the present Admiral Sir John Borlase Warren, who was exceedingly kind to, and, at length, actually purchased a commission for him. On his arrival in America he was noticed by General Howe, then Commander-in-chief, and advanced to the rank of lieutenant; but he was soon cut off during the war."

the other is still alive. I have been repeatedly assured by himself, that he had more than once tasted the bounty of the late Princess Dowager of Wales, who compassionated his misfortunes and those of his family. There is also some reason to believe that her Royal Highness was partly induced, from certain *political motives*, to patronise him; for it was rumoured at that time, that the Duke of York, brother of his present Majesty, had conceived the idea of becoming King of Corsica."

This curious *rôle* of managing delicate negotiations was not unprofitable in those days; and the two dissipated princes, then in difficulties, were glad to have recourse to any adroit person who would raise them money. The colonel was employed by the Prince of Wales and his brother of York to try and raise a loan at Antwerp; and the affair was completed, and their bonds put in circulation. A very awkward business followed, which has never been quite cleared up. It seems certain that the princes received a good deal of the cash, but the bonds were repudiated. And when the creditors began to press, and became clamorous, the Alien Act was set in motion by Government, and the inconvenient creditors sent out of the country. Colonel Frederick was despatched to Antwerp, to arrange the business. This would appear to have been the De Beaune Loan for £100,000, made in 1790, and which is fully explained in Huish's "Life of William IV." There was for sale not long since a letter of Colonel Frederick, in reference to this matter, in which he declares, "I could a tale unfold."

"After an absence of a few months on the Continent, Frederick returned to London with a riband in his hat. He also occasionally appeared in a green uniform richly laced with silver, and long German epaulets; and, as he was said to have obtained the brevet rank of colonel from the late Duke of Würtemberg, and also the *Croix de mérite*, he was ever after recognised by that appellation. Although not formally acknowledged as his highness's agent in this country, it is well known, however, that he transacted business of a diplomatic nature in his name, and helped him to dispose of a regiment of his subjects to the English East India Company. Towards the latter end of the American war, the colonel also tendered the service of a body of Würtembergers, ready disciplined and accoutered; and he was accustomed to assert that the premier, having cheerfully acceded to the proposition, the troops were actually put in motion, and considerable expenses incurred. On being countermanded, soon after this, by an order from Great Britain, the colonel preferred a claim for bat and forage money, pay and subsistence, amounting to many thousand florins; and his pretensions were backed by repeated memorials, addressed to all the different administrations that have succeeded each other since that period until 1797.

TO THE LORD CHANCELLOR.

"September 26th, 1793.

"Your lordship's constant silence to my repeated supplications for some redress to the grievances which I humbly stated in the petition to the King, gives me the concern it ought; for, as my claim is founded on the principles of honour and equity, and I am persuaded that no passion has any influence over your lordship's rectitude, I attribute your silence to wrong suggestions.

"I beg, therefore, in the name of what is sacred in heaven, and most dear to you on earth, that your lordship will be pleased to order a fair inquiry into the facts stated in that petition, which, if they should be found true, as I trust they will, there is no doubt but his Majesty, on your lordship's representation, as the keeper of his conscience, would be graciously pleased to grant me such relief as in his great goodness he shall deem me entitled to.

"The voice of humanity, my lord, pleads also the cause of a man well born, liberally educated, and whose conduct he hopes to be without reproach; a man who, in consequence of the service rendered to the King, stated in the petition alluded to, is reduced so low as to want literally bread, who has had the honour to be your instructor, has given proofs of his disinterested attachment to your person, and is with profound respect,

"Your lordship's, etc."

He thus wearied out successive officials with his importunities, but at last succeeded in extracting £100.

He was ever good-natured and sympathetic, as his visiting the unfortunate Dr. Dodd proves. The latter wrote to him from his prison :

"Accept, dear sir, my best thanks for your very humane and consolatory visit, and permit me to assure you that I have conversed with few whose sentiments have been so satisfactory to me, and so familiar to my own. Life has no charms amidst this dreadful shipwreck which I have brought upon myself; and death, through my unshaken confidence in redeeming mercy, few terrors.

"Yet I think it my duty to do all I can to preserve that life; and I will, from the depth of my soul in sincerest truth declare to you, that my first and chief wish for its preservation springs from an ardent desire to perfect my repentance, and to show to mankind the sincerity of that repentance by a conduct the most humble, holy, and exemplary. Deeply convinced and humbled to the dust for my manifold offences, nothing wounds my heart so much as the sad sense of public scandal and offence to our divine religion! And I unceasingly beg of God to grant me a little time to show to all the world that I am, indeed, not more sensible of my sins than solicitous to wipe away every stain they have occasioned.

"Pardon, dear sir, this effusion of my sentiments drawn forth by a sympathetic interest you kindly discover for my welfare. At such a dreadful hour as this it is impossible to dissemble; and I bless God that I live every moment, as I wish to live every future moment, always in His presence and always most thankfully resigned to His will. I shall be extremely happy to see you again, sir, whenever your humanity will permit you to visit so doleful a mansion as this; and if in the meantime you would be so indulgent to me as to favour me with a copy of the King of Prussia's lines, which you repeated (and to ask for which was indeed the only cause of this trouble), you will greatly oblige,

"My good sir, one of the most unfortunate
and truly distressed of men,

"W. D.

"April 27, 1777."

"His dress was plain, but neat; he usually wore a blue coat with a red cape, white cloth waistcoat and breeches, and in winter a pair of military boots, with a loose blue great coat. Sometimes he put on a black suit, manufactured abroad, the dye of which he was accustomed to commend as infinitely preferable to that of England; and it must have possessed some extraordinary properties, as it had retained the undiminished lustre of its original tint for at least ten or fifteen years.

"There is scarcely a coffee-house in the city of Westminster in which the Colonel's face was not familiar, and he visited two, and sometimes three, every day, particularly the Salopian, the Cannon, and Mill's in Gerrard Street. He lived for many years in Northumberland Street, in the Strand, and had a number of little harmless peculiarities. He never put on a pair of shoes until the maid had scrubbed the house in them and worn them for a fortnight. If he dined at one place he was sure to take his tea at another. He was wonderfully abstemious both in eating and drinking; his reckoning was accordingly proportionately small, seldom exceeding two shillings and sixpence. He never was seen with more than half-a-guinea at a time; and, on being asked the reason by a friend, he replied: 'that this great town was full of distressed men, many of whom he knew; and if he was discovered with anything worth borrowing he should be asked for it, and could not refuse.'

"His finances, during many years, were in a

deranged state; and, for some time before his demise, he had been occasionally supplied with little sums from various friends. Being a great economist, his expenses were small; but, notwithstanding this, he had contracted several trifling debts, and one in particular to an amount which subjects a man's body to the rigours of a jail. In short, he was in daily danger of being arrested; and thus became prevented from frequenting those places and persons rendered dear to him by custom.

"Another object, of no small concern to a feeling mind, occupied and agitated his thoughts. This was the situation of his daughter, Mrs. Clark, a lady who had also her full share of misfortunes. His grand-daughters too were grown up, but remained wholly unprovided for. It had been the colonel's custom to visit them frequently, and on all occasions, when it suited his convenience, he was sure to make little presents to the family.

"As it now became dangerous to remain any longer at his lodgings in Northumberland Street, in the Strand, where he had resided during many years, he repaired to Waghorn's Coffee-house, under the House of Lords, and communicated his fears to a woman, who permitted him during that night to sleep in another house belonging to her in the neighbourhood. In the morning he repaired to the attorney of the plaintiff, who had issued out a writ against him, to solicit a little delay; but he was refused this in a brutal manner. He then asked a friend for the loan of twenty pounds; but receiving a plain refusal became distracted at his situation. His misfortunes now multiplied every hour, and his calamities became at length so great that he determined to put an immediate end to his existence. It was at this critical moment that he is supposed to have written the following melancholy note on a slip of paper:

"All the curses in the tragedies are fallen upon me: without a house, without a country, without a friend; having for enemies even those men whom I have obliged; incumbered with debts, and so poor that I live only from day to day; and sometimes I have nothing to live on.

"To these I have opposed magnanimity to distress, nature to law, and reason to the troubles of the soul.

"Having procured and loaded a pistol, and being no longer apprehensive of the myrmidons of the law, whose power he could now set at defiance, he arose at the usual hour in the morning of Wednesday, February 1st, 1796, and walked out in his customary manner, without exhibiting any signs of agitation, or betraying any symptoms of his dreadful purpose to those whom he accosted.

"Towards the afternoon he proceeded to Storey's Gate Coffee-house, Westminster, a place often frequented by him, where he dined. He then called for his half pint of port—a quantity he rarely exceeded, looked over the morning papers, asked for and perused an evening one, and departed at eight o'clock with his accustomed serenity.

Having then repaired straight to the gate of Westminster Abbey, which is in the immediate vicinage, he pulled out the instrument of destruction from his pocket, and applying it to his temple, drew the fatal trigger, and in a moment ceased to exist."

Such was the sad fate of father and son—the stage king and his son—both dying in want and despair.

LADY HAMILTON.

LADY HAMILTON.

ADMIRERS of Romney have noticed a kind of conventional female head among his conceptions—a coaxing, beseeching face turned to the left, as if looking into some pitiless countenance which it was trying to fascinate. It may be seen at the National Gallery. In annuals, in mezzotints, as Nymph, or Grace, or Bacchante, this one face often recurs. It is that of Emma, Lady Hamilton, one of the most remarkable women that ever lived, and on whose character the prestige and honour of England rested in a way that has been little suspected. The face seems to signify little more than passive influence—the influence of soft and seductive and imploring looks, showing little of the woman of mind and intellect. In most of Romney's pictures it lurks in a sort of sly ambuscade. His nymphs, goddesses, maidens, all imperfectly disguise Emma Lyons. She perfectly infatuated three men of mark—Romney, Sir William Hamilton, and the greater Nelson.

A woman who had been painted no less than three-and-twenty times by an artist of the powers of Romney—who had sat twice to Sir Joshua, twice to Hoppner, twice to Lawrence, and three times to Madame Le Brun—might excite interest and curiosity. Such a face must have had some irresistible charm; and admirers of Nelson might appeal to it as some faint excuse for his weakness.

England was represented at Naples, for many years at the end of last century, by Sir William Hamilton, a man of good connections and of remarkable tastes. He was the foster-brother of George III., a collector, in days when collectors of antiquities were few; and a diligent inquirer into geology, and in accordance with principles of accurate observation which belong to the modern school. Mount Vesuvius was one of his hobbies, which he was said to have visited and explored some twenty times. The "Transactions" of the day are full of his researches; and he gives us a good idea of the *dilettante* of his time, who employed the artist and collector as his deputies. He thus acquired a magnificent collection of Greek vases, which became famous over Europe; all which he had engraved and published in one of those sumptuous works by which rich amateurs loved to prove their genuine passion for art. To this fashion we owe those noble " Galleries," whose grand plates, paper, and type are now a feast for the eye, and by which means the fortunate owners of a picture-gallery or museum made those in far-off countries admire and envy what they could not hope to visit. In course of time, however, it was discovered that the English ambassador was combining his taste and knowledge with profit. He sold his own collection to the country he represented for 7000*l.*, and immediately began collecting a fresh one, which was by-and-by offered over Europe, backed by the prestige of one great country having already purchased his first gallery. Wedgwood reproduced these models in his admirable ware, and declared that its sale abroad had brought three times that sum into England. It was scarcely dignified, and not surprising that the French should sneer, and say that it was not so much that he protected the arts as that they protected him. He was, besides, a musician of taste, and an ardent sportsman of the English type—a taste thoroughly congenial to the strange monarch at whose court he was accredited. We learn from the many travellers who passed by Naples how eccentric were the royal proceedings: how the queen held the gayest court in Europe, indulging in odd freaks and strange partialities, thinking of nothing but amusement; and how the king, half boor, half devotee, gave himself up to sports and tremendous *battues*, and would make any letter he wrote to his wife nothing but a simple game list.

Sir William arrived there in 1764, and with his first wife added to the *agréments* of the place. She was a famous performer on the pianoforte or harpsichord, giving the best concerts, and at which she had the finest musicians. A clever and friendless young Irishman, Kelly, sent to study music in Italy, was kindly patronised by her, and made to sing that "genteelest of tunes," "Water parted." When a song from the "Duenna" introduced him to the palace, Ferdinand asked with a wise air, "Was he a Christian?" He had one refined taste, however, and could act in private theatricals with the queen, and was considered to play with spirit; not, however, on every stage, as all who came to him on business, or to ask a favour, were told to "speak to the Lady."

Thus busy with his vases and music, the ambassador passed many years. That agreeable Frenchman, Dutens, author of the "Voyageur qui se repose," recalled pleasant evenings at this house. But by 1782 wife and daughter were dead, and Sir William was left a widower. Shortly afterwards he repaired to England, after an eighteen years' absence; and when he came out again, some amazement, though no scandal, was caused by his being accompanied by a lady who was not his wife. At any other court, the matter would have ended in the withdrawal of the ambassador;

and certainly it seems strange that a purist court like that of England should allow itself to be thus represented. But at Naples it was only a few smiles and shrugs; and the face that had been painted by so many artists was held to be the best excuse for the Adonis of fifty.

This was the famous Emma Lyons, whose history up to this period had best be hurried over as quickly as can be. She was born in 1764, and was the daughter of very poor people, who were colliers, in Wales. Her mother, left a widow, went to live with her own family, colliers also; and it was said that the little girl had been often seen walking beside a donkey laden with coal for sale. In some short memoir, which she was said to have dictated or inspired, she said Lord Halifax had her educated in a superior manner—a statement refuted by that indifferent spelling and English which she never got rid of to the end of her life. At thirteen we find her a sort of child's governess or maid, at the house of a Mrs. Thomas. Three years later she got to London as a shop-girl, in St. James's Market, where she soon attracted attention, and a lady took her for a maid—a Mrs. Budd, who lived in Chatham Place. It is curious that at this Mrs. Budd's there should have been a fellow-servant, who afterwards went on the stage, and acquired great reputation as Mrs. Powell. Not less singular is it to read of the renewed friendship of this pair of former servants. A letter written when both were in the height of their prosperity, has been preserved:

"Dear Lady Hamilton," wrote the actress, "I cannot forbear writing a line to inform your ladyship I am at this place (Southend), and to tell you how much your absence is regretted by all sorts of people. Would to Heaven you were here to enliven this, at present, dull place! Please remember me to all at Merton."

Mrs. Budd's was a gay house, where balls and parties were always going on—something more like what she longed for. Here she read novels, and paid stolen visits to playhouses, and was presently turned away. She was next seen at a tavern frequented by artists and actors, where she acquired that wonderful dramatic taste and pantomimic action for which she became so celebrated; and, like Garrick when a youth, she would go through a whole series of attitudes and declamations for her histrionic admirers at the tavern. It was there that "the female of whom we are speaking"—to use the valet-like phrase of the person who put together her memoirs—heard of the impressment of a young Welshman whom she liked; and she went to Captain Payne—afterwards the Admiral Payne, so well known as a man of pleasure, and friend of the Prince of Wales—to intercede for her friend. Such intercession was only too successful, and fairly started her on the career that suited her.

The idea of her having assisted to illustrate the quack Graham's lectures is considered to be completely disproved by dates.* Graham exhibited during the years 1780–84. Now Emma Lyons (or Harte) was at the time servant to the Mrs. Budd we have named, and had also been in the houses of Captain Payne and Sir H. Featherstonehaugh. But these numerous employments within so short a space do not at all disprove, but rather confirm, the story, as one more employment might have been readily found in addition to the others; and this same argument might have been used to show she could not have been at Captain Payne's. The story is indeed very likely to be true, when we consider that she was Romney's permanent model, and that she acquired celebrity for her shawl-dance "attitudes."

Angelo, the fencing master, gives a sketch of this quack:

"When that rage and curiosity which encouraged Doctor Graham, about the year 1783, at his temple of health, Pall Mall, began to subside, he imposed on the credulous part of the public with his earth-bath exhibition in Panton Street, Haymarket. I was present at one of his evening lectures upon the benefits

* Mr. Paget, in his paper on Lady Hamilton ("Paradoxes," etc., p. 228), and Dr. Doran, take this view.

arising from earth bathing (as he called it), and in addition to a crowded audience of men, many ladies were there to listen to his *delicate* lectures. In the centre of the room was a pile of earth, in the middle of which was a pit, where a stool was placed: we waited some time, when much impatience was manifested, and after repeated calls, 'Doctor, Doctor!' he actually made his appearance *en chemise*. After making his bow he seated himself on the stool; when two men with shovels began to place the mould in the cavity; as it approached to the pit of his stomach he kept lifting up his shirt, and at last he took it entirely off, the earth being up to his chin, and the doctor being left *in puris naturalibus*. He then began his lecture, expatiating on the excellent qualities of the earth-bath. Whether it was that the men felt they had had quite enough of his information, which had lasted above an hour, or the hearers got tired, or some wags wished to make themselves merry at the doctor's expense, we cannot say; but there was a cry of 'Doctor, a song, a song!' The doctor nodded assent, and after a few preparatory hems, he sang, or rather repeated:

> Ye fair married dames, who so often deplore,
> That a lover once blest is a lover no more,

Mrs. Abingdon's song in 'The Way to keep Him.' The doctor was a tall, handsome man, about forty, his manners pleasing, and much information was derived from his lectures, in their way. It will perhaps hardly be believed that such an exhibition would have been permitted in what is called an enlightened country; it was, however, not only tolerated, but received much encouragement from persons who possessed great influence in the fashionable world."

But there was this sign of grace shown in Emma's character: almost as soon as she was established "in splendour," she sent for her mother—the former servant—and at once established her as "Mrs. Cadogan;" and from that time was never separated from her. In this, as in many other instances, she bears a curious likeness to Peg Woffington; having the same good heart, the same spirit, the same accomplishments, and a dramatic power, though of far lower degree.* She had the wild but good heart of the clever actress, who also was careful of her mother.

Mr. Timbs quotes a curious letter of hers to an old friend. "Mrs. Burt," he says, "the lady to whom the letter is addressed, was well acquainted with Emma Lyons when she was a barefooted girl residing at Hawarden, near Chester, and gaining a livelihood by driving a donkey, laden with coals and sand for sale. Mrs. Burt, having occasion to come to London,

* Why Mrs. Lyons became "Mrs. Cadogan" does not appear. There was a gentleman of that name who figured in the arrangements after the death of Lady Hamilton.

brought Emma with her at the request of Mrs. Lyons, then occupying some situation in the household of Sir W. Hamilton. (Emma is also said to have begun life in the metropolis as a barmaid, at The Coach and Horses Inn, in Flood Street, Westminster, but to have been discharged for misconduct.) When, in the course of time, the little barefooted girl became Lady Hamilton, she, during her absence from England, occasionally wrote to her old friend and former protectress; but so far as is known, this is the only one of those letters now in existence, and is in the possession of a grandson of Mrs. Burt. It is addressed: 'Mrs Burt, at Mr Boberts, no. 16 upper John' Street, Marlebone, London.'

"Caserta, near Naples, dec^{br} 26th 1792.

"My dear Mrs. Burt, I Receved your very kind Letter this morning & am surprised to hear my poor dear grandmother can be in want, as I left her *thirty pound* when I Left england besides tea sugar & several thing' and it is now five weeks since I wrote to a friend of ours, & endeed a relation of my husbands to send twenty pound more so that my Grandmother must have had it on cristmas day, you may be sure I should never neglect that dear tender parent who I have the greatest obligations to, & she must have been cheated or she never cou'd be in want, but you did very Right my dearest friend to send her the four

Guines which I will send you with enterest & a thousand thanks endeed I Love you dearly my dear Mrs Burt & I think with pleasure on those happy days I have pass'd in your Company, I onely wait for an answer from our friend with the account of my grandmothers having Receved her twenty pounds & I will then send you an order on him for your money, & I send a piece of Silk to make you a gown we send it in the ship Captain newman, who sails for england this month, but my next letter I will send you a bill of Loading. I wrote you a Long Letter Last march, but I am affraid you never got it, which I am sorry for as their was a Long account of my reception at the Court of naples, endeed the Queen has been so Kind to me I cannot express to you she as often invited me to Court & her majesty & nobility treats me with the most kind and affectionate regard. I am the happiest woman in the world my husband is the best & most tender of husbands & treats me and my mother with such goodness & tenderness, endeed I love him dearly, if I cou'd have my dear grandmother with me, how happy I shou'd be, but gods will be done, she shall never want & if she shou'd wish for any thing over above what I have sent her Let her have it & I will repay you with entrest and thanks, you see my dear Mrs Burt in a year and 2 months she will have had fifty pounds theirfore I have nothing to Lay to my charge, I write to Mrs Thomas who Lives on the spot, & who I hope will see she is kindly used, I enclose this in a friends Letter to save you the postage which is very dear. I will write to you as soon as we have Receved the answer that the twenty pounds are receved & I then will say more about Mr Connor, my dear mother desires her best Love to you & your Brother, & pray present my Compliments to him & when you write to Michell say every thing thats kind from us to him. Miss Dodsworth, Mrs Greffor now, is brought to bed & the King was god father and made her a present of a Gold watch set in pearls twelve Sylver Candlesticks, a Sylver tea board & Sylver coffey pot Sugar Basen, &c. &c. She is a very good wife and Mr Greffor is a good man & the King is very fond of him when the Court is at Caserta we go with them and I see Mrs Greffor often. Sir William is now on a shooting party with the King, the Queen is at Caserta & our family is now there we onely Come to naples for a few days. I am now at Caserta, we have a good many english with us the duchess of ancaster Lord & Lady cholmondly Lady plymouth Lady webster Lady Forbes, &c. &c. they all dined with me yesterday. I expect Sir William home to night. God Bless you my dear Mrs Burt, & thank you for all your goodness write soon & believe me your ever true *and affectionate friend*

"EMMY HAMILTON.

"Direct for Lady Hamilton at naples."

The original is written in a bold hand, but not with the freedom of a practised writer.

It is to the credit of Lady Hamilton, that in her prosperity she was neither ashamed of her origin nor unmindful of her friends. Young Burt, the son of Mrs. Burt, and articled to an engraver, was a frequent guest at Merton, where he sat at table with the great Nelson himself, and has heard Lady Hamilton delight her company with songs celebrating the deeds of the hero, and amuse them with reminiscences of her village life.

We may pass over the various unpleasant shifts and changes in her history—a disagreeable subject. She enjoyed the favour and "protection" of various gentlemen of fashion, and thus gradually struggled out of the depths of poverty. She at last, as we have seen, attracted the notice of Sir William Hamilton, the ambassador, whom she was eventually to marry, and with him repaired to Naples.

She was thus withdrawn from public notice, and devoted herself to improving her mind and repairing the defects of her education. Her wonderful gifts soon began to develop; and at private parties given by Sir William she sang in a manner that delighted all. The most curious performance was what might be called her *poses plastiques*, when she would stand up in the drawing-room, and snatching a shawl or a piece of stuff, would, by a series of striking and intensely dramatic attitudes, convert herself into a Roman matron, a bayadere, a nymph, or represent grief, joy, or terror. This was also a favourite effect of Garrick's, who would stand up and "go through his rounds," as he called it. Her elderly patron was the most enraptured of all the delighted spectators; and he employed a German artist, named Rechberg, to sketch all these various attitudes in outline, like the drawings of Flaxman's figures. These were published in a large volume, and are curious, though not very remarkable. The rage for caricature which then prevailed in England could not let so tempting an opportunity pass; and later a series of plates, of the same size, appeared, representing the same attitudes as performed by a very stout lady.

Goethe, at this time on his Italian travels, came to Naples; and, ever susceptible to female charms, gives this enraptured description of her: "She is very handsome, and of a beautiful figure. The old knight has had made for her a Greek costume, which becomes her extremely. Dressed in this, and letting her hair loose, and taking a couple of shawls, she exhibits every possible variety of gesture, expression, and look; so that at last the spectator almost fancies it is a dream. One beholds here, in perfection, in movement, in ravishing variety, all that the greatest of artists have rejoiced to be able to produce. Standing, kneeling, sitting, lying down, grave or sad, playful, exulting, repentant, menacing, anxious —all mental states follow rapidly one after the other. With wonderful taste she suits the folding of her veil to each expression, and with the same handkerchief makes every kind of head-dress. *The old knight holds the light for her, and enters into the exhibition with his whole soul.* He thinks he can discern in her a resemblance to all the most famous antiques, all the beautiful profiles of the Greek coins—ay, of the Apollo Belvedere itself. This much at any rate is certain: the entertainment is unique. We spent two evenings on it with thorough enjoyment."

This performance of hers, the shawl-dance, she always gave with great fire and piquancy. Feeling, however, that she had greater gifts than these, and longing for a field more worthy of her talents, she made all these fascinations turn to the one end— that of an honourable position; and at last prevailed so far, that in 1791 they set off for England with the intention of being married. It has been generally repeated that this marriage took place at St. George's, Hanover Square; but Mr. Paget discovered that it was celebrated at St. James's Church, Marylebone, having found the registry. The witnesses were the Marquis of Abercorn and Mr. Dutens. This ceremony took place in 1791, and characteristically enough, the signature to the registry runs, "Amy Lions." The lady was twenty-seven; her husband, sixty.

Great efforts were made to have the new Lady Hamilton presented at court; but this was sternly refused. Even on the day of the marriage Sir William had a private interview with the King, who mentioned the report of the marriage, and said he hoped it was not true. The minister answered that it had taken place that morning. The fashionable world, however, gathered round, once she had secured her "patent," and flocked about her; and for them she went through her little performance. Gallini, of the Opera-house, offered her two thousand a year and two benefits.

The greatest homage to her influence was the extraordinary passion with which she inspired Romney, the fashionable painter, then living in Cavendish Square. Her face, or some reminiscence of it, is found in nearly all his pictures. Her vanity and satisfaction at this sort of homage must have been excessive, when we find, as we have related, that she sat to her admirer for so many picture-portraits—for Bacchantes, Calypso, wood-nymphs, Magdalenes, and even for the devotional St. Cecilia. Some irresistible spell forced his brush to limn this one face. This extraordinary and almost unique passion of Romney's was to offer a very pitiable contribution to the history of such infatuations. His friend Hayley, the original of the æsthetic school now in fashion, has frankly recorded the stages of this weakness: his delight when the goddess was in good humour, his despair when she was the reverse. It must be said his representations of her are charming; and he seems to have had a particular gift for representing the mouth, which was exquisitely formed, short, and round. A few extracts from the painter's letters will show how he was affected.

"August 8th, 1791.

"In my last letter I think I informed you that I was going to dine with Sir William and his lady. In the evening of that day there were collected round people of fashion to hear her sing. She performed in both the serious and comic to admiration, both in singing and acting; but her 'Nina' surpasses everything I saw, and I believe as a piece of acting nothing ever surpassed it. The whole company were in an agony of sorrow. Her acting is simple, grand, terrible, and pathetic. My mind was so much heated that I was for running down to Eastbourne to fetch you up to see her. But, alas! soon after, I thought I discovered an alteration in her conduct to me; a coldness and neglect seemed to have taken the place of her repeated declarations of regard for me. They left town to make many visits in the country; I expect them again the latter end of this week, when my anxiety—for I have suffered very much—will be either relieved or increased, as I find her conduct.

It is highly probable none of the pictures will be finished, unless I find her more friendly than she appeared the last time I saw her. I had it in contemplation to run down for a day or two, and bring you up with me; and I mentioned it to her. She said, 'Do so,' but in a cold manner; though a fortnight before, when I said I should do so, she was very desirous I would bring you to town."

Things brightened a little by August the 29th. "Cassandra came to town on the 16th, and I did not see her till the 20th; so you may imagine how my feelings must have suffered. She appointed to sit on the 23rd, and has been sitting almost every day since. When she arrived, she seemed more friendly than she had been. I began a picture of her, as a present for her mother. I am very successful with it; for it is thought the most beautiful head I have painted of her yet. Now, indeed, I think she is as cordial with me as ever.

"I think it excessively kind in you to enter so deeply into my distresses. Really, my mind has suffered so very much that my health was much affected; but, since she has resumed her former kindness, my health and spirits are quite recovered. She performed at my house last week, singing and acting, before some of the nobility, with the most astonishing power. She is the talk of the whole town, and really surpasses everything, both in singing and acting."

After this divinity had returned to Naples, the painter reverted to his avocation; but he soon sank into ill-health and dejection of mind. He was invited to pay his friends a visit at Naples, but could not go. When they came to him in 1800, he was suffering too much to renew their old intimacy. "The pleasure," he wrote, "I should receive from a sight of the amiable Lady Hamilton would be as salutary as great; yet, I fear, unless I should enjoy more strength and better spirits, at a better time of the year, I shall never be able to see London again."

He died soon after; but his pictures remain, and have helped, in the most important way, to give immortality to his Emma.

When we think that this woman had been lifted out of the very mud and dregs of London, and was now an ambassadress performing the part of the affectionate wife, the friend and adviser of the queen, and no more than twenty-eight years old, the riddle of her character becomes more and more perplexing. A kind and affectionate disposition, however, is often a good guide and guarantee for reform; and it is certainly in her favour that every one, including all the bold sea-captains and admirals held her in regard. Lord St. Vincent begs "she will continue to love him," and assures her that no man respects and esteems her more. Sir A. Ball protests: "I cannot help loving and esteeming you very much, though you have proved such a false gipsy." Trowbridge thinks "she will spoil them all." These "sea-dogs" were not attracted by her charms, but felt she was a true Englishwoman, and, like themselves, was fighting for the country with an undaunted spirit. Her affection, too, for her coarse, old, unpresentable mother—whom she never would separate from—is another evidence of a good heart. And yet, when we think of the really noble character of Nelson—his sense of duty, his courage, his love of his country, his really heroic nature, and even his strong sense of natural piety—one is drawn to apply a less harsh measure to his folly, and to presume that there must have been some extenuation unknown and unseen. One motive, certainly, was the belief in the loyal exertions of his friend, which, like his own, were devoted to his country, and, like his own, exerted with extraordinary success.

"Another of Lady Hamilton's chief attractions," says Mr. Pryce Gordon, "was her hair, with which, it is well known, she played wonderful tricks in her attitudes. I have more than once witnessed these exhibitions. On one occasion, being desirous to astonish a gentleman who had just arrived, and had not heard of her ladyship's attitudinal celebrity, she dropped from her chair on the carpet, when sitting at table after dinner. The comb which fastened her superabundant locks had been removed, and nothing could have been more classical or imposing than this prostrate position. Sir William started up to open a little of the curtain in order to admit the proper light, while the stranger flew to the sideboard for water, with which he plentifully sprinkled the fainting dame, before he discovered that it was a *scena* (and not a fit, as he thought) which had been got up. 'You have spoiled, my good friend,' said the knight, 'one of the most perfect attitudes that Emma ever executed—how unlucky!'" "She is the most extraordinary compound I ever beheld," wrote the agreeable Sir Gilbert Elliott in 1796. "Her person is nothing short of monstrous for its enormity, and is growing every day. She tries hard to think size advantageous to her beauty, but is not easy about it. Her face is beautiful; she is all nature, and yet all art; that is to say, her manners are perfectly unpolished, of course very easy, though not with the ease of good-breeding, but of a barmaid; excessively good-humoured, and wishing to please and be admired by all ages and sorts of persons that come in her way; but besides considerable natural understanding, she has acquired, since her marriage, some knowledge of history and of the arts, and one wonders at the application and pains she has taken to make herself what she is. With men her language and conversation are exaggerations of anything I ever heard anywhere."

In September, after she and Sir William had left England to return finally to Naples, she at once took up a remarkable position. Another adventurer—Acton, an Englishman of good family, had extraordinary influence at court, and with him she took care to cement a firm alliance; but with the Queen she became a favourite in the most extravagant sense of the term.

They had a charming villa, commanding a panorama of the bay, in full view of the volcano, which Sir William had explored so patiently; and there some of the gayest parties and junketings went forward. Sir Nathaniel Wraxall found his way to Naples when wandering from court to court, and gives a very graphic description of the strange society. He describes Sir William as a tall, meagre man; very dark, and with an aquiline nose. Miss Knight describes him as "a little man." He was indefatigable in vigorous sport—up all night at balls, yet the next day away hunting and shooting with the King, harpooning fish in the rivers—and yet past sixty years of age.

The partiality of the Queen for his wife increased every day. They affected the liking of sisters, dressed in the same colours, slept in the same room. She had the right of *entrée* at any hour, and without announcement. It was scarcely wonderful that the jealousy of the court ladies should have been aroused, or that they should have at last worked up the Queen to resent her too arrogant exercise of such privileges. One day the visitor was stopped at the door by one of the royal pages, and informed that her Majesty was engaged. An extraordinary scene was said to have taken place; and not an improbable one, considering the character of these two women. Lady Hamilton forced her way in, and began to reproach the Queen for this affront. The other, indignant, burst into fury. Billingsgate could hardly supply the terms which the two ladies showered on each other. The whole culminated in a blow from the Queen, promptly returned by the ambassadress, who had not forgotten her training at the tavern. The King was present, and roared at the scene, which ended in a renewed friendship.

With such a society the whole tone of the place may be guessed. Sir William himself was a sort of elegant professor of natural religion, and would write to his wife in this comfortable strain: "The whole art is to live all the days of our life; admire the Creator and all His works, to us incomprehensible; do all the good we can on earth, and take the chance of eternity," etc. Under these convictions the name of Lady Hamilton might never have reached beyond the humble notoriety of being recorded in a traveller's note-book or memoirs as the free but attractive ambassador's wife, had not the great name of Nelson been coupled with it; and it certainly had been well for the fame of the hero had his duty kept him anywhere but in those Italian waters. Visitors to the court brought away curious stories about the King's strange humours; but it would seem that, with all these eccentricities, he combined a sort of taste for letters and an earnestness for more serious matters which was redeeming. Proof of this is a very curious little red volume, with its vile Italian printing and viler paper, which appears to be a code of rules for a sort of religious and moral confraternity. The King's name is on the title-page as author. But equally curious is the inscription at the beginning: "Given to me by the King of Naples at Belvidere or S. Leucio, the 16th May, 1793, where Sir William and I dined with his Majesty and Duchess of Devonshire, Lady Plymouth, Lady Besborough, Lady E. Forster, Sir George Webster, Mr. Pelham.—EMMA HAMILTON."[*] It will be noted that the old defects of spelling had not been cured, though Nelson would

---

[*] There is a letter in the beginning of Grenville Sharpe's book stating this to be one of the "most interesting pieces" he had ever met with. He thought of translating it. A copy of this little royal volume, with the note of Lady Hamilton on the fly-leaf, is in the British Museum.

reassure her in this seamanlike fashion: "You lie *(what your goodness often told me)*; I can read and perfectly understand every word you write."

The power of fascination which this singular woman exerted over everyone she met, was indeed extraordinary. We have seen how she affected the unhappy painter. But the devotion of her husband was quite as remarkable. His letters to her are full of a deep affection, tempered with much good sense and a strain of excellent advice, without any attempt at lecturing or "preaching." Thus, when he went away with the King on one of his shooting expeditions, he would write to her a vast number of these agreeable letters, describing the dejection of his Majesty when no game was found: "another long-faced day," he would add. Thus, from Persano, in 1792, we find him sending her the following:

"I was sorry, my dear Em, to leave you in affliction. You must harden yourself to such little misfortunes as a temporary parting; but I cannot blame you for having a good and tender heart. Believe me, you are in thorough possession of all mine, though I will allow it to be rather tough. Let us study to make one another as comfortable as we can, and 'banish sorrow 'til to-morrow,' and so on every day. You are wise enough to see the line you ought to take, and have, hitherto, followed it most rigorously; and I can assure you, that I have not the least doubt of your continuing in it."

Again:

"I am glad all goes on so well. I never doubted your gaining every soul you approach. I am far from angry at your feeling the loss of me so much; nay, I am flattered; but believe me, the time will soon come that we shall meet. Years pass seemingly in an instant. Why then afraid of a few days?

"It was not your white and silver alone that made you look like an angel at the Academy. I will allow, however, that a beautiful woman, feeling herself well dressed, will have a sort of confidence which will add greatly to the lustre of her eye; but take my word, that for some years to come, the more simply you dress, the more conspicuous will be your beauty—which, according to my idea, is the most perfect I have yet met with, take it all in all. . . .

"I am glad you have been at the Academy, and in the great world. It is time enough for you to find out that the only real comfort is to be met with at home. I have been in that secret some time. You are certainly the most domestic young woman I know; but you are young and most beautiful, and it would but be natural if you did not show yourself in public. The effusion of tenderness with regard to me, in your letter, is very flattering. I know the value of it, and will do all I can to keep it alive. . . .

"You did admirably, my dear Em, in not inviting Lady A. H. to dine with the Prince, and still better, in telling her honestly the reason. I have always found that going straight is the best method, though not the way of the world. In short, always consult your own good sense; and do not be in a hurry, and I am sure you will always act right. Adieu, my lovely Emma."

In the month of September, 1793, Captain Nelson arrived in the Bay of Naples. He was married to a good and indulgent wife, to whom he was deeply attached. Long after, he owned that his wedding-day had been the happiest of his life. On this occasion — his first acquaintance with the English minister and his wife—he found the former "a good-natured friendly man." Sir William was much struck by the future hero. He made the prophecy—which has often been repeated—about the "little man" who would one day astonish the world. It is quite plain that no very great impression was made upon Nelson at this time. He had not yet achieved his series of victories, and his love for his wife was still fresh and strong. Of Lady Hamilton he wrote to his wife: "She has been wonderfully good and kind to Josiah. She is a young woman of amiable manners, and who does honour to the station to which she has been raised."

When the curtain next rises the revolutionary spirit was strong everywhere, and the crown of Naples insecure. Nelson was eagerly looking for the French; and it was then that this bold woman performed a remarkable service, namely, procuring news of the secret intentions of Spain to declare war on England, and sending it home. The story ran that Lady Hamilton had noticed the emotion of the King of Naples on receiving this letter, and had bribed a page, or obtained the aid of the Queen, to get it from his pocket. It is just as likely that she heard the news from the Queen. Sir William, talking with Wraxall, assumed the credit of the discovery—which, of course, as a discreet diplomatist, he would do; but the news not having come through such an official channel, ministers at home might naturally decline to recognise such irregular service, which could not be publicly dealt with. Nelson, in his will, declared that she was entitled to the credit of the proceeding; and gave a solemn charge to the British people not to let it go unrewarded. This expression of the wish of so faithful and gallant a servant should have been enough, without prying too closely into the niceties, or the probability that so infatuated a lover would have accepted and believed any story told him by the woman who had enslaved him. It is certain, however, that the warning was received through the agency of the British minister at Naples; and it must be assumed to be no more than a praiseworthy and zealous exercise of his duty.

She sent a copy home by express to Lord Grenville, at a cost out of her own pocket of four hundred pounds, and that nobleman at once availed himself of her information.

Two or three years more passed by, and then came round that exciting time for the great sea-captain, when the French fleet proved as bewildering a mystery as the Flying Dutchman; when no one could tell where they were lurking—or "skulking," as the British tar would say—and Nelson was distracted with the uncertainty. Nearly all the ports were shut to the English; and even friendly nations had about as much dread of sheltering or harbouring an English war-ship as respectable people would have of giving asylum to anyone under the ban of the law. Nelson wrote a good deal to his friends at Naples, sometimes a note to both—to Sir William and Lady Hamilton—but oftener to Sir William, and without any allusion to Lady Hamilton. Then came that crisis, when it was safety or destruction for Nelson that he should have liberty to victual his ships in Italian ports, as the treaty with France forbade the admission of more than two ships into any Neapolitan port. He was just starting on that famous chase which ended only in the great battle that destroyed the French navy; and the timorous Ferdinand was trembling through dread of the "Corsican ogre."

This scene is truly dramatic. One morning the brave Trowbridge roused Sir William from his bed, with a letter from Nelson, begging that leave would be got for him to provision his ships, otherwise he would have to make for Gibraltar, and thus miss the French. It was all important. A council was hastily summoned by the King; but the fear of the French was too strong, and they decided that nothing could be done. Then it was that the spirit of the intrepid Emma rose. Falling on her knees to the Queen, she prayed, wept, argued, and at last succeeded in obtaining a letter of permission, with which Trowbridge set off. The splendid well-known battle followed; yet this brave woman—she who performed this service—was suffered by her country to die in want and exile.

Sir Harris Nicholas refuses to allow Lady Hamilton any share in this transaction, and while giving admission to letters that seem to prove it, insinuates they have been forged. This prejudice blinds him even to understanding the case. His grounds are these: when Nelson was leaving the port, he wrote to the Hamiltons that all his wants had been supplied; but he was "tormented because no private orders have been given by the Government for the admission of my ships. But, *thanks to their exertions*, he had victualled and watered." Now, Sir Harris Nicholas says there is an inconsistency between this acknowledgment and the other passage about "no private orders being given," and says the one was most likely fabricated to found a claim for Lady Hamilton. But he has confounded two different things—the admission into the port, and the difficulty of victualling; and Nelson's complaint only referred to the former. In the codicil to his will he distinctly gives her the whole credit of the matter. And, finally, there is Lady Hamilton's MS. note in the letter-book: "The Queen's letter, privately got by me, got him and his fleet victualled and watered in a few days."

When Nelson returned triumphantly after this his great victory, in September, 1798, a series of dazzling scenes awaited him; and the Circe of the place seemed then called on to exert her charms to enslave the hero and conqueror. The whole city had been in a fever of expectation as to the result of the battle. When the news arrived, the enthusiastic ambassador jumped from his carriage to stop a cardinal with whom he was not acquainted—no other indeed than the Cardinal York—with a certain lack of delicacy. In a few days the English fleet was approaching, and King and Queen, ambassador and wife, all went out to greet the hero. The scene was most dramatic, the greeting enough to turn any head. Nelson wrote the whole in a sort of excited way to his wife. The news of his coming had been "imprudently told to her: it was like a shot; she fell apparently dead." This incident had of course only been related to him. "Alongside came my honoured friend. . . . The scene in the boats was terribly affecting: up flew her ladyship, exclaiming, 'O my God, is it possible?' *and fell into my arms more dead than alive.*' This remarkable letter is leavened with some passages to allay the reasonable misgivings of a wife. 'What must this be to my dearest wife, my friend, *my everything* which is most dear to me in the world! I hope," he goes on, 'to have one day the pleasure of introducing you to Lady Hamilton. She is one of the best of women in the world; she is an honour to her sex.'"

The name of Nelson appeared everywhere; and the whole service of china bore his initials, "H. N." There was nothing but feasts and revelry, with the one hero and heroine moving through the gay throng. Lady Hamilton wrote an obsequious letter to the absent wife, full of news about Nelson, recounting the honours paid to him, enclosing an ode. The King had his picture painted and set round with diamonds; a whole service painted with views of his great battles. Sir William is in a rage with ministers for not having made Lord Nelson a Viscount. "*Hang them, I say!*" she added; and in this familiarity to a lady she had not seen and did not know, the old vulgar copper comes through the plating. But this deprecation was not of much avail. Already rumours and open talk had reached England of the strange proceedings at Naples, of the follies of the commander of the English fleet. Good-natured friends wrote to him delicately and considerately; and one hinted at Lady Nelson's uneasiness, "who swears she will join you at Naples." However, he could stoop to write back letters about his pride in being her husband. But all had little effect. He still lingered on in these dangerous waters until near another year had gone by.

At that birthday-ball a scene took place which should have awakened Nelson to the folly of his proceedings. A young fellow, a son of Lady Nelson by a former marriage, had long secretly resented this treatment of his absent mother, and whether from wine or Nelson's conduct, broke out publicly with some violent language against Lady Hamilton. The brave Trowbridge was at hand, and got him away; but in any other court there had been a scandal. Something should be done; and later the lady herself undertook to soothe this ungracious man. Nelson wrote home to his wife the happy result of these efforts, and their joint obligations to Lady Hamilton!

When the French came to punish the violation of

the treaty, it was this intrepid woman that planned the escape of the pitiably helpless royal family. It was she who explored the subterranean passages through which the jewels and property were conveyed away; and it was she who showed a true courage and gallantry in the most perilous situation.

We now come to the execution of Caraccioli, discussed with so much temper and partisanship. The events of the story are well known. The royal family had fled from the revolution; but Cardinal Ruffo and the royal troops had nearly reduced the insurrection when Nelson entered the bay. He annulled the capitulation, which had been almost concluded, and, on the recapture of the old chief had him tried and hanged the same day. There were a violence and an indecorous hurry in his proceedings excusable in so decisive a commander, but which become significant when we think of the infatuation and influence which were working on him. The partisanship of the English ambassador and his wife was unbecoming the representative of a foreign nation, they being more the hated partisans of the King at whose court they were. They were with Nelson; and no English commander before or since has volunteered to act as executioner for the ally whom he was assisting.

All the steps in the business point to some influence that was not like the character of Nelson.

His own officer, Captain Foote, had joined in the armistice; and yet he turned on him and branded what he had done as "infamous." Cardinal Ruffo, a true fighting patriot, was for the capitulation; and a remarkable scene took place between him and Nelson on board the vessel, with Lady Hamilton and Sir William acting as interpreters, and, it was said, putting strange words into the cardinal's mouth. There was a firmness about the latter, on the side of mercy and honour, which nothing could shake, and which contrasts strongly with the blustering which seems like the consciousness of having acted wrongly.

This question of Lady Hamilton's being "present" at the execution of Caraccioli, and being rowed with Nelson "to take another look" at the unfortunate man then swinging from the yard, has been matter of discussion. For this story Mr. Paget maintains that there is not the least foundation; and quotes Sir Francis Collier, who was in the *Foudroyant* at the time, and who says it was "an arrant falsehood;" also a declaration of Lord Northwick's to Mr. Mulready that he was sitting at dinner with Lady Hamilton in the cabin of the *Foudroyant* when they heard the gun announce the execution. But surely there are fair foundations for saying that "she was present." She was on board one of the vessels from which the execution could be seen. She was a devoted partisan of Nelson's and of the Queen. It was unlikely that she would shut herself up in the cabin to avoid the spectacle, while, if she appeared on deck at all, it would naturally be said she was "looking on."

"A ludicrous circumstance," says Mr. P. Gordon, who, moreover, vouches for the story of going to see the body of Caraccioli, "occurred at dinner on the day of the execution, which I had from Mr. L——, consul-general, who was present. There was a roast pig at the bottom of the table, which was dissected by the admiral's secretary, and when the *head* was *cut off*, Lady Hamilton fainted! On recovering, she said, sobbing: 'That it put her in mind of her dear Caraccioli.' Her ladyship, however, who was an *amateur* of this savoury dish, ate heartily of it—ay, and even of the brains!"

The scene of pleasure that followed—the junketings, galas—in which the great admiral figured like some Antony, and lingered on with his indignant tars and fleet, is truly humiliating. There were fancy balls, where Lady Hamilton appeared as Victory, her dress embroidered with the names of Nelson's victories. The Sicilians even gave him a nickname. The English men-of-war were made to form processions for pleasure-parties, with the barges and galleys tricked out for theatrical shows. Now she appears in the admiral's own boat dressed as Cleopatra; he sitting beside her, and twelve tars rowing with scarcely concealed contempt. Even the King declined to take part in the show; but went in a boat by himself, shooting at the birds! What a picture! At one of the banquets in his ship's cabin, something like shame at the degrading part he was playing made Nelson start up and hurry to the deck, which he paced in great agitation; but he was followed by the siren and soothed back again. It was no wonder that the honest Trowbridge should write him a manly and touching appeal, speaking as it were for the fleet. His sincere esteem, he said, was his excuse; then goes on bluntly: "I know you can have no pleasure sitting up all night at cards. . . . Why sacrifice your health, purse, comfort? *Your lordship is a stranger to half that happens, or to the talk it occasions.* If you knew what your friends feel for you! . . . I beseech your lordship, leave off." Such an expostulation might well have brought a blush to his cheek; but it seems to have had no effect. The "talk it occasions" referred to the hiring of Italian boats for stores, etc.—transacted, it was said, through the favourite—and "bits of patronage" in her hands.

It was scarcely wonderful that the envoy, or possibly his wife, should have been recalled. Sir William was eager to arrange for a handsome pension of 2000*l.* a year. He considered himself badly treated, and wrote to Nelson complaining, and talking of "my poor Emma."

"On his return to Naples," says Mr. Gordon, "he

was surprised to read in the French *Moniteur* 'that a peace had been concluded,' of which he knew nothing! This apathy at last roused our cabinet, and Mr. Wyndham, the envoy at Florence, was despatched to Naples to investigate into this extraordinary measure. The knight was discovered to be (what had been long known) an elderly gentlewoman, incapable of filling any official situation, and was ordered home, Mr. Paget being sent out as his successor; but the revolution at Naples detained him some time longer in office. He emigrated with the court to Sicily, of which he made a profitable job; Lord Nelson having given him a large vessel to transport his furniture and effects to Palermo, and an officer to superintend the embarkation of every article contained in his hotel." We still find Nelson writing to the lady as "the first of her sex:" "You never ask favours but for your friends; in short, from every point of view, from ambassadress *to the duties of domestic life,* I never saw your equal."

It was said that the Queen was very eager to detain Lady Hamilton, offering her a large pension. A statue of her was executed in marble for the King, as a Venus or nymph. A more singular honour was the gift of the Cross of Malta from the emperor, the first time such an honour was paid to an English lady. She wrote to her own government for permission to wear it, but was treated with a mortifying silence

Indeed, at home, eyes were being opened, rather late, to the proceedings of the minister and his wife; and there was great talk of compromised interests and moneys wasted. All this, it will be seen, would only tie tighter those conventional "silken fetters" in which Nelson was bound. It also explains some of the grumbling and complaints against ".the way he was treated" by those in authority.

That progress home is unpleasant to think of. The Queen, Sir William and Lady Hamilton, and the admiral, with the agreeable diarist, made up the strange party. They came by way of Leghorn, and made for Vienna; where the unhappy English admiral was dragged through a series of fêtes at the skirts of this extraordinary woman. Great honours were paid him. The whole party were entertained by Prince Esterhazy with almost barbaric honours. Miss Knight's bombastic ode, " Britannia's Leader gives the dread Command," was put into Haydn's hands to set to music; and it was performed before a large company. Not so honourable a position for the *gran maestro* was his having to sit at the harpsichord and accompany Lady Hamilton while she sang it in honour of the hero.

A bookseller of Leicester Square has a little volume of Molière, with the following extraordinary inscription, which he has been kind enough to copy. It illustrates our heroine's character in the most singular way:

"Given to me by Miss Knight, whom I thought good and sincere. We succoured, cherished, and protected her and her mother, Lady Knight, and brought them off from Naples to Sicily, when Lady Knight died. My dear mother took Miss Knight to our house, Sir William and self being then at the re-taking of Naples, with Nelson. We gave shelter to Miss Knight for near two years; we brought her, free of expense, to England. What has she done in return? Ingratitude—God forgive her!—for, although she is clever and learned, she is dirty, ill-bred, ungrateful, bad-mannered, false, and deceiving. But my heart takes a noble vengeance—I forgive her.

"EMMA HAMILTON."

The book is marked " E. C. K.," in gilt letters on the cover outside, and has Miss Knight's own name, " Ellis Cornelia Knight," written on the title.

Her passion was gambling, which was marked by various observers. " Nelson and the Hamiltons were there," says the young Lord FitzHarris ; " we never sat down to dinner or supper less than sixty or seventy persons, in a fine hall, superbly illuminated; in short, the whole in a most princely style. Nelson's health was drunk with a flourish of trumpets and firing of cannon. Lady Hamilton is, without exception, the most coarse, ill-mannered, disagreeable woman I ever met with. The Princess, with great kindness, had got a number of musicians, and the famous Haydn, who is in their service, to play, knowing Lady Hamilton was fond of music. Instead of attending to them, she sat down to the faro table, played Nelson's cards for him, and won between 300*l.* and 400*l.* He told me he had *no thoughts of serving again;* in short, I could not disguise my feeling, and joined in the general abuse of her.

"Nelson and the Hamiltons all lived together, in a house of which he bore the expense, which was enormous, and where every sort of gaming went on half the night. Nelson used to sit with large parcels of gold before him, and generally go to sleep, Lady Hamilton taking from the heap without counting, and playing with his money to the amount of 500*l.* a night. Her rage is play; and Sir William says when he is dead she will be a beggar. However, she has about 30,000*l.* worth of diamonds from the royal family, in presents. She sits at the councils, and rules everything and everybody."

Mr. Rushout, who was on board the flagship of Lord Nelson when the royal family emigrated, gives us a lively description of the disasters which occurred. The King, he said, seemed quite reconciled to his fate when he embarked, continued on deck till midnight, and conversed familiarly with the officers, who knew Italian or French. Shortly after they got unde weigh, the wind shifted to the *tramontana* (north), when his Majesty observed to Sir W. Hamilton: "We shall have plenty of woodcocks, *cavaliere;* this wind will bring them—it is just the season, and we will have rare sport (*bella caccia*). You must get your *cannone* ready;" and, summoning his principal *cacciatore* (gamekeeper), the two entered into a long discussion about woodcocks. The wind, however, increased with heavy squalls, accompanied by vivid flashes of lightning, the sure forerunner of a storm in the Mediterranean. At length it blew so hard that the sails were split into atoms, the sea rose mountains high, and the ship was considered in such danger during the hurricane, that preparations were made to cut away the mainmast, after the loss of the foreyard. The terror and consternation of the royal party and their followers may be easily imagined. The youngest prince, a child six years old, actually fell a victim to fright, having died in convulsions. The Queen and Lady Hamilton, soothed by the kind care and attentions of the gallant admiral, conducted themselves with firmness.

Mr. Pryce Gordon was in Italy at this time, and saw and heard a good deal of this strange party during these exciting scenes. Some of his recollections have grotesque airs, as, for instance, his introduction to Lady Hamilton:

"The *cavaliere* retired, but shortly returned, entering by a *porte battante*, and on his arm, or rather his shoulder, was leaning the interesting Melpomene, her raven tresses floating round her expansive form. What a model for a Roman matron! but alas! poor Emma was indisposed, 'dying,' she said, 'of chagrin for the loss of her beloved Naples;' yet the roses on her cheek prevailed over the lilies, and gave hopes that her grief would not prove mortal. The ceremony of introduction being over, she rehearsed in a subdued tone a *mélange* of Lancashire and Italian, detailing the catalogue of her miseries, her hopes, and her fears, with lamentations about the dear Queen, the loss of her own charming *palazzo* and its precious contents, which had fallen into the hands of the vile republicans. But here we offered some consolation, by assuring her ladyship that every article of the ambassador's property had been safely embarked in an English transport, and would be despatched in a few days. All this, we afterwards learned, she knew, as the vessel had actually arrived. During this interesting conversation the lady discovered that she was Lord Montgomery's *cousin*, and, appealing to her husband, said 'A'nt us, Sir William?' His lordship made his bows and acknowledgments, and we were invited to dinner, her ladyship regretting 'that her small house could not accommodate him;' (it was a place of fifty rooms at least). The hero of the Nile now came forth from a corner where he had been writing, and cross-examined us about Naples. After a few trifling queries about the burning of the gunboats, Lord Nelson said to me: 'Pray, sir, have you heard of the battle of the Nile?' I thought this a strange question, and could not help imagining for a moment that the great hero meant to quiz me; but I replied with equal gravity, 'that I had heard of *two* battles *of the Nile*, and that I had perhaps done more honour to them and to his lordship than any other individual as far as wine could testify loyalty; for I had quaffed at least half-a-dozen bottles on the occasions,' adding, 'that having been at Pisa in July, an account had been sent from Leghorn of a great victory at the mouth of the Nile, which was celebrated by a party of Englishmen, when it was discovered that the news was a fabrication, and I got a headache for nothing; but this did not deter me from assisting at the celebration of the glorious victory, when it did happen, a few weeks after.' I know not what his lordship thought of this speech, but he replied: '*That* battle, sir, was the most extraordinary one that was ever fought, and it is *unique*, sir, for three reasons; first, for its having been fought at night; secondly, for its having been fought at anchor; and thirdly, for its having been gained by an admiral with one arm.' To each of these reasons I made a profound bow; but had the speech been made *after* dinner, I should have imagined the hero had imbibed an extra dose of champagne. It is very singular, however, that he made the very same harangue to the Lord Mayor of London the following year, when a sword and the freedom of the city were presented to him."

"Shortly after our arrival we dined with our ambassador. In the evening a stranger was announced as having arrived, bearing a despatch from the Emperor Paul of Russia: the messenger was a Turk. Lady H., with her usual tact, recommended Lord Nelson, for whom the despatch was destined, to clothe himself in his pelisse and aigrette to receive the Turk. This was done in a moment. The party moved to a *salle de réception.* The folding-doors were thrown open, and the Mussulman entered. The moment he caught a glance of his lordship's costume, the slave was prostrate on the earth, making the grand salaam. This was the scene her ladyship had anticipated, and it was got up with stage effect. The credentials being delivered were found to contain an autograph letter from Paul, complimenting the hero on the glories he had achieved; and, in testimony of his Majesty's regard, the Emperor of all the Russias desired his acceptance of a gold snuff-box, on which was the imperial portrait. The letter (in French) was read to the assembly, and the present exhibited. It was superb, of chaste gold; the portrait was set with large brilliants—a gift worthy of an Emperor. Lady H——, by means of a Greek interpreter belonging to the embassy, flirted with the Turk, a coarse savage monster; and he was invited to dinner the following day to drink the health of the Emperor.

"The only memorable event which occurred at the minister's entertainment was this warrior getting drunk with rum, which does not come under the prohibition of the prophet. The monster, who had the post of honour at her ladyship's side, entertained her, through the interpretation of the Greek, with an account of his exploits; among others, that of having lately fallen in with a French transport, conveying invalids and wounded soldiers from Egypt, whom he had brought on board his frigate; but, provisions and water having run short, he found it necessary to get rid of his prisoners, and amused himself by putting them to death. 'With this weapon,' said he, in his vile jargon, and drawing his shabola, 'I cut off the heads of twenty French prisoners in one day! Look, there is their blood remaining on it!' The speech being translated, her ladyship's eye beamed with delight, and she said : ' Oh, let me see the sword that did the glorious deed!'" It was presented to her; she took it into her fair hand, covered with rings, kissed it, and handed it to the hero of the Nile. Had I not been an eye-witness to this disgraceful act, I would not have ventured to relate it.

"Mrs. C——s L——e, the beautiful and amiable wife of our consul-general, was sitting *vis-à-vis* to the

Turk, and was so horrified at the scene (being near her accouchement) that she fainted, and was taken out of the room. Her ladyship said it was a piece of affectation, and made no efforts to assist her guest; the truth is, she was jealous of her beauty, and insinuated that, being a sister of the late Lord E—— F——, she must necessarily be a Jacobin. N.B.—She wore green ribbons. The toadeaters applauded, but many groaned and cried 'shame' loud enough to reach the ears of the admiral, who turned pale, hung his head, and seemed ashamed. Lord M—— got up and left the room, and I speedily followed. Poor Nelson was to be pitied; never was a man so mystified and deluded!"

Mrs. St. George, mother of archbishop Trench, gives some lively and even amazing sketches of the "doings" that went on at this time.

" *Oct*. 3.—Dined at Mr. Elliot's, with only the Nelson party. It is plain that Lord Nelson thinks of nothing but Lady Hamilton, who is totally occupied by the same object. She is bold, forward, coarse, assuming, and vain. Her figure is 'colossal, but, excepting her feet, which are hideous, well-shaped. Her bones are large, and she is exceedingly *embonpoint*. Her eyebrows and hair are dark, and her complexion coarse. Her expression is strongly marked, variable, and interesting; her movements in common life ungraceful; her voice loud, yet not disagreeable. Lord Nelson is a little man, without any dignity. Lady Hamilton takes possession of him; and he is a willing captive, the most submissive and devoted I have seen. Sir William is old, infirm, all admiration of his wife, and never spoke to-day but to applaud her.

"*Oct.* 7.—Breakfasted with Lady Hamilton, and saw her represent in succession the best statues and paintings extant. She assumes their attitude, expression, and drapery with great facility, swiftness, and accuracy. Several Indian shawls, a chair, some antique vases, a wreath of roses, a tambourine, and a few children, are her whole apparatus. She stands at one end of the room, with a strong light to her left, and every other window closed. Her hair (which, by-the-by, is never clean) is short, dressed like an antique, and her gown a simple calico chemise, very easy, with loose sleeves to the wrist. She disposes the shawl so as to form Grecian, Turkish, and other drapery, as well as a variety of turbans. Her arrangement of the turbans is absolute sleight-of-hand, she does it so quickly, so easily, and so well. It is a beautiful performance, amusing to the most ignorant, and highly interesting to the lovers of art. The chief of her imitations are from the antique. Each representation lasts about ten minutes. It is remarkable that, though coarse and ungraceful in common life, she becomes highly graceful, and even beautiful, during this performance. It is also singular that, in spite of the accuracy of her imitation of the finest ancient draperies, her usual dress is tasteless, vulgar, loaded, and unbecoming. Her ruling passions seem to me vanity, avarice, and love for the pleasures of the table. She shows a great avidity for presents, and has actually obtained some at Dresden by the common artifice of admiring and longing.

"*Oct.* 8.—The Electress will not receive Lady Hamilton, on account of her former life. She wished to go to court, on which a pretext was made to avoid receiving company last Sunday, and I understand there will be no court while she stays. Lord Nelson, understanding the Elector did not wish to see her, said to Mr. Elliot: 'Sir, if there is any difficulty of that sort, Lady Hamilton will knock the Elector down.' She was not invited in the beginning to Madame de Loss's; upon which Lord Nelson sent his excuse, and then Mr. Elliot persuaded Madame de Loss to invite her.

"*Oct.* 9.—A great breakfast at the Elliots', given by the Nelson party. Lady Hamilton repeated her attitudes with great effect. All the company, except their party and myself, went away before dinner, after which Lady Hamilton, who declared she was passionately fond of champagne, took such a portion of it as astonished me. Lord Nelson was not behindhand, called more vociferously than usual for songs in his own praise, and after many bumpers proposed the Queen of Naples, adding, 'She is *my* queen; she is queen to the backbone.' Poor Mr. Elliot, who was anxious the party should not expose themselves more than they had done already, and wished to get over the last day as well as he had done the rest, endeavoured to stop the effusion of champagne, and effected it with some difficulty; but not till the lord and lady, or, as he calls them, Antony and *Moll* Cleopatra, were pretty far gone. Lady Hamilton expressed great anxiety to go to court, and Mrs. Elliot assured her it would not amuse her, and that the Elector never gave dinners or suppers. 'What!' cried she, 'no guttling?' Sir William also this evening performed feats of activity, hopping round the room on his backbone, his arms, legs, star and ribbon all flying about in the air."

"*Oct.* 10.—Mr. Elliot saw them on board to-day. The moment they were on board there was an end of the fine arts, of the attitudes, of the acting, the dancing, and the singing. Lady Hamilton's maid began to scold in French about some provisions which had been forgot, in language quite impossible to repeat, using certain French words which were never spoken but by *men* of the lowest class, and roaring them out from one boat to another. Lady Hamilton began bawling for an Irish stew, and her old mother set about washing the potatoes, which she did as cleverly as possible. They were exactly like Hogarth's actresses dressing in the barn."

After these scenes, who can deny that the influence of such a creature could have had no effect on the simple character of the hero? The mind that could be reduced so low must have found its views of everything, even of what is heroic, coloured by such a medium.

At last they arrived in London. Now came a still deeper sinking into the mire for all parties concerned, with a prying and scoffing audience to look on. They all put up at the same hotel, and from that time began a series of follies. The position of Lady Nelson was truly pitiable—forced into a sort of countenance of the proceedings, this being the homage most welcome to the intruder, the husband requiring some such *amende* for what he considers unworthy suspicions. He took a house in Dover Street, and there the odious pill was forced down her very throat. Sometimes her restraint gave way; and it was told at the clubs how she had fainted at the theatre, and had to be carried out. A more painful scene still was reported, where the unfortunate wife was made to go and fetch a shawl for her rival. There is not chapter and verse for these stories; but in such episodes they are, as it were, common forms.

It is sad to think of him as the hero of such a scene as the following: The Hamiltons had taken a house in Piccadilly looking into the Green Park. Before they entered into possession, a lawyer and a clerk went to make a schedule of the fixtures, and found themselves attended round the house by an emaciated weather-beaten man, very shabbily dressed, and who seemed to them like one of the French refugee priests who were then wandering about London in crowds. They no doubt made small account of him, and still less of a jesting request "to include him in the fixtures." Afterwards they found that this was Lord Nelson! Such a state of things could not long continue. Sir William, now growing old, seemed equally infatuated by his wife as was Nelson, and could not see what was going on. It was artfully put before him again and again that Nelson was unhappy at home—misunderstood, miserable; in fact, it was urged at last, without a home to lay his head in. "Without a home?" said the other; "let him come here—ours is large enough." And in a short time the London gossips heard the trio were all living together in Piccadilly. From this time Nelson seems to have quite given himself up to this thraldom; and it was said grew irritated by the remarks made on the affair, and determined to support Lady Hamilton. It may be questioned whether the influence of his relatives could have made much effect; but it makes the picture complete to think that that influence and countenance should have been turned in another direction. His aged father—a man of eighty—did not take part with his daughter-in-law; and a man who has since acquired a notoriety—the clerical brother, William Nelson, D.D., was foremost in his obsequious homage and devotion to the woman who was ruining his brother's name. Disgraceful, too, was the fashion in which the genteel world crowded to her rooms—were eager to be admitted to the *soirées*, where she went through her old round of *poses* and antics.

In 1800, when the hero and his party landed at Yarmouth, his friends held up his wife to disdain, because, poor lady! instead of rushing down to that port to welcome him, she remained to meet him in London. There she is said to have received him. The hero and his wife occupied a house in Dover Street, with the heroine, making the *rôle* of the wife rather difficult to play with dignity. The scene is described in her "Memoirs"—a catch-penny thing, as it is called, but which has a grand air of *vraisemblance*. A lady of high rank, a duchess it was said, had called on them, and, during the visit, persistently ignored the presence of Lady Hamilton, devoting all her attentions to Lady Nelson. On her departure she was roundly abused, both by Nelson and his Emma; and, as Lady Nelson said nothing, she was rated by her husband as if she was to blame for the neglect; with other scenes of the same painful kind. Two months were passed in this fashion, of which Nelson later wrote: " Sooner than live the unhappy life I did in London, I would stay abroad for ever." His confidential business adviser related, so lately as 1846, how he had been present at the crisis. He had come to breakfast. A cheerful conversation was passing on indifferent subjects, when Lord Nelson spoke of something that had been said or done by *dear Lady Hamilton,* upon which Lady Nelson rose from her chair, and with much vehemence exclaimed: "I am sick of hearing of 'dear Lady Hamilton,' and am resolved you shall give up either her or me." Lord Nelson with perfect calmness said: "Take care, Fanny, what you say. I love you sincerely; but I cannot forget my obligations to Lady Hamilton, or speak of her otherwise than with affection and admiration." Without one soothing word or gesture, but muttering something about "her mind being made up," Lady Nelson left the room, and shortly after drove from the house.

"I believe," adds this friendly adviser, "he took a formal leave of her before joining the fleet; but, to the day of her husband's death, she *never made any apology* for her abrupt and singular conduct."

The poor, long-suffering lady may not have been ordered to quit, and may have departed of her own motion; but the causes that impelled her are clear. Unhappily, the hero himself, with the candour which belonged to his character, openly bore testimony against himself. His assurance at parting was: "I call God to witness there is nothing in your conduct I wish otherwise." On his return, not long afterwards, he wrote to Mr. Davidson, to signify to his wife, "I expect, and for which I have made such a very liberal allowance (1200*l.* a year), *to be left to myself, without any inquiries from her.*"

The attitude of Sir William Hamilton, when this had been going on for so many years, was a puzzle to many. Of his worshipping attachment for Nelson, almost equal to that of his wife, there can be no doubt. He was a diplomatist of at least ordinary shrewdness and observation, and must have seen or suspected, or found friends to hint or speak openly to him. This infatuation may have led him to think that he might trust the hero, as he showed, indeed, in his will, where he bequeathed an enamel of his Emma to "my dearest friend, Lord Nelson; a small token of the great regard I have for his lordship, the most *virtuous, loyal, and truly brave character* I ever met with. God bless him; and shame fall on those who do not say, Amen!"

A blush must have come to the now pallid cheek of Nelson, as he read this testimonial of his foolish, doting friend. "The most loyal!" Alas!

The brother of Lord Nelson was truly a singular character; and there is something almost comic in the open manner in which he *exploité*'d his famous relation's services to forward his own interests. Not less droll is the placid manner in which the good-natured Nelson accepted the situation, and used every possible exertion to forward his promotion. Lady Hamilton the cleric overwhelmed with civilities and attentions. "I send you," he wrote in 1801, "a *hunted* hare. . . . Your letters," he adds, "always give an additional zest to our breakfast-table." He has just had a letter from his great and beloved brother, "who has sent his letter to the new Lord Chancellor. God grant it may have the desired effect!"

"Another," says the *Edinburgh Review*, "equally noble, though as yet only reverend correspondent, survives, who surely cannot have forgotten how often he was her 'obliged and faithful servant;' called her 'his deary;' condescended to write jocose and free letters to her of a Sunday morning, between morning and evening service; looked to her, as his 'best and truest friend,' for protection and advancement; engaged her to obtain prebends 'with six hundred a-year, and good houses;' and enclosed a list of five deans, 'all old men.' To him, and to such as him, who are wallowing in riches, and have given her claims on their gratitude, she is certainly entitled to look for assistance; not to the public, of whom she has deserved ill, and never more so than by the present publication."

"I am told there are two or three very old lives, prebends of Canterbury, in the Minister's gift—near six hundred a-year and a good house. The deans of Hereford, Exeter, Lichfield, and Coventry, York and Winchester *are all old men*."

He could be obsequiously jocular too: "Now this morning comes your roguish, waggish letter, about love, courtship, marriage, throwing the stocking, going to bed; quite shocking to write to a country parson." He, however, evidently furnished amusement to, and was the *farceur* of, the singularly assorted party. We find the poor blinded Sir William writing in 1801, after the victory, from Piccadilly: "You would have laughed to have seen what I saw yesterday. Emma did not know whether she was on her head or her heels; in such a hurry to tell your great news that she could utter nothing but tears of joy and tenderness. Your brother, Mrs. Nelson, and Horace dined with us. Your brother was more extraordinary than ever; he would get up suddenly and cut a caper, rubbing his hands every time, as the thought of your fresh laurels came into his head."

Dr. Nelson, who was so free and pleasant in his allusions, used to invite Lady Hamilton and Mrs. Billington down to Canterbury, where the ladies sang duets together in a manner that ravished the very limited circle that listened; for, as may be conceived, the decorous Canterbury folk were much scandalised at his having such a pair mixing with his family; and when they asked him, took care to put on the card, "Not Lady H——." The prudent ecclesiastic recked little of their prudery; he had set his mind on the coveted preferment, through the agency of "my heroic brother," operated on by Lady Hamilton. ("No beggarly stalls.")

Writing to the worthy Mr. Greville, she complains bitterly of this ignoring of her society, and that "our private characters are to be shattered in the dark. First it was said Lord Nelson and Sir William fought; then, that we played and lost. First, Sir William and Lord Nelson live like brothers; next, Lord Nelson never plays; and this I give you my word of honour. So I beg you will contradict any of these vile reports."

"Whatever you do for my charge," wrote Nelson, "I must be pleased with. Probably she will be lodged at Merton, when she can have the benefit of our walks. It will make the poor mother happy, I am sure. I do not write to her to-day, as this goes through the Admiralty; but tell her all I would say; you know my unchangeable thoughts about her." Most extraordinary and inexplicable is his question: "*Have we a nice church at Merton? We will set an example of goodness to the parishioners.*" Later, however, he more reasonably anticipates a cold reception from the parishioners of Merton :

"No person at Merton can take amiss our not visiting; the answer from me will always be very civil thanks, but that I wish to live retired. We shall leave our sea friends."

"Never mind the great bashaw at the Priory." (This referred to Lord Abercorn at Stanmore). "*He be damned!* If he were single, and had a mind to marry you, he could only make you a marchioness; but as he is situated, and I situated, I can make you a duchess."

"Everything you tell me about my dear Horatia charms me. I think I see her, hear her, and admire her; but she is like her dear, dear mother."

After this, a separation was thought best for all parties. Nelson chose the moment of his departure on the Danish expedition to inform his wife of this step; and he was escorted to his ship by Sir William and Lady Hamilton, and the obsequious and reverend brother.

Then came fresh naval glories, all through which a stream of letters was kept up. Sir William was commissioned to purchase an estate, and Merton was accordingly secured—in truth, to furnish means for a provision for the lady.

News of the Copenhagen *coup de main* had reached London on the 15th of April, 1801, and with it came letters for Lady Hamilton. Wraxall gives a curious picture of the celebration at their house, and shows us at the same time how this woman was countenanced by the world of fashion. On that night she gave a party to celebrate the victory, and Sir Nathaniel repaired there at ten o'clock, and found a very distinguished circle, that included the Dukes of Gordon and Queensbury, Lord W. Gordon, Calonne (the French minister), Mr. Kemble (the actor), the Duc de Noïa (a Neapolitan grandee), together with the Rev. Dr. Nelson. She was the life and soul of the party, and in more than her usual spirits. She played the harpsichord, sang, and finally proposed to dance the "Tarantella" in the fiery Neapolitan fashion. She commenced it with Sir William, who soon had to give way; and was succeeded by the Italian duke, who in his turn retired; and a maid-servant was sent for to succeed him; and after the maid-servant was tired down, a black Copt woman—"a present," says Wraxall oddly, "from Nelson"—succeeded. It seems to have been a most extraordinary performance, and to have suggested to those present the curious antics of the Eastern dancing girls—full of screams, starts, and languishings, accompanied by castanets and tambourine; in short, as the baronet says, "certainly not of a nature to be performed except before a select company." Truly, reading such records as Selwyn's and Angelo's memoirs, we may be reasonably amazed at the tone of London fashionable life, which seemed to anticipate the scandalous orgies of the French empire.

During this time, too, he was writing those strange letters, which were so shamefully published, according to the inevitable Nemesis, which great men when committing themselves to such declarations should bear in mind. He tells her she was a nonpareil; there is not one fit to wipe her shoes; he had rather hear her call "Cupidy! Cupidy!" or her "little story of the hen getting into a tree, than all the speeches made in Parliament."

Through all, too, he shows a rooted dislike to the unfortunate lady who was his wife, and plainly expresses his wish to be rid of her.

Not content with this exhibition of the hero, "the people of England," she said, "must see the man who had upheld the glory of the British flag:" and such was her influence over him, that she persuaded him to quit his family and to exhibit himself at all the corporate and manufacturing towns in the island, attended of course by her and the *ci-devant* ambassador. Where there was a theatre, she conducted him thither, well knowing with what applause he would be received, of which she would come in for her share. Public balls, dinners, etc., were given him, with city freedoms, presented in gold and silver boxes. Poets and minstrels sang his praises, from Falmouth to John-o'-Groat's.

"But at length John Bull, who is at bottom a moral character, recollected that his hero had a wife, and began to marvel that he preferred showing himself to the people accompanied by the spouse of another rather than by his own. The murmurs increased, and, before the tour was completed, his popularity was on the decline. The press attacked this wandering party, insinuating that they moved about for show; and that the public exhibition of a sea-captain, such as Nelson, in the character of an Italian *cavaliere servente*, ought not to be encouraged. The last act of the drama was performed in the theatre, Wellclose Square, where he appeared, dressed in all his orders, and with the sword which had been in the morning presented to him by the Lord Mayor. The enthusiasm of the people on this occasion was less than on any similar one. The 'gods' played off their wit at her ladyship's expense, and she prudently retired. This was her last appearance in public."

These two letters (unpublished) are truly characteristic:

"You cannot think, my dear sir, how sorry we are for poor Dodd's death; but anything we can do to assist the poor widow we will. I am very sorry you are not with us to keep the Hero of heroes' birthday, the 29th; but you will drink his health. Sir William begs his compliments. We have had a most charming tour, which will burst *some* of them. So let all the enimies (sic) of the greatest man alive bless his friends. So I will finish with saying, God bless you."

"MERTON, *February.*

"MY DEAR SIR,

"We are very happy to hear you are better. Lord Nelson has been very uneasy about you; and not hearing from you alarmed us very much. Take care of yourself; avoid hurry and company; do not be persuaded to go out of night; take care of yourself for a month, and you will do very well. But you are in the midst of friends and relations; therefore, I need not say more. Poor Langford has been with us. The *Jesuit* has promised Lord Nelson to make him; but we don't much rely on his word, although I think he cannot well be off. Lord Nelson had an interview with him the other day, and told him his own, and he was as humble as possible. Sir Thomas rules the roast. How long this reign may last I do not know. Great changes are spoken of. Nelson—the glorious Nelson—is the truly great man. In his retirement he seldom goes to town, and for that reason he is much desired and sought for. Keeping men off you keep them on, will do for men as well as women. If ever he is employed—which he will be if there is a new war—you will be one of his select, for such he calls you; but he will not take such a command as he had last year. Shame on them for giving it him; but Nelson is a being of a superior class; the most trivial command he makes of importance, and I look on the attack off Boulogne as the bravest thing we have done. It was not his fault it did not succeed. Alas, the poor brave little Parker! but we must not dwell on such ideas. The Grand-Seignior has sent our Nelson a riband to wear with his star of the crescent, and a very handsome letter through Lord Elgin. The medals for Copenhagen are not yet given. These vagabonds in power are not worthy of great victories. I had some lines sent me the other day on seeing the medal of Julius Cæsar '*Veni, vidi, vici*':

> " Two-thirds of Cæsar's boasted fame
> Thou, Nelson, must resign;
> To come and see is Parker's claim,
> To conquer only thine.

" Are they not very neat?

"Nelson is still with us. We are very busy planting, and I am as much amused with pigs and hens as I was of the court of Naples' ambassador."

Next came a tour in Wales, the party consisting of Nelson, Sir W. and Lady Hamilton, and the brother, Dr. Nelson. Returning home by Blenheim, either by accident or intention the family did not appear to the party, which Nelson took in high dudgeon, and refused the refreshments offered. The lady who had inspired such high-handed treatment of the Neapolitans was not inclined to put up with this affront, and her voice was heard in protest against the ingratitude which denied the hero a place " to which Blenheim should be a kitchen-garden." This scene is another of those painful ones which put him so low.

At last, in 1803, died the foolish old Sir William, as blinded and infatuated in his own way as the admirer; and his last act was to commend "his incomparable Emma" to the care of his dear Nelson, with a declaration that she had never offended him during her life. The duty was willingly undertaken, and was needed, as only a trifle was left to her. Sir William's nephew—the elegant Greville, her early ally and patron—entered on his inheritance with indecent haste, and in money matters behaved with a Shylock-like severity.

Yet this improvident woman had small claims to the public assistance she was so clamorous for. On the ground that she was amply provided for, Sir William left the bulk of his property to Mr. Greville, subject to a charge of 700*l.* a year for her. This old friend and patron seems to have at once turned her out of her London house. This disposition excited the indignation of Nelson, and seems to have at once turned him against his old friend; for we find him writing to the Queen of Naples, reminding her of her obligations to Emma, in this strain: "Your Majesty never had a more attached, sincere, and real friend than your dear Emma. You will be sorry to hear that good Sir William did not leave her in such comfortable circumstances as his fortune would have allowed. He has given it away to his relatives. But she will do honour to his memory, though every one else of his friends calls loudly against him on that account." He was not slow to compensate her for the disappointment; he settled 1200*l*. a year on her. Writing to her he says: "As for old Queensberry, he may put you into his will, or scratch you out, as he pleases; I care not. If Mr. Addington gives you a pension, it is well; but do not let it fret you. Have you not Nelson?" In his will he provided for her amply, and there are numerous codicils adding more and yet more—all Merton, the house and lands; then 4000*l*.; then 2000*l*.; then 500*l*. a year out of Bronte, which, it is to be presumed, never was paid to her, as he never received anything. The last codicil was significant of her grasping nature. It was drawn up to give her "all the hay on the ground," at Merton.

This reference to "Old Queensberry," discloses

an oddly humorous side to the business, for they were both "cultivating" that old jaded creature with a view to his leaving Emma a handsome legacy. The hero is solicitous in sending over wine, etc., such as the old duke likes, promising her to send so many bottles.

She was persuaded to make a humble application to Government for the continuance of even a portion of her husband's pension. In her letter she speaks of her "irreparable loss," her ever-honoured husband, and her dear Sir William, and signs herself with "a respect more than she can well utter." This was refused. She next took a house in Clarges Street, where she began a round of dissipation quite congenial to her temper.

By this time the servile Dr. Nelson had obtained a stall in Canterbury—evidently the reward of his obsequious attendance on Lady Hamilton—and hoped for a richer prize.

The lady is later found living at Nelson's place in Merton, where her extravagance and waste knew no bounds. From a distance he would write to her of the wife with whom he "had no fault to find": "I beg you will never mention that person's name." He was looking forward impatiently to that person's death, when he could be joined by "a nearer tie in law"!

In due time Nelson returned, and the old devotion was signalised by a yet greater infatuation. She had been with him in all his thoughts; and the great commander had, according to precedent, been moved to rhyme verses "in a gale"—some bold, fresh, seamanlike lines, with, however, a significant declaration :

>Though Emma's polish'd verse superior shine,
>Though sensibility grace every line,
>Though her soft Muse be far above all praise,
>And female tenderness inspire her lays:
>>Deign to receive, though unadorn'd
>>By the poetic art,
>>The rude expressions which bespeak
>>A Sailor's untaught heart!
>
>A heart *susceptible*, sincere, and true;
>A heart, by fate, and nature, torn in two :
>One half, to duty and his country due ;
>The other, *better half*, to love and you !
>
>>Sooner shall Britain's sons resign
>>The empire of the sea,
>>Than Henry shall renounce his faith,
>>AND PLIGHTED VOWS, TO THEE !
>>And waves on waves shall cease to roll,
>>And tides forget to flow,
>>Ere thy true Henry's constant love
>>Or ebb, or change, shall know.

When Nelson was fighting his last battle, the Rev. William Nelson, his wife and family, were living with Lady Hamilton. The character of this gentleman has been shown; but it will be enough to mention that this ecclesiastic had entrusted his daughter for some six years to the care of such a directress as Lady Hamilton. The reason for this confidence is too apparent. He doubtless felt that such a proof of trust would be the most flattering token he could give her of belief in her reputability. But in return for this scandalous service he was continually pressing her to exert her interest for his promotion: "Now we have secured the peerage we have only one thing to ask, and that is my promotion in the Church, handsomely and honourably, such as becomes Lord Nelson's brother and heir-apparent to the title. *No put-off with beggarly stalls.* Mr. Addington must be kept steadily to this point." No put-off with beggarly stalls!

The day before the tremendous conflict, Nelson wrote to his daughter Horatia this last letter:

"*Victory*, October 19th, 1805.

"MY DEAREST ANGEL,

"I was made happy by the pleasure of receiving your letter of September 19th; and I rejoiced to hear you are so good a girl, and love my dear Lady Hamilton, who so dearly loves you. Give her a kiss for me. The combined fleets of the enemy are now reported to be coming out of Cadiz, and therefore I answer your letter, my dearest Horatia, to mark to you that you are ever uppermost in my thoughts. I shall be sure of your prayers for my safety, conquest, and speedy return to dear Merton and our dearest, good Lady Hamilton. Be a good girl."

Here, again, is seen this extraordinary jumble of affection and piety, with the still more singular unconsciousness that he was doing aught but what was fitting, moral, and becoming.

His last letter, before the battle, was addressed to Lady Hamilton, and is full of strange presentiment:

"The signal has been made that the enemies' combined fleet are coming out of port. . . . May the God of battles crown my endeavours with success! At all events, I will take care that my name shall ever be most dear to you and Horatia, both of whom I love as much as my own life; and, as my last writing before the battle will be to you, so I hope in God that I shall live to finish my letter after the battle. May Heaven bless you, prays your—NELSON AND BRONTE."

This was found lying unfinished on his table after the battle.

When it first broke on her that she was to be

sacrificed and abandoned—she, having fancied that, as Nelson's legacy to the nation, she would be loaded with favours and benefactions—the revulsion was bewildering; she could not realise it. What her feelings were is shown in an outburst to Dr. Scott, Nelson's chaplain, in her own passionate, uncompromising style. It is dated September, 1806:

"How hard it is, how cruel, this treatment to me and Horatia! That angel's last wishes neglected, not to speak of the fraud that was acted to keep back the codicil. . . .

"You know the great and virtuous affection he had for me, the love he bore my husband; and, if I had any influence over him, I used it for the good of my country. Did I ever keep him at home? Did I not share his glory? Even this last victory it was I bid him go forth. Did he not pat me on the back, call me brave Emma, and said, 'If there were more Emmas there would be more Nelsons'? Does he not in his last moments do me justice, and request, at the moment of his glorious death, that the King and nation will do me justice! And I have got all his letters, and near eight hundred of the Queen of Naples, to show what I did for my King and country, and prettily am I rewarded!

"Psha! I am above them; I despise them, for, thank God, I feel that, having lived with honour and glory, that glory they cannot take from me. I despise them! my soul is above them, and yet I can make some of them tremble by showing how he despised them—for, in his letters to me, he thought aloud. Look at ——, courting the man he despised, and neglecting those whose feet he used to lick! Dirty, vile groveller!"

It is melancholy to have to relate that the prodigious friendship of the Queen of Naples for her English friend did not stand the test of adversity. These violent delights have ever violent endings; and it is said that an application for assistance made to her by Lady Hamilton in her distress was taken no notice of. The latter states, as we have seen, that she had no less than *eight hundred* letters from this royal personage.

The last scene in Nelson's life has been often described, as well as that remarkable codicil to his will, written on October 21st, 1805, "then in sight of the combined fleets of France and Spain," distant about ten miles, and which is devoted entirely to Lady Hamilton. In the preamble, he states that her "eminent services" have never been rewarded by "our king or country;" and he recapitulates them minutely, viz., the obtaining the letter in 1796, and the order for victualling the fleet. He also recommends his daughter Horatia to his king and country. An air of romance has been cast about this last solemn act, and his gallant and truly heroic end, together with the smoke of that glorious victory, has blinded the world to the extraordinary character of the proceeding. If by some accident the French fleet had got away, and the engagement had not taken place, what sort of judgment would have been pronounced on the matter? First, the complacent prayer "to the great God whom I worship" for a blessing to descend upon him and crown his efforts. "He was not alone then," says the writer of an extraordinary article in *Blackwood*; "for One whose 'good and faithful servant' he had always been was with him!" Surely one with the most elementary notions of piety would have thought that at such a crisis, and after such a prayer, some *amende* was due to the outraged law of morality, and to his deserted and injured wife. Even that appeal for Lady Hamilton was not justifiable; for he knew that he had provided for her at the sacrifice of those who had legitimate and honourable claims on him. He had given her Merton, and made a settlement on her of his Sicilian estate, and she had 700*l*. a-year from Sir William. His reason, therefore, for begging from his "King and country" an ample provision to maintain her rank in life must have been his knowledge of her reckless extravagance, to support which her handsome fortune would have been inadequate. It seems ungracious and unbecoming to scrutinise the last act of such a hero—one who has laid this nation under an eternal weight of obligation.

As to the legacy, there can of course be but the one opinion—that it should have been religiously carried out by the country. Indeed, the late history of that codicil is disgraceful in every view. It was given to Captain Blackie, and handed by him to the Rev. Doctor Nelson. Not a word was heard of it until the day after parliament had voted 120,000*l.* for the heirs of the dead hero. Dining with Lady Hamilton, the fortunate earl threw it to her across the table, and said she might do what she liked with it. Such a story of elaborate ingratitude and baseness would seem incredible. It is not even disputed; and the worst part is, that the scheme succeeded perfectly. The suppression could not be repaired; the money was voted, and the matter could not be reopened. There was a natural disinclination to discolour the national glory and Nelson's glory with such a *tache* as Nelson's frailty. The strangest part, however, was that in this matter the Government was curiously impartial in its slight, and in this settlement passed over the injured wife as well as Lady Hamilton. For this there could be no justification or excuse of precedent, as, in Abercrombie's instance, the wife had been included in the limitations. On the whole, never were the *laissez-faire* principles of an English Government carried so far.

The rest of Lady Hamilton's history is the history of a miserable descent — embarrassments, beggings, borrowings, and straits of every kind. Her debts were 18,000*l.*; and she had the charge of her daughter Horatia, bequeathed as a legacy to the country, and shifted from the legatee to her. It was said she had her taught some of her own *poses* and attitudes as the beginning of an education; but this may have been one of the many stories circulated about her. She herself, indeed, could not get rid of her old theatrical associations; and as she had long played the part of the hero's "love," she must now play the hero's mourner.* When in one of Mr. Braham's new operas that amazing piece of declamation, so dear to robust tenors, "The Death of Nelson," was introduced, Lady Hamilton attended in a box at the theatre; and when the singer was vociferating, "Then England confessed that every man," etc., she fainted away. Some indulgence might be felt for this exhibition; but when it occurred a second time, and was repeated, it became a matter of just amusement. But she had more serious things to think of. She was being pressed by creditors of all kinds. She implored the old profligate Duke of Queensberry, who had been her admirer, and whom the hero was anxious

---

* There was a lady living not long ago who went to see her at this time, and found her in bed, with the sheets trimmed with black.

should be her admirer, to purchase the estate Nelson had bequeathed to her; but he refused. Then came executions and sales. The Patriotic Fund and Lloyd's did what the nation would not do, and made her liberal grants. But this was of no use; and there was presently the scandalous spectacle of an execution sale, with all Nelson's presents and articles belonging to him, such as the box containing the freedom of the city of Oxford. No one cared to interfere to save Nelson's memory from the slur.

The death of the hero and her own extravagances left Lady Hamilton in a miserable condition both of mind and body. It is to her credit that her first thoughts were not for herself, but for his family, left quite unprovided for. Mr. Rose was then in office, and seems to have taken a good-natured interest in her fortunes, even to the end of her disastrous career, in spite of the lady's erratic doings. He seems to have dreaded her publishing the papers and letters, which would have been fatal to her interests, on which she wrote him this characteristic letter from her bed, where she says "she had ever been since the fatal sixth of this month (November, 1805)":

"Believe me, then, when I assure you I do not see anyone but the family of my dear Nelson. His letters are in the bed with me; and only to the *present Earl* did I ever read one, and then only a part. It is true he is leaky, but I believe would not willingly tell anything; but I have been told something like some of my letters have been printed in some paper. I never now read a paper, and my health and spirits are so bad I cannot enter into a war with vile editors. Of this be assured, no one shall ever see a letter of my glorious and dear departed Nelson. It is true I have a journal from him ever since he came up to Naples to get provisions for our troops in Toulon, when he was in the *Agamemnon;* but his letters are sacred, and shall remain so. My dear sir, my heart is broken. Life to me now is not worth having; I lived but for him. His glory I gloried in; it was my pride that he should go forth; and this fatal and last time he went I persuaded him to it. But I cannot go on—my heart and head are gone; only, believe me, what you write to me shall ever be attended to. Could you know me you would not think I had such bad policy as to publish any thing at this moment. My mind is not a common one; and having lived as a *confidante* and friend with such men as Sir William Hamilton, and dearest, glorious Nelson, I feel myself superior to vain tattling women. Excuse me, but I am ill and nervous."

The brave Hardy was no less zealous in her cause, and, as soon as he landed in England, waited on Mr. Rose to press her claims, showing him Nelson's last entries in his pocket-book, recommending her to his country. Mr. Rose engaged to mention the matter to Mr. Pitt, though he feared her case was now too remote, and was properly in the Department of Foreign Affairs. Mr. Pitt died without anything being done for her. Mr. Rose, however, pressed Mr. Canning to do something, who promised that he would consider it carefully. The result, however, was but little encouraging.

With " such earnest entreaties " as he could use, Rose implored him to let her have a sum of some 6000*l*. or 7000*l*. from the Secret Service Fund. But this was found out of the question, and the most that could be looked for was a trifling pension " for the child who lives with her, and was recommended also by Lord Nelson in his last moments "—a phrase that supports the theory of Horatia being Nelson's daughter.

Lord Grenville, when the matter was referred to him, would do nothing; and both he and Mr. Canning resorted to some ingenious official objections in support of their disinclination.

" I do assure you," wrote the latter, " that I should be very sincerely disposed to gratify your anxious wishes in behalf of Lady H. if I could do so. But Lord Grenville's letter, as you yourself seem aware, does not help me at all; on the contrary, it is worded with the coldest caution, and would, I think leave it quite open to him, and is intended to leave it open to him, to say that though Lady Hamilton's services deserved reward, yet the Foreign S. S. Fund was not the proper fund out of which that reward should come.

"I confess I am myself of this opinion. I do think that a pension might be well bestowed on Lady H. But I do *not* think that, *even at the time*, the influence of a foreign minister's wife with the court where her husband resides, is a fit subject for compensation by secret-service money. There is still, however, another consideration more embarrassing, particularly in the times in which we are acting. The S. S. fund is, by express designation, for *secret* services—services that *cannot be explained or avowed.* Now *here* is a service published not only in Lady H.'s memorials, and known to every person whom she has solicited, but printed in extracts of a will registered in Doctors' Commons, and accessible to all mankind. What reason upon earth is there, it will be said, that if this service is remunerated *at all*, it should be remunerated *secretly?* or how *can* it be remunerated *secretly* in fact? Would not everyone whom Lady H. has solicited, and every member of opposition high and low, know that Lady H. *had* received the reward of those services, and received it from a fund not brought to account? And why not bring to account a matter so notorious? Do you not see the multitude of inconvenient questions to which this transaction would give rise?"

When Nelson was setting out on his last voyage, he was visited on board the *Victory* by Mr. Canning and Mr. Rose, who dined with him in the cabin of the *Victory*. On this occasion he had implored Mr. Rose to press Lady Hamilton's claims on Mr. Pitt. The hero seems to have taken a sanguine view of the assurances given him, for he wrote to her that *both* had assured him that Mr. Pitt had engaged to take care of her. Unfortunately there was a misconception here, as Mr. Canning declared that no conversation on the topic had taken place, and Mr. Rose insisted that he had done no more than promise to use his influence. Nothing, however, was more likely than that the most handsome and most abundant assurances would have been given that all Nelson's wishes should be attended to, and it *does* seem probable that he would have mentioned the matter to Canning. The result, however, was that nothing was done. A petition was presented to the Prince Regent, but with the same result.

Eight years after Nelson's death she was arrested, and consigned to the King's Bench, with her daughter. The heroine of the fêtes at Naples, the beautiful wife of the English minister, the Queen's companion, the adored of Nelson, now to be in the hands of tipstaffs and bailiffs! While she was in duress, appeared those volumes of letters, the publication of which excited such a storm of abuse and reviling. For these she was said to have received 1000*l*. It must be confessed that, for an unfortunate creature rejected by all the friends who had courted her when she was prosperous, sneered at by the public, who disbelieved in her claims of friendship with Nelson, it seemed the readiest means of vindication; and, if worse than indiscreet, it was an excusable indiscretion. To read the letters of the Queen of Naples, of English admirals and officers, all fawning on her, and affecting to be devoted to the Neapolitan cause, because they followed the cue of their admiral, thus pandering to his infatuation, is a humiliating thing, and deserved exposure. Worse were the flattering deans, bishops, and clergy, with other great people. We can almost sympathise in the singular character of this publication, and enjoy the confusion it occasioned. The unfortunate woman affected to deny having sanctioned the publication, by advertisements in the papers and other ways; and it was stated on her behalf, that it had been done by some scribe or hack whom she had taken into her house to prepare a statement of her case, and who had surreptitiously taken copies of the letters.

There is one often-debated subject connected with this episode, namely, that of Horatia, Nelson's "adopted daughter" as he styles her in his will. This lady eventually married, in 1822, the Rev.

Philip Wand, and died only a short time since. In Nelson's letters she is always spoken of as Thompson, and was christened by that name, though her proper one was added later. Sir Harris Nicholas, in his vast collection of Nelson letters, discusses the question as to who were her father and mother, propounding many theories. She was born on October 29th, 1800. Nelson's confidential solicitor assured Sir Harris Nicholas that he knew Lady Hamilton was not her mother. Sir T. Hardy told Mr. Locker, of Greenwich Hospital, that she was not Nelson's or Lady Hamilton's daughter, but the daughter of a petty officer named Thompson. Lady Hamilton herself declared that she was Nelson's daughter, but her mother was a "great personage." Mr. Paget in his interesting essay, declares that "the character of Lady Hamilton's intimacy with Nelson will ever remain an enigma." Unfortunately, the matter is only too clear, and no one who examines the matter, can have a moment's doubt that Horatia was their daughter. The letters of Nelson, published by her, are admitted to be genuine, and there is one letter of August 26th, 1803, pp. 175-8, which, in spite of the omissions, is really convincing. It was natural that Lady Hamilton should so studiously deny the relationship. But there was a more particular reason still in the fact that she was pressing her claims on the Government, which would seriously damage them all, about "the adopted daughter." This curious trickery was carried on in various shapes. Thus, among Lady Hamilton's papers was one to this effect:

"She is the daughter, the true and beloved daughter, of Viscount Nelson; and if he had lived, she would have been all that his love and position could have made her; for nature has made her perfect, beautiful, good, and amiable. Her mother was TOO GREAT to be mentioned, but her foster-mother and Horatia had a true friend in Emma Hamilton."

Of her she wrote to Miss Nelson in that vehement, excited style to which she was prone:

"Although her parents are lost, yet she is not without a portion, and I shall cherish her to the last moment of my life, and *curse* them who *curse her, and Heaven bless them who bless her!*"

The daughter's opinion of her was more measured. "With all Lady Hamilton's faults—and she had many—she had many fine qualities, which, had she been placed early in better hands, would have made her a very superior woman."

At last a generous alderman named Smith came to her assistance. He procured her release; and, before fresh detainers could be lodged, she got away to Calais, then the happy sanctuary for the distressed and broken-down, and there joined the English herd of unfortunate exiles. She was to live there, however, but eighteen months.

Characteristically enough, she put up at that most expensive of hotels, the famous Dessein's, which almost deserves to have its history written, so many strange characters have stopped there. She immediately wrote over that she was educating her child. She gave her the best masters the place could furnish; she sent her to a ladies' day-school, where she remained from eight to one, and was taught piano, harp, and all the accomplishments. "*Not any girls but those of the first families go there,*" wrote the poor broken creature. What the "first families" of the Calais of that day were may be imagined. They went to *fêtes champêtres* outside the town; and, indeed, it was no wonder, as she said almost pathetically, she "felt so much better from change of climate, food, air, large rooms, and *liberty,*" that she began to hope to see her dear Horatia grow up. But in truth she was in wretched health, and was growing unwieldy from dropsy and other causes. An English interpreter there (De Rheims) let to her a small meanly-furnished apartment. But from this she had later to remove to something meaner. And from that time it became a miserable struggle, as she sank lower and lower, until her last sickness came on. There is something tragic in the incidents of these closing scenes; and her whole history is to be added to the list of almost dramatic reverses which point many a moral and adorn tales. An English lady ordering meat for her dog at the butcher's was told by this honest De Rheims that he knew of a lady who would be glad of even a scrap from the dog's portion. He would not divulge the name, as he was bound to secrecy, and the fallen creature was too proud to receive charity. The lady then—a true Samaritan—bade him furnish wine, and anything else that was required, at her charge, and as from his own bounty. When the outcast was almost at her last, he begged of her to see the lady who had been so good; and on his stating that she was not a person of title, she consented, received this Mrs. Hunter—whose name should be preserved—thanked and blessed her.

A mean little house belonging to one Damy, now No. 111, Rue Française, saw the close of this strange career, which must have seemed to her clouding faculties like a dream, and which, in spite of all the brilliant scenes between, had ended nearly as it had begun. It was noticed too that, as her end approached, some of the old beauty came back; and on the 15th of January, 1815, an hour after noon, the deserted exiled outcast ended her life.

Her burial was in keeping, though the account is not very consistent. Mrs. Hunter, it is said, wished to have her interred according to English custom. For this she was only laughed at, and poor Emma was put into a deal box without any inscription. "She was only allowed to contribute a pall, which she made out of a black silk petticoat." Yet the "deal box" must have taken the shape of a coffin; and there was no English clergyman in Calais to read any service; so what English custom was refused, except the inscription, it is hard to see. She was, moreover, interred in unconsecrated ground, formerly the garden of the Duchess of Kingston, and later converted into a timber-yard. There an Irish half-pay officer read the service over her for whom bishops were once proud to officiate.

There were many stories about her last sickness: that "she had fallen into intemperate habits and become a Catholic; that she was pursued with remorse for her share in Caraccioli's death." The story was not improbable from her long residence in Italy. The "intemperance," it has been seen, was not so improbable.

An inventory was drawn up of her miserable little property, which is still to be seen at the municipal office. It was valued at about nine pounds. There were also a few pawn-tickets for trinkets, etc. She owed money to the tradesmen. They wished to detain the unhappy Horatia; but she was got on board ship, and escaped their greedy hands. The Rev. Earl Nelson, it was said, appeared on the scene, actually, with a meanness that seems fatuity, to claim any little trinkets which he fancied might have belonged to his late brother. But when he was presented with the pawn-tickets he declined to pay any expenses, and returned home. The good city alderman, however, took this on himself.

Some drafts of a will found among her papers, unexecuted, reveal to us the warm, passionate nature of this woman, more sensitive to petty wrongs than to great ones, and scarcely yet able to appreciate the incredible bitterness of the thought that Nelson's countrymen would allow Nelson's Emma to sink in neglect and even starvation before their eyes. There is a curious natural quaintness in the phraseology; and the passages I have underlined are curious.

"Merton, October 7th, 1806.

"I, Emma Hamilton, being in sound body and mind, leave this as my last will and testament. I beg, as the virtuous and dear Nelson wished me to be buried near him, that, if it is possible, I may be; but if it cannot be, then let me be buried at Merton ; but if it is possible, let me rest near my ever-beloved Nelson. I give to my dear mother, formerly Mary Kidd, then Lions, and after *Mary Doggen, or Cadogan, however she may be called,* all my property, let it be either in wearing apparel or furniture, gold, silver, jewels, pictures, wine, and everything in the house at Merton, and seventy acres, which the glorious Nelson left me, and two acres and a half which I have bought since, added to it, all of which I give to my dear mother for her natural life; and, after her death, I give all I have mentioned to my dear Horatia Nelson Thompson, or properly, Horatia Nelson, and her children for ever. . . . Also, I beg to leave to my dear Horatia Nelson that she pays the above yearly pensions: one hundred a year, and fifty pounds, to Sarah Reynolds and Caroline Connor. *I do not leave anything to Ann, or Mary Ann Connor, as she has been a wicked, story-telling young woman, and tried to defame her best friends and relations.* I leave Horatia Nelson a ward in Chancery, and I beg my dear friends, George Mathison and his wife, to have the goodness to see after her education, and that she is properly brought up after her mother's death. *If they see to this Nelson's and Emma's spirits will look down on them and bless them.* My dearest mother I leave executrix with full power. If I have not mentioned everything, I leave all I am possessed of and have to my mother for her natural life, and after to Horatia Nelson, she being six years old."

Two years afterwards she writes another paper, in which she recurs yet more bitterly to her treatment by Mrs. Connor. It is dated

"October 16th, 1808.

" If I can be buried in St. Paul's, I shall be very happy to be near to glorious Nelson, whom I loved and admired, as once Sir William Nelson (Hamilton ?), and I had agreed we should all be buried near each other. This would have been that three persons, who were so much attached to each other from virtue and friendship, should have been laid in one grave *when they quitted this slanderous, ill-natured world. But 'tis past; and in Heaven I hope we shall meet.* If I am not permitted to be buried in St. Paul's, let me be put *where I shall be near my dear mother, when she is called from this ungrateful world.* But I hope she will live to be a mother to Nelson's child, Horatia. I beg that Merton may be sold, and all debts paid; and whatever money shall be left after all debts are paid, I give to my dear mother, and, after her death, to my dear Horatia Nelson. I also give all I am possessed of in this world to my dear mother, Mary Doggen, or Cadogan, for her use; and, after her death, to Horatia Nelson. I hope Mr. George Rose will be my executor, and take care of my dear mother and Horatia; and if he should not be living, I hope his eldest son will perform this last favour and see justice done to Nelson's daughter; and also I beg His Royal Highness the Prince of Wales, as he dearly loved Nelson, that His Royal Highness will protect his child, and be kind to her; for this I beg of him, for there is no one I so highly regard as his Royal Highness. Also my good friend the Duke of Queensberry, I beg of him, as Nelson beseeched of him to be kind to me, so I recommend my dear mother and Horatia to him. *I have done my King and country some service; but as they were ungrateful enough to neglect the request of the virtuous Nelson in providing for me, I do not expect they will do anything for his child; but if there should be any administrating at my death, with heart and feeling I beg they will provide for Horatia Nelson, the child who would have had a future if he had not gone forth to fight his country's battles; therefore, she has a claim on them."*

There is a rude, burning eloquence in these words —an inexpressible bitterness. Not less characteristic is the sudden turn to the Connor grievance, and the language is not less excited:

"I declare before God, and as I hope to see Nelson in heaven, that Ann Connor, who goes by the name of Carew, and tells many falsehoods that she is my daughter, but from what motive I know not; I declare that she is the eldest daughter of my mother's sister Sarah Connor, and that I have the mother and six children to keep, all of them except two having turned out bad. I therefore beg of my mother to be kind to the two good ones, Sarah and Amelia. This family having by their extravagance almost ruined me, I have nothing to leave them; but I pray God to turn Ann Connor's, *alias* Carew's, heart. I forgive her; *but there is a madness in the Connor family.* I hope it is only the effect of this disorder that may have induced this bad young woman to have persecuted me by her falsehoods."

What a beginning! what a finale! Anyone standing before the charming face at South Kensington —its grace, *enjouement*, elegance—would not credit such a history.

THE BEAUTIFUL GUNNINGS.

THE BEAUTIFUL GUNNINGS.

This may be thought an old and familiar story, but it is well worth relating at greater length than it has hitherto been told; indeed, little more than the outline of the romantic history of these two girls is known to the general reader.

About the middle of the last century, there was a certain Irish country gentleman living down in the west of Ireland, who is set down in the books of heraldry as "John Gunning, Esquire, of Co. Roscommon." Mr. Gunning fulfilled the customary function of many Irish gentlemen of that day, shooting snipe, and perhaps Irish gentlemen, and certainly never dreamed of the destiny that was in store for his two little daughters. He had made a good connection, marrying a sister of Lord Mayo's, so that the obscurity of the little girls is not such as has been represented, nor their rise so extraordinary. They were born at

Castlecoote, their father's place; Maria, the eldest, in the year 1733; the other, Elizabeth, a year later. The family consisted of one son and five daughters— namely, John, Mary, Elizabeth, Catherine, Lizzy, and Sophia. John grew up from being "a sweet little boy," as one who knew him called him, entered the Army, fought with distinction at Bunker's Hill, became a major-general, and Sir John Gunning. The first girl was to be hereafter Countess of Coventry and titular belle of the English court; the other was to wed successively the Duke of Hamilton and Duke of Argyll, and become the mother of four dukes—elevations which, however striking, have been paralleled. Not so, however, that union of beauty, fortune, rank, and romance. There were, indeed, *three* beautiful sisters; and, looking at the prints, it would not be difficult to award the palm. Lady Coventry was the most attractive. Her sister, who made a comparatively obscure marriage to Mr. Travis, was almost as handsome, having the same small mouth and elegant features. The Duchess was of a graver cast.

"John Gunning, Esquire," does not appear to have risen with his children, nor would public curiosity be likely to be much excited in his behalf. He had come up to Dublin, and had lived in that gay capital during one of its gayest epochs, until he could reside there no longer; and, as we are naïvely told, had been "obliged to retire into the country, to avoid *the disagreeable consequences that must ensue.*"

An odd, irregular actress, who about this time had an engagement at Mr. Sheridan's theatre in Dublin, happened to be one day returning from rehearsal. When at the bottom of Great Britain Street, she heard what she called "the voice of distress." These were the times when sentiment was fast coming into fashion, both before and behind the curtain. So, on hearing "the voice of distress" in Britain Street, the actress at once turned in the direction, entered a house, and, without ceremony, proceeded upstairs. Strange men, however, stood at the door, and in the parlour she found a distressed family, consisting of "a woman of a most elegant figure," and who was the centre of a group of "four beautiful girls" and "a sweet boy of about three years." The united voices of this young family had joined in the mournful chorus which had so irresistibly attracted the actress in Britain Street.

The "woman of a most elegant figure" proved to be Mrs. Gunning, wife of "John Gunning, Esquire, Co. Roscommon;" she received her guest very politely, and complimented her "upon possessing such humane sensations." She then entered upon an explanation of her position—how they had lived beyond their income, and how John Gunning, Esquire, had been obliged, as before mentioned, "to retire into the country, to avoid the disagreeable consequences that must ensue." Some hopes had been entertained that Lord Mayo, her brother, would have come forward, "listening to the dictates of fraternal affection," and have done something for Mr. Gunning and his family; but this hope had turned out quite futile; and the ill-looking officials at the door were actually preparing to carry out their stern duty, in virtue of the powers confided to them by the high sheriff. The future countess and double duchess were awaiting with tears this indignity in what is now one of the obscurest streets in the city. But what shall be said of Mr. John Gunning, who had "withdrawn into the country," to avoid the inconveniences of this proceeding, and left his family to face bailiffs and executions?

The actress and the lady, however, soon arranged a practical plan. It was resolved that, when darkness set in, the actress's man-servant should be despatched to Britain Street, to stand under the drawing-room, and catch any light articles that should be thrown down to him, that something might be saved.

Further, the good-natured actress actually agreed to take in the whole of the young family and their servant until some arrangement could be made. Not long after, "Miss Burke, Mrs. Gunning's sister, a lady of exemplary piety who had passed her probation in the community of Channel Row," sent for the younger children; but the two remained with the actress. Maria, the elder, seems to have been "all life and spirits," a sort of boisterous hoiden; the other was "more reserved and solid."

This charitable actress was the well-known George Anne Bellamy, who has left behind her some outspoken, rather vulgar memoirs, but which are yet natural and characteristic, tinged also with garrulity, so as to become very entertaining. These were services which should have left a sense of obligation.

After this odd incident the actress was drifted away to London, and became lost in the whirl of theatrical intrigue. How the Gunning family were finally extricated does not appear; but Maria, our heroine, wrote her benefactress a letter—strange both in orthography and composition—but which seems so overdone in its mistakes as to excite reasonable suspicion. It is known, however, that these beauties were sadly illiterate, and so the letter is to a certain degree in keeping. It was addressed to "Miss Bellamy in England."

The following are some characteristic extracts:

"I rec^d my dearest Miss Bellamy letter at last; after her long silence, indeed I was very jealous with you, but you make me *amen's* in Letting me hear from you now. it gives me great joy and all our *faimley* to hear that yr Dear mama and your Dearest self are in perfect health to be sure that yr Relations where fighting to see which of them shod have you last and Longest with y^m. . . . I am very unfortunate to be in the country when our Vaux Hall was. If I was in Town I shod be thear and I believe I should be much more delighted than at a publicker diversion. . . . I don't believe it was Mr. Knox you read of at Bath for he is hear. Dublin is the stupites place. . . . I believe Sheredian can get no one to play with him is doing all he can to get frinds for him sef to be sure you have hread he is marrd for sirtain to Miss Chamberlan. a sweet pare.

"I must bid a due and shall only say I am my D^r your ever affe^{cnat}

"M. GUNNING."

After all, this spelling was hardly exceptional at the period. Mr. Sterne's MSS. are full of faults almost as gross; and he talks of "opening a dore."

What became of the "sweet little boy" has been mentioned. Of the three sisters, one, who is unknown to fame, Catherine, married an undistinguished gentleman who, as we have mentioned, has only come down to posterity as "Robert Travis, Esquire." The account of the undistinguished portion of the family was written by an ancient parish clerk, in a letter to a Mr. Madder, of Fulham, and, appropriately enough, was adorned with spelling quite as unorthodox. "I take the freedom," says this odd document, which is dated from Huntingdonshire, "in wrighting to you from an information of Mr. Warrington, that you would be glad to have the account of my Townswoman, the Notefied, the Famis, Beautifull Miss Gunnings, born at Hemmingfordgrey, tho they left the Parish before I had knoledge enough to remember them, and I was born in 32. But I will give you the best account I can, which I believe is better than any man in the country besides myself, though I have not the Birth Register for so long a Date, and since Dr. Dickens is dead, I don't know where it is." He then tells of the two elder sisters; and recollects distinctly seeing the Portrait of the wife of Robert Travis, Esq., in a print-shop, "I beleeve in St. Poul's Churchyard;" and who had acquired a sort of reflected reputation from her sister's fame. This was an oval after Cotes, with a scrap of doggerel underneath :

> This youngest grace, so like her sister's frame,
> Her kindred features tell from whence she came :
> 'Tis needless once to mention Gunning's name.

This is probably an hallucination of the worthy clerk's, as the sisters appear certainly to have been born in the sister country; but which the memory of the ancient parish fashioned into something more elaborate :

> The youngest of these Beauties here we have in view,
> So like in person to the other two;
> Whoever views her person and her fame,
> Will see at once that Gunning is her name.

"Which," he adds, "is the best account I can give of them three; but then there was two more, which perhaps you don't know anything about; which I will give you the true Mortalich Regester off, from a Black mavel which lies in our chancel, as follows."

The "black mavel" tells the story of the lives of little Sophia and Lizzy, in a pretty inscription.

By-and-by the two belles, now grown up, were taken over to London, and almost instantly caused a success and sensation, for which a parallel, in that department, can scarcely be found. They had no fortune, they had slender connections; but fashion in these days was more or less republican. In a society a little wild and frank in tone, and where men of the stamp of Lord March, Selwyn, Mr. Wilkes, and Sir Francis Dashwood were leaders, the claims of dazzling beauty were not to be resisted. They took the town by storm. They burst upon the metropolis in the early months of the year 1751. Walpole, that most full and delightful chronicler, made this appearance a leading item in his next budget for Florence. The wranglings of ministers, he wrote to his friend, were regarded with utter indifference. The Miss Gunnings were in everybody's mouth, "being twenty times" more talked of than the Newcastle family and Lord Granville. These, he says, are "two Irish girls of no fortune, who are declared the handsomest women alive. I think," says the critical Horace acutely, "their being *two* so handsome and such perfect figures is their chief excellence, for singly I have seen much handsomer women than either."

Many stories flutter about as to their first entry on the gay London social boards. Mrs. Gunning was not likely to step from Great Britain Street into the Mayfair of those days without some trick of honourable society being specially contrived for her. One legend was, that some cruel wag sent them sham cards for a great lady's masquerade, but which the Irish mother was skilful enough to detect, and which she "improved" with the wit and daring of her country. She waited on the noble lady in person, taking care to bring with her one of her matchless daughters. She told of her false card. The eyes of the noble lady fell upon the daughter. She thought of her masquerade, and, as may be imagined, substituted a genuine for the forged invitation.

The new belles received a shape of homage that

was almost inconvenient; for when they went forth upon the public *prado,* and took the air in the parks at fashionable hours, they were attended by such admiring crowds that it soon became impossible to pursue their walk. The public admiration was not restrained by any feeling of delicacy, and was perhaps the more acceptable as an honest testimonial. That was in June. In August they were still cynosures, and "make more noise than any of their predecessors since the days of Helen." No wonder Mrs. Montagu spoke of them as "those goddesses the Gunnings."

But their fresh *naïveté,* and, it must be said, rough *brusquerie,* laid them open to all manner of strange stories and ill-natured remarks. An odd legend went round the clubs. They went down to see the paintings at Hampton Court, and having passed into what was called the Beauty Room, where are the questionable shepherdesses of King Charles, they heard the housekeeper show another company in with this introduction, "Ladies, here are the Beauties." The wild pair, assuming this to be directed to themselves, flew into a violent rage, asked her what she meant—that they came to see the palace and paintings, not to be shown themselves.

They were adopted into the best society. About Christmas in the same year it was not surprising that each should have a distinguished adorer. James, Duke of Hamilton, a wild *roué* Scotch nobleman, "equally damaged in his fortune and person," says the bitter Horace, met her at a masquerade, and fell desperately in love with Elizabeth, the younger. Lord Coventry, "a grave young lord of the patriot breed," was the professed admirer of the other. Everyone watched the progress of the business eagerly. The malign Lord Chesterfield was inclined to think it would end doubtfully for the honour of the lady.

She and her mother played a bold but skilful game. They appeared everywhere with the noble suitor. When he had to move the address in the House of Lords the brilliant girl sat beside him, and thus caused him to be agitated by the two passions of fear and love. Her mother told Lord Granville afterwards that "the poor girl was near fainting with agitation." The duke vaguely proposed marriage some time in the spring.

Lord Chesterfield presently gave a magnificent assembly, at which every person of quality was present, who were to be amused with the spectacle of the duke's frantic courtship. He sat at one end of the room, and played faro and carried on a disorderly flirtation with the young beauty who was at the other end. Three hundred pounds was on each board; so, in a very short time, by these tactics, he was a loser of nearly 1000*l.* The Honourable Horace Walpole was among the company, taking sarcastic notes. "I own," he said, "I was so little a professor in love that I thought all this parade looked ill for the poor girl, and could not conceive, if he was so much engaged with his mistress as to disregard such sums, why he played at all."

Two nights afterwards, the strange *dénouement* came about. Her mother and sister were away at Bedford House, and the duke found himself alone with the belle. A sudden ardour—whether of wine or affection—seized on him, and he insisted on having the ceremony performed at once, and on the spot. A parson was promptly sent for, but, on arriving, refused to officiate without the important essentials of a license or a ring, neither of which had been thought of. The duke swore, and talked of calling in the archbishop. Finally, the parson's scruples gave way before his impatience; the license was overlooked, and the lack of the traditional gold ring was happily supplied by the *ring of a bed-curtain!* Thus the ardent duke was at last lawfully married, at midnight, in Mayfair Chapel, on February 14th, 1752.

This adventure threw all London into an uproar. The Scotch were furious; "the women mad that so much beauty has had its effect" (thus the bitter Horace); and, better than all, it had a stimulating effect on the admirers of her sister; for Lord Coventry at once gave out that he intended marrying the sister; and, within three weeks, on the 5th of March, 1752, she was, according to the suitable phrase, "led to the hymeneal altar." This rise in their fortunes brought about a perfect *furore*, both of curiosity and of enthusiasm. The public, who had crowded before to see them as "the Gunnings," with the true instinct of a mob, became frantic to see them again in their new and higher station. We see in the old music-books a Lady Coventry's minuet. When the duchess was presented at court, the noble persons at St. James's actually climbed up on tables and chairs to have a good stare, like a mere vulgar crowd. When they came out to their chairs to go to parties, they found immense mobs gathered. There was a rush to take places at the theatres if it became known they were going.

The critics, however, were not unanimous. The Duchess of Somerset thought her "too tall to be genteel, and her face out of proportion to her height." Her dress, too, was thought rather to savour of the ballet than of an English lady of quality. To the duchess, Lady Di Egerton and Mrs. Selwyn appeared quite as pretty and a good deal more modest.

In a few weeks their lords took the brides down to their respective castles, and, says Walpole, "one hears no more about them," save this simple fact, which amounted to a good deal, that when the duchess put up one night at a Yorkshire inn, no less than seven hundred people sat up all night round it to see her get into her post-chaise in the morning! She was always good-natured, and gave Tate Wilkinson benefits at his country theatre.

When the season came round again there were no signs of a reaction. But a new beauty had appeared in the horizon, and comparisons began to be made. The world was talking of Lady Caroline Petersham. Mrs. Grenville, writing to her husband, tells him, as a little bit of gossip, that the "Morocco ambassador" —whose standard of beauty, however, would have been directed by barbaric canons—actually preferred Lady Caroline to Lady Coventry. Both were now being taken over to another metropolis, to confound our hereditary enemies—or allies?—in their own capital. The Gunnings arrived with a vast prestige. A lucky shoemaker of Worcester was making her a pair of shoes, and actually "turned" two guineas and a half, in pennies, for showing them! Still the old *gaucherie* was not softened down; rather it became more conspicuous by their high position; and the ill-natured public indemnified itself for its insane freaks of admiration by circulating all manner of what are called *spropositos*. "I can't say," even Mr. Walpole must admit, "her genius is equal to her beauty." It would be unreasonable to expect such a combination.

Looking at the brilliant mezzotint which once hung in the print-shops, we can gather a faint notion of those wonderful charms which once so dazzled the London lieges. Something very bright, very spiritual, very dazzling; but what all agree was the greater charm is, of course, lost. This was the extraordinary play of expression, which comes from wild spirits, and which may still be seen in many Irish girls. Mrs. Delany saw her often, and noted this special attraction. "She has a thousand dimples and prettinesses in her cheeks, her eyes a little drooping at the corners, but fine for all that; she has a thousand airs, but with a sort of humour that diverts me." There was a good deal of the hoiden about her, with much of that polite sauciness which is more or less the titular belle's prerogative. The pretty elegy, in which the Rev. Mr. Mason bewailed her loss, touches very happily on these charms, and, with the aid of her picture, sets her before us.

> Whene'er with soft serenity she smiled,
>   Or caught the orient blush of quick surprise,
> How sweetly mutable, how brightly wild
>   The liquid lustre darted from her eyes!
> Each look, each motion, waked a new-born grace
>   That o'er her form a transient glory cast;
> Some lovelier wonder soon usurp'd the place,
>   Chased by a charm still lovelier than the last.

Mr. Mason's lines were greatly relished at Cambridge. They were got by heart and adapted to the charms of university seamstresses and bed-makers.

This was the figure that the Parisians now saw at

all their leading fêtes ; but, as might be expected, the French refused to confess the admiration, or, at least, would not allow themselves to be dazzled. It is natural, indeed, that when a beauty or singer comes, with heraldings and flourishes, their patents should be looked into jealously. Lady Caroline Petersham they dismissed contemptuously, not crediting that she had ever been handsome. Lady Coventry was admitted to be passable. But there was a native belle in the field, one Madame Brionne, to whose charms even the English abroad testified; and French beauty, fortified with the graces of French wit and training, and refined by the associations of the most elegant court, was scarcely fair competition. The Roscommon girl, as her friend Walpole remarked, "was under piteous disadvantages." For she was "very silly, ignorant of the world," and could not speak a word of French ; and was not to be redeemed as to any of these failings by her husband, who was the best illustration in the world of what the French call *bête*. He is described as being "silly in a wise way, ignorant, ill-bred, and speaking very little French himself —just enough to show how ill-bred he is." He was a sort of titled, fox-hunting squire. He was, besides, very jealous—a fatal and unpardonable *sottise* with the French—and almost childish in his treatment of her. He would not tolerate any rouge or powder upon her cheeks, adornments then so fashionable, and which was indeed an excusable stretch of conjugal tyranny.

At a large dinner-party at Sir John Bland's, he fancied he perceived the presence of this forbidden cosmetic on her cheek, and instantly rose, chased her round the table, caught her, and with a napkin, actually "scrubbed it off by force"—it may be imagined to the intense amusement and surprise of the persons of quality then assembled. He then set off in a pet, and told her publicly that since she had deceived him and broken her promise he would take her back to England.

It does not appear that she was presented at the court of the gallant monarch who then ruled France; at least, that scrupulous courtier, Dangeau, who registered every presentation, makes no mention of her. The French, however, were very anxious they should stay for the grand fêtes at St. Cloud that evening, but her lord said he was obliged to return, as he said he would not like to miss a musical meeting at Worcester. There were some fireworks at Madame Pompadour's, to which she was invited, but she excused herself on the ground of her music-master coming at that hour. The Duc de Luxembourg, the pink of French quality, when they were having some party, came to tell him that he had called up Milady Coventry's coach, upon which my lord said, " *Vous avez fort bien fait.*" The *comble* to these joint *bêtises* was when the Maréchale de Lowendahl admired an English fan of Lady Coventry's, who, upon that, presented it to her. But next morning there came a letter, asking it back, and saying that it had been presented by my lord before marriage, and that parting with it would cause an "irreparable breach." An old one was sent instead. On this, the beautiful stranger went round telling her wrongs to everybody, saying, it is "so odd my lord should treat her in this way, when she knew he would die for her, and he had been so kind as to marry her without a shilling." It may be imagined what the polite but amazed Frenchmen thought of these confidences. It must, however, be recollected she was no more than eighteen.

They then returned to London. The year after Mrs. Delany saw her at a party—a party where the Duke of Portland wore "a coat of dark mouse-coloured velvet," and a vest of "Isabella velvet"— and described her as "looking in high beauty."

In the November of the following year, one Sunday afternoon, a ducal friend brought the famous countess from church to visit Mrs. Delany—"To feast me; and a feast indeed she was." Her dress was "a black silk sack, made for a large hoop, which she wore without any, and it trailed a yard on the ground." She also wore "a cobwebbed lace handkerchief, a pink satin long cloke, lined with ermine mixed with squirrel skins." That wonderful face was adorned with "a French cap that just covered the top of her head—of blonde—and stood in the *form of a butterfly with wings* not quite extended." The whole was completed by lappets tied under the chin with pink and green ribbons; a headdress, in short, which charmed the Dean of Down's lady. Still she was struck by "a sort of silly look at times about her mouth;" and in the portraits there are traces about that feature of a little weakness.

After all, she seems to have had a sort of unsophisticated good-nature, which all the extravagant worship she was paid did not impair. She was not a "hollow" beauty, and had friends as well as admirers. One of the prettiest stories about her, is her behaviour to a young hoiden (a belle also, whom fickle London was already beginning to talk of) who had naïvely asked to have her pointed out to her.

A grand masquerade had been given at Somerset House, at which was this little Irish beauty—a Miss Allen—an unsophisticated "lively sort of a fairy," says Mrs. Delany. She went up to Lady Coventry, and, looking at her very earnestly, said, "I have indeed heard a great deal of this lady's beauty, but it far surpasses all I have heard." "What!" said the other Irish belle, "did you never see me before?" The young girl's *naïveté* amused everybody. A gentleman then took her about, showed her everything, got her a good seat at supper—everyone, to the astonishment of the young girl, bowing and making way for them. At the end of the night he turned out to be the Duke of York. The story has quite a Cinderella air.

Horace Walpole testifies to this good-humour under certainly trying circumstances. "If she was not," he says, "the best-humoured creature in the world, I should have made her angry." It was at a great supper at Lord Hertford's, and the beauty was asked to take some more wine. She answered "in a very vulgar accent, if she drank more she should be *muckibus!* 'Lord!' said Lady Mary Coke, 'what is that?' 'Oh!' said Mr. Walpole, 'it is only Irish for sentiment.'" Lady Mary Coke, we may be sure, would not be slack to point attention to the odd phrase.

Her short race was but for eight years; and yet, to the last, London training seems to have had but little effect on the old wild nature. In one sense, this is a good testimony to her disposition. Even the year before her death Mr. Jenkinson filled in a corner of one of his letters with a story about her which was then amusing all London—"a silly action" he calls it. Walking in the Park, the mob had been disrespectful, incited by her airs. It came to the ears of the King—that good-natured King to whom she had said, that of all the sights in the world, " she longed to see a coronation"—and on the followng Sunday evening he sent her a guard, to attend her as she walked. A discreet person would have declined the questionable honour, but the saucy countess exulted in her escort, and made a triumphant progress with "two sergeants in front carrying their halberds, and twelve soldiers following behind, and the whole guard held ready close by to turn out at a moment's notice." Thus attended, the gay countess continued her promenade from eight until ten o'clock, the mob also forming part of the procession, and not restrained by the military force from uttering some plain truths—so plain, indeed, that "Fielding's men" had to take up a few. As an illustration of that "silliness in the mouth" which Mrs. Delany remarked, this is worth a whole essay.

So her short butterfly life passed. We have glimpses of her down at Crome, the family seat, with a house full of company, and "Gilly Williams," one of the Selwyn set (whose letters should be more known), and "old Sandys;" while the Earl good-naturedly held a faro bank every night, which "we have as yet," writes Gilly, "plundered considerably." There was a certain captain there who is mentioned as "studying a pretty attitude for the countess." She was then "in· high spirits and great beauty." Poor countess!

But in August, 1760, she fell sick. That bourgeois husband of hers was not altogether so foolish in his generation when he chased her round the Paris dining-room and rubbed the paint off her cheeks with a napkin; for she had since had her own way, and used to daub her cheeks profusely with white lead. To this abominable custom—one of the sacrifices which Moloch fashion then demanded—she is said to have fallen a victim. She was living down at her own place, and a Doctor Wall, who attended on her, wrote to Mr. Selwyn an account of her sickness, making, as he said, "no excuse for being minute, because I believe that it would be most agreeable to you that I should be so." For the profound wit was one of her admirers.

The doctor gives a touching and graphic account of this last illness.

"Crome, August 8th, 1760.

"Sir,

"I have spent almost all my time at this place since my lord went to London; and, indeed, Lady Coventry has been so extremely ill, so much worse than when you saw her last, that she wanted all the attendance I could give her. For two or three days the oppression on her breast and the sickness at her stomach were excessive; but these were at last happily removed by some medicines, which, indeed, operated a little roughly; but it was a necessary severity, for she could not have lived without it. She has now for two or three days complained of a pain in her side and across the breast, which I look upon to be muscular, and a sort of spasmodic rheumatism. Excuse me for using terms of art, but I don't know how to express myself without them. Her pulse, notwithstanding this, has for three days last past been very remarkably slower, her feverish heats less than usual. She is extremely weak. Yesterday morning a letter came from the Duchess of Hamilton, directed for Lord Coventry. She knew the hand, and unluckily opened it.

Hinc illæ lachrymæ!

"The duchess had too plainly explained her sentiments of Lady Coventry's condition; had lamented her as a sister whom she should never see; had entirely given her up, expressing her concern as for one already in the grave.

"You, who know how apt Lady Coventry is to be affected, may easily conceive the anguish which such a letter would occasion. Indeed, it did almost kill her. I was called to her, and found her almost fainting and dying away. However, she soon after recovered, and I took my leave; but after I was gone the same scene was several times renewed. Her attendants thought her expiring. In their hurry they despatched an express to my lord, who, I suppose, will, in consequence of that, be here this evening. However, she has had a very good night, and is tolerably well this morning. I make no excuse for being so minute, because I believed it would be most agreeable to you that I should be so."

It is really painful to read how she was affected by the news of her approaching end. She was never without a pocket-glass in her hand, and this sad truth-teller betrayed to her the ravages of disease. She seems to have lost all hope and spirit, took to her bed permanently, allowed no light in the room but "the lamp of a tea-kettle," and actually took things in through the curtains without suffering them to be withdrawn.

> "Odious in woollen! 'twould a saint provoke!"
> Were the last words that Narcissa spoke.
> "No; let a charming chintz and Brussels lace
> Wrap my cold limbs and shade my lifeless face;
> One would not, sure, be frightful when one's dead;
> And, Betty, give this cheek a little red."

But on October 1st, 1760, she died. Mr. Walpole was affected at the news, and wrote to his friend: "The charming countess is dead at last; and, as if the whole history of both sisters was to be extraordinary, the Duchess of Hamilton is in a consumption too, and going abroad directly. Perhaps you may see the remains of these prodigies. You will see but little remains: her features were never so beautiful as Lady Coventry's, and she has long been changed, though not yet, I think, above six-and-twenty. The other was but twenty-seven."

Her worthy lord soon recovered her loss, and in 1764 wedded Miss Barbara St. John.

"An odd event," writes Mrs. Harris to her son, "happened the day they were to have been married. His lordship had not got a license; they were at Lady St. John's house in the country; my lord was obliged to come up to Doctors' Commons to swear to his own age, and also to Miss St. John's, and then to send to Lambeth for the license; but, unfortunately, his grace was not at home. So it was agreed that they had better eat the dinner rather than it should be spoilt; so to dinner they went, and sat all the afternoon, dressed in their white and silver, expecting every moment the express from Lambeth; but nothing came. The same reason still held good for eating a supper as for eating the dinner; and, in short, they supped and sat till after two; and then, by mutual consent, dismissed the parson, and all retired. About four the license came, but they were not married till eleven that morning."

It was curious that the marriage ceremony was attended by almost the same embarrassment that had accompanied that of the Duke of Hamilton to Lady Coventry's sister. One of the wild and witty comrades —Gilly Williams—saw them on their honeymoon, and his report has a bitter significance.

Lady Coventry had left two little girls—Maria and Nanny—in whom both Gilly Williams and Selwyn were interested.

"You will certainly want to know how the children relish their new relation. I will give you a trait of Nanny that pleased me. When mademoiselle broke it to them, Maria cried, and the little one said: 'Do not cry, sister. If she is civil to us, we will be civil to her; if not, you know, we can sit up in our own rooms, and take no notice of her.' There is a degree of philosophy in this infant that I do not think age can improve."

"My dear George,

"You may talk as you please of what you have seen and heard since we parted, but I would not have given up my last night's supper for the whole put together. The earl brought his new countess to Margaret Street. You know him so well that I dare say you are perfectly master of his words and actions on such an occasion; and as for her ladyship, it was all prettiness, fright, insipidity, question, and answer, which neither gold stuffs, diamonds, a new chair with a very large coronet in the centre, like the Queen's—neither of these, I say, had power to alter; and as my friend was never cut out for decent and matrimonial gallantry, a very awkward air made them both as entertaining a couple as ever I passed an hour with. They are to be introduced at court on Sunday, and to set out for Crome the next day."

In another letter the same author describes what he saw when visiting the "happy pair;" and his report is in the vein of true comedy.

"I like," he says, "the behaviour of the children much, and likewise the propriety of Bab's behaviour to them; but you would have laughed to have seen what a hearty kiss the little one would often give mademoiselle (their governess), as looking upon her as the only real friend she had in the family. There is no possibility of saying more of *her* at present, than that she is very pretty; the rest is all grimace. But as to his lordship, he certainly surpasses all you can conceive of him; his plantations, his house, his wife, his plate, his equipage, his—etc. etc. etc.—are all topics that call forth his genius continually. We went to church with them, and the curiosity of all the neighbouring parishes would not have displeased you. I thought I could hear, among the crowd, some odious comparisons; and these were all in favour of our old friend" (the late beauty), "who lies very quietly in the neighbourhood. I do not love to dea in horoscopes, but his lordship will certainly tire of this plaything, as he has done of all he has hitherto played with, and be plagued with the noise of the rattle when he is no longer pleased with blowing a the whistle. He means to instruct by lectures in his table-talk, and by drawing pictures of good and bad wives. You know how he succeeded in the last; God grant him better success in his present plan!"

The Rev. Mr. Mason wrote the following touching lines on the departed beauty:

> Yes! Coventry is dead. Attend the strain,
>   Daughters of Albion! ye that, light as air,
> So oft have tripp'd in her fantastic train,
>   With hearts as gay, and faces half as fair.
> For she was fair beyond your brightest bloom
>   (This Envy owns, since now her bloom is fled);
> Fair as the forms that, wove in Fancy's loom,
>   Float in light vision round the poet's head.
> Whene'er with soft serenity she smiled,
>   Or caught the orient blush of quick surprise,
> How sweetly mutable, how brightly wild
>   The liquid lustre darted from her eyes!
> Each look, each motion waked a new-born grace,
>   That o'er her form a transient glory cast;
> Some lovelier wonder soon usurped the place,
>   Chased by a charm still lovelier than the last.
> That bell again! It tells us what she is!
>   On what she was no more the strain prolong;
> Luxuriant Fancy, pause: an hour like this
>   Demands the tribute of a serious song.
> Maria claims it from that sable bier,
>   Where, cold and wan, the slumberer rests her head;
> In still small whispers to Reflection's ear
>   She breathes the solemn dictates of the dead.

We now turn to her sister, who had lost her husband, the Duke of Hamilton, in 1758. But in 1759 she was married, a second time, to Colonel

Campbell, who afterwards became Duke of Argyll. Her former husband had shown more than the average Scotch pride; and it was reported that the duke and duchess used to sit in grim and solitary state in their great Scotch castle, waited on by all their servants; and, when they had guests, walked in together before their company. It is unprecedented that a simple Irish girl, without fortune beyond her face, should have lived to be the mother of four dukes—of James George and Douglas, seventh and eighth Dukes of Hamilton; of George William and John Douglas, sixth and seventh Dukes of Argyll. She was, moreover, created a baroness in her own right; and, besides, was the mother of Lady Charlotte Campbell, one of the most beautiful women of her day, and as lively and witty as she was beautiful. One of the most dramatic and even picturesque passages in "Boswell's Tour to the Hebrides" is his account of his visit to Murray Castle, in 1773; and of his treatment by this haughty dame, then Duchess of Argyll.

"I told Dr. Johnson I was in some difficulty how to act at Inverary. I had reason to think that the Duchess of Argyll disliked me, on account of my zeal in the Douglas cause; but the Duke of Argyll had always been pleased to treat me with great civility. They were now at the castle, which is a very short walk from our inn; and the question was, whether I should go and pay my respects there. Dr. Johnson, to whom I had stated the case, was clear that I ought; but in his usual way, he was very shy of discovering a desire to be invited there himself. At the same time he was, I believe, secretly not unwilling to have attention paid him by so great a chieftain and so exalted a nobleman. He insisted that I should not go to the castle this day before dinner, as it would look like seeking an invitation. 'But,' said I, 'if the duke invites us to dine with him to-morrow, shall we accept?' 'Yes, sir;' I think he said, 'to be sure.' But, he added, 'He won't ask us!' I mentioned that I was afraid my company might be disagreeable to the duchess. He treated this objection with a manly disdain. '*That*, sir, he must settle with his wife.' We dined well. I went to the castle just about the time when I supposed the ladies would be retired from dinner. I sent in my name; and, being shown in, found the amiable duke sitting at the head of his table with several gentlemen. I was most politely received, and gave his grace some particulars of the curious journey which I had been making with Dr. Johnson. When we rose from the table, the duke said to me: 'I hope you and Dr. Johnson will dine with us to-morrow.' I thanked his grace; but told him my friend was in a great hurry to get back to London. The duke, with a kind complaisancy, said, 'He will stay one day; and I will take care he shall see this place to advantage.' I said I should be sure to let him know his grace's invitation. As I was going away, the duke said: 'Mr. Boswell, won't you have some tea?' I thought it best to get over the meeting with the duchess this night; so respectfully agreed. I was conducted to the drawing-room by the duke, who announced my name; but the duchess, who was sitting with her daughter, Lady Betty Hamilton, and some other ladies, took not the least notice of me. I should have been mortified at being thus coldly received by a lady of whom I, with the rest of the world, have always entertained a very high admiration, had I not been consoled by the obliging attention of the duke.

"When I returned to the inn, I informed Dr. Johnson of the Duke of Argyll's invitation, with which he was much pleased, and readily accepted of it.

"*Oct.* 25.—My acquaintance, the Rev. Mr. John M'Aulay, one of the ministers of Inverary, and brother to our good friend at Calder, came to us this morning, and accompanied us to the castle, where I presented Dr. Johnson to the Duke of Argyll. We were shown through the house; and I never shall forget the impression made upon my fancy by some of the ladies'-maids tripping about in neat morning-dresses.

"When we came in before dinner, we found the

duke and some gentlemen in the hall. The duke placed Dr. Johnson next himself at table. I was in fine spirits; and though sensible that I had the misfortune of not being in favour with the duchess, I was not in the least disconcerted, and offered her grace some of the dish that was before me. It must be owned that I was in the right to be quite unconcerned, if I could. I was the Duke of Argyll's guest; and I had no reason to suppose that he adopted the prejudices and resentments of the Duchess of Hamilton.

"I knew it was the rule of modern high life not to drink to anybody; but that I might have the satisfaction for once to look the duchess in the face, with a glass in my hand, I with a respectful air addressed her: 'My lady duchess, I have the honour to drink your grace's good health.' I repeated the words audibly, and with a steady countenance. This was, perhaps, rather too much; but some allowance must be made for human feelings. The duchess was very attentive to Dr. Johnson. 'I fancy you will be a *Methodist.*' This was the only sentence her grace deigned to utter to me; and I take it for granted, she thought it a good hit on my *credulity* in the Douglas cause.

"Dr. Johnson talked a great deal, and was so entertaining, that Lady Betty Hamilton, after dinner, went and placed her chair close to his, leaned upon the back of it, and listened eagerly. It would have made a fine picture to have drawn the sage and her at this time in their several attitudes. He did not know, all the while, how much he was honoured. I told him afterwards. I never saw him so gentle and complaisant as this day.

"We went to tea. The duke and I walked up and down the drawing-room, conversing. The duchess still continued to show the same marked coldness for me; for which, though I suffered from it, I made every allowance, considering the very warm part that I had taken for Douglas, in the cause in which she thought her son deeply interested. Had not her grace discovered some displeasure towards me, I should have suspected her of insensibility or dissimulation.

"Her grace made Dr. Johnson come and sit by her, and asked him why he made his journey so late in the year. 'Why, madam,' said he, 'you know Mr. Boswell must attend the Court of Session, and it does not rise till the twelfth of August.' She said, with some sharpness, 'I *know nothing* of Mr. Boswell.' Poor Lady Lucy Douglas, to whom I mentioned this, observed: 'She knew *too much* of Mr. Boswell.' I shall make no remark on her grace's speech. I indeed felt it as rather too severe; but when I recollected that my punishment was inflicted by so dignified a beauty, I had that kind of consolation which a man would feel who is strangled by a *silken cord*. Dr. Johnson was all attention to her grace. He used afterwards a droll expression, upon her enjoying the three titles of Hamilton, Brandon, and Argyll. Borrowing an image from the Turkish empire, he called her a *Duchess* with *three tails*."

It is noteworthy that a descendant of this remarkable woman was herself one of the famous beauties of her day; and many still recall the charms and brilliant talents of Lady Charlotte Campbell, who lived till the year 1861.

THE ROMANTIC STORY OF SIR PHILIP FRANCIS.

VOL. I.

THE ROMANTIC STORY OF SIR PHILIP FRANCIS.

A CHARACTER or career in many points suggestive of Hugh Elliot was that of Philip Francis, the accepted author of "Junius." Both had the same impetuosity of temper, the same dash, and a good deal of the same brilliancy. But here the likeness ends. One was Scotch, the other Irish. Elliot knew how to manage men; Francis was impracticable and unsuccessful in his treatment of critical questions. On the other hand, Francis was a trenchant and brilliant writer, whose great "Letters" were efficient, to an extraordinary degree, in producing the effect demanded. The name of Elliot is but little known to "the general," while that of Francis will long be celebrated.

Francis was born in 1740, and even as a boy he showed a good deal of the spirit which later distinguished him. Taken one night by his father to Drury Lane Theatre, they met the courtly Lord Chesterfield. "The noble paragon of courtesy and fine words, indulging in polite conversation with the Doctor, as usual paused for some felicitous word. In one of his lordship's stops young Philip promptly supplied the properly-considered word—the noble lord adopting it—with the preface of a bow and the remark, 'As the young gentleman has most correctly said.'"

When a young man in London he figured in the theatrical riots which were set on foot to the annoyance of Garrick, and prompted some of Churchill's bitterest verses. It is curious that, like Elliot, he had a taste for amateur military work; and when sent, in a civil capacity, on the expedition to Cherbourg, was reprimanded for going into the trenches to see some of the fighting. He engaged in several other missions, as secretary, etc. In 1762 he made an early and improvident marriage—of course, in defiance of the wishes of his father and his relatives. He soon obtained a clerkship in the War Office, and began writing letters to the papers, in the style of the more famous "Junius" attacks. These were under various signatures, and contrast with his letters to his wife, which have been preserved, and which show that this fierce assailant was of an affectionate and even uxorious nature. Thus:

"This post is very convenient, for though we are above seventy miles off, I hear this morning how you did yesterday. This is so great a pleasure to me that I wait with impatience for the hour of the post; and woe be to you if you disappoint me! I am perfectly satisfied that you will not dance with any but a proper person; but that was not what I meant. I am apt to suspect that the general run of the company is not of the best; therefore, would wish you not to make yourself too cheap among them. Whom did you dance with? The time till my dearest Betsy returns seems full as tedious to me as it can do to you. . . . My sweetest Betsy, I hope you think of me, and that you really wish to be with me again; if you do not, you are ungrateful to the last degree. Haven't you fixed the day yet for your return? As you are such a constant bather, I should imagine your stay might be shortened. But all this I leave to yourself. As I write constantly twice a week, you ought to be contented, though I don't complain of your wishing to hear oftener from me. I wish Sally would do me the favour to say a few words; can't you persuade her to write a line or two to me?— Yours, my dearest Betsy, for ever, P. F."

In 1769 appeared the first Junius letter in the *Public Advertiser;* and the best evidence of their being his work, apart from innumerable other cogent reasons, is that their interruption coincided with his own movements, absences from town, illnesses, etc. And in 1772, when he was absent from England, the letters ceased to appear. At last, in 1774, he was appointed to the Indian Council at Bengal.

When he reached his new sphere of action, he found himself in perpetual conflict with Hastings, and engaged in embittered disputes with members of the council, which was split into factions. This animosity raged for some time until, in 1777, Hastings sent home his resignation, and was presumed to have given up the struggle. When the letter of the directors arrived accepting it, with the appointment of a successor, a series of extraordinary and dramatic scenes followed.

Hastings repudiated the authority of his agent, and refused to acknowledge the acceptance of a resignation which he denied himself to have tendered. Clavering endeavoured to seize on the supreme power by violence. "The General," says Macaulay, "sent for the keys of the fort and of the treasury; took possession of the records,. and held a council, at which Francis attended. Hastings took the chair in another apartment, and Barwell sate with him. . . . It seemed that there remained no way of settling the dispute except by an appeal to arms; and from such an appeal, Hastings, confident of his influence over his countrymen in India, was not inclined to shrink. He directed the officers of the garrison of Fort William, and of all the neighbouring stations, to obey no orders but his. At the same time, with admirable judgment, he offered to submit the case to the supreme court, and to abide by its decision. . . . Clavering and Francis, after some delay, unwillingly consented to abide the award of the court. The court pronounced that the resignation was invalid, and that therefore Hastings was still Governor-General under the Regulation Act; and the defeated members of the council, finding the sense of the whole settlement against them, reluctantly acquiesced in this decision."

At last, in 1780, matters came to a crisis. After many violent scenes at the council board, the Governor declaring that " he would not bear it," etc., a dispute arose between them on a point of good faith, Hastings charging Francis with having made an honourable agreement and departing from it.

"The issue," he wrote, " to which Mr. Hastings has agreed to bring the question between us, prevents me from answering the paper I received from him on Monday night in the manner in which I otherwise should have answered it. Nor indeed have I sufficient time to spare from other duties, at this juncture indispensable. If I should fall, I hope the following declaration made now, with the most solemn appeal to God Almighty for the truth of it, will not only satisfy my friends, but clear my character and honour in the opinion of the world.

"I declare, then, I never was a party to the paper quoted by Mr. Hastings, nor did I ever, directly or indirectly, give my assent to it."

Hastings enforced his view in an offensive minute. When they met at the board on August 15th, Francis took him into another room and thus addressed him:

"'Mr. Hastings, I am preparing a formal answer to the paper you sent to me last night. As soon as it can be finished, I shall lay it before you. But you must be sensible, sir, that no answer I can give to the matter of that paper can be adequate to the dishonour done me by the terms you have made use of. You have left me no alternative but to demand personal satisfaction of you for the affronts you have offered me.'

"As soon as I had read the preceding words to Mr. Hastings, he said he expected the demand and was ready to answer it. We then agreed to meet in the morning."

"On the 17th," says Francis "we arrived at the ground near Belvedere, near an hour before Mr. H., who comes about six, with Colonel Pearse. Watson marks out a distance, about fourteen common paces, the same, he said, at which Mr. Fox and Mr. Adam stood. My pistol missing fire, I changed it. We then fired together, and I was wounded and fell. I thought my backbone was broken, and of course that I could not survive it. After the first confusion had subsided, and after I had suffered great inconvenience from being carried to a wrong place, I was at last conveyed to Major Foley's house on a bed. The surgeon arrived in about an hour-and-a-half from the time I was wounded, and cut out the ball, and bled me twice in the course of the day.

"Mr. Hastings sends to know when he may visit me.

"18th.—In these two days the pain I suffered was very considerable.

"19th.—Desire Colonel Watson to tell Mr. Hastings as civilly as possible that I am forced to decline his visit."

The triumphant Hastings was continued in his office, and Francis had soon to return to England. Before he departed, however, he had part in a very curious sort of romance, which it will be found interesting to recount.

Warren Hastings was a rather brilliant adventurer. The glittering scene in which he figured, the barbaric oppression of which he was accused, his wonderful administration, the celebrated trial which was itself a drama, the glittering pages of Macaulay, in which his story is set out, all combine to lend fascination to the whole. To make the whole a suitable picture of an adventurer's career, there is the contrast between the brilliant sovereignty, the enormous wealth, the diamonds, and the close of his career in fallen state, disgrace, and comparative want.

There was living in England, shortly after George III. came to the throne, a German portrait-painter and his wife, of the name of Imhoff, who were friends of the well-known Keeper of the Wardrobe to the Queen, Miss Burney's Mrs. Schwellenberg. Through this channel the Queen was induced to patronise them, and, through the same agency, leave was obtained from the East India directors for their going out to Madras. For such was the despotic rule of these magnates, that no one could establish themselves in the cities or territory without their sanction. This was in 1768.

It happened that there was embarking in the same Indiaman that took out the Imhoffs, Mr. Hastings, who was just appointed to the council at Fort St. George. The *Duke of Grafton* was the name of the vessel. Mrs. Imhoff has always been described as singularly interesting and of fascinating manners. She was a native of Archangel. At that time Hastings had never seen or heard of her; but, shortly after sailing from England, accident, which had brought them into the same ship, also made them personally known to each other. Wraxall describes what occurred on the voyage, which, as Macaulay says, might have furnished romance for a good three-volume novel.

"Hastings having engaged the room denominated the round-house for his own exclusive accommodation, Mrs. Imhoff, believing him to be on the quarter-deck, without previously ascertaining the fact, mounted by the stairs of the quarter-gallery to that apartment. Their surprise at meeting was mutual; and she made, from the first instant of his seeing her, a deep impression on the future Governor-General. In the course of their voyage, Hastings formed a very strong attachment to her, and, his passion acquiring strength by time, he continued to visit her with great assiduity while she and her husband resided at Madras; but, always with such precautions and under such restrictions as not to compromise her. About the time when Hastings was appointed to the government of Bengal, in January, 1772, a termination of her marriage with Imhoff took place; which union, as having been originally celebrated in Germany, was asserted to be capable of dissolution by mutual consent. This amicable divorce was not, however, effected without the aid of money, Hastings having, in fact, paid to Imhoff a sum considerably exceeding 10,000*l.*; with which acquisition the fortunate painter quitted India, and, returning to his native country, there bought an estate. Mrs. Imhoff followed her lover to Calcutta, and, as soon as her former husband had transmitted authentic intelligence that the divorce was obtained, the new Governor-General of India legalised his connection by the solemnities of wedlock.

This extraordinary transaction has been described by one of Hastings's biographers as "wise and judicious;" but it was, in truth, a scandal.

On July 19th, 1777, Francis wrote to one of his friends:

"There is no answering for the resolutions of such a timid, desperate, distracted being as Hastings. To complete the character, as it will probably conclude the history of this extraordinary man, I must inform you that he is to be married shortly to the supposed wife of a German painter, with whom he has lived for several years. The lady is turned of forty, has children grown up by her pretended husband, from whom she has obtained a divorce under the hand of some German prince. I have always been on very good terms with the lady, and do not despair of being invited to the wedding. She is an agreeable woman, and has been very pretty. My Lord Chief Justice Impey, the most upright of all possible lawyers, is to act the part of a father to this second Helen, though his wife has not spoken to her this twelvemonth."

But in the year following, the person who penned these lines was himself to be the hero of an extraordinary adventure. In 1778, a Swiss gentleman, M. George F. Grand, came, with his wife, to Chandernagore (where he seems to have been established in business) and in Calcutta. His wife, only sixteen, was the daughter of a M. Worlée, at the French settlement of Pondicherry, where she was born.

"She was," says a writer in the *Calcutta Review*, "very young and very charming. Her picture, painted by Zoffany, now (1844) adorns the walls of Mr. Marshman's residence at Serampore. There is more of feminine softness than of strength of character in her fair countenance; the sensual prevails everywhere over the intellectual."

With the Swiss gentleman's lady, Francis fell desperately in love, and the husband told the public, in print, what followed:

"On December 8th, 1778, I went out of my home the happiest, as I thought myself, of men, and between eleven and twelve o'clock returned the same night to it as miserable as any being could well feel. Scarcely had I sat down to supper at my benefactor Mr. Barwell's society, who required of his friends to join him every fortnight at this convivial meeting, when a servant came and whispered to me that Mr. Francis was caught in my house and secured by my jemmadar. I rose up from table, ran to the terrace, and sent for a friend out, whom I requested to accompany me. On my way I called on my friend Mr. Palmer, and requested the use of his sword, and to attend me as a friend. We repaired to the spot. The porter, hearing my voice, opened the gate; and in my lower apartments my friend and I beheld with astonishment the present Sir George Shee bound to a chair, and endeavouring to obtain from my servants his release, with Mr. Shore, now Lord Teignmouth, and the late Mr. Archdekin, companions to him, joining in the same prayer and entreaty. My jemmadar, however, told a plain tale. It was that he had secured Mr. Francis, until Mr. Shee, assisted by the other gentlemen, upon a loud whistle sounded by Mr. Francis, had scaled the walls of my compound, rushed furiously on him, and in the scuffle occasioned Mr. Francis to escape. I ordered their release, and leaving my house to the care of my faithful jemmadar and servants, I retired to Major Palmer's.

"I anxiously awaited the morning, to require from the undoer of my happiness the satisfaction which the laws of honour prescribe. I wrote to Mr. Francis that, void of every spark of principle and honour as I deemed him, still I trusted he would not deny me the meeting to which I summoned him. His reply was laconic and easy: 'That, conscious of having done me no injury, and that I laboured under a complete mistake, he begged leave to decline the proposed invitation.' I now returned home, occupied the lower apartments of my house, whilst Mrs. Grand remained in the upper, and on the Sunday following everything was arranged for Mrs. Grand's returning to live under her relatives' mansion and protection. An interview was entreated, and could not be denied. It lasted three hours, interrupted with the most poignant lamentations. I pitied her from my heart. I sincerely forgave her, and with a sorrow approaching to distraction, we parted.

"A course of law alone remained open. This I had recourse to—not without experiencing great difficulty, most of the complaisant advocates of the supreme court having either been retained by him, or intimidated from acting. At length I succeeded with one who brought the process to a successful issue. By the testimony of Mr. Shee, Mr. Archdekin, and others, the trespass was fully proved, and the trespasser was condemned by the bench of judges in damages of fifty thousand sicca rupees, with costs of suit."

Francis's own account of the adventure as related to his wife, is like a scene in one of the old comedies, say, "The Suspicious Husband:"

"Mrs. Grand was at that time the most beautiful woman in Calcutta. She was tall, most elegantly formed, the stature of a nymph, a complexion of unequalled delicacy, and auburn hair of the most luxuriant profusion; fine blue eyes, with black eyelashes and brows, gave her countenance a most piquant singularity. This beautiful creature had the misfortune to be married to a dirty, sordid old Frenchman, who treated her very ill, and having lost a good deal of money at play—which was then carried to a great extent at Calcutta—looked out for the best opportunity of repairing it, and was not very particular about the means. Mr. F. soon distinguished this fair lady, and, though not displeased to be admired, threw him into despair. His contempt for the husband and regret for the ill-fated beauty made such an addition to his passion that he fell into a fever which lasted him six months. Her pity so far worked upon her for her to consent to his coming one night — when her husband was absent—to her house, accompanied by a friend. He went to the house," the narrative proceeds, "accompanied by his friend Ducarel, who waited outside, when he was surrounded by a set of ruffians with whom her husband, who had been only absent as a plot to draw Mr. Francis into the house, had seen him go in, having previously laid the plot. Had Mr. F. had his sword on, he said, some of them would have paid dearly for their attack; but they having taken care to possess themselves of it, and being armed, forced him into another apartment, where they held him down in a chair whilst Mr. G., with all the airs of injured honour, called for a pistol to take away the life of the man who had dared to attack it. Nevertheless, the lady called out of the window to Mr. Ducarel, 'For God's sake come; they are murdering him.' Mr. Ducarel, without waiting for another word, very resolutely rushed into the house among the gang, who, seeing another gentleman sword in hand, and not knowing whether there might not be more, relaxed their hold and began to prepare for their defence. Upon seeing Ducarel, his friend threw off those about him, who were glad to take refuge in flight; and the two adventurers made an orderly retreat."

Now to follow the extraordinary future career of the heroines; and it is remarkable that these two ladies, obscure personages in Calcutta society, should have been both destined, through themselves or their husbands, to have a European celebrity.

We next hear of the beautiful Madame Grand at Paris in 1796, when we find Talleyrand writing to Barras to release her from arrest, she being charged with conspiring for the emigrants.

"C'est la personne," he wrote, "d'Europe la plus éloignée et la plus incapable de se mêler d'aucune affaire. C'est une Indienne bien belle, bien paresseuse, la plus désoccupée de toutes les femmes que j'aie jamais rencontrées. Je vous demande intérêt pour elle. Je l'aime : et je vous atteste à vous, d'homme à homme, que de sa vie elle ne s'est mêlée et n'est en état de se mêler d'aucune affaire. C'est une véritable Indienne ; et vous savez à quel degré cette espèce de femmes est loin de toute intrigue."

When the Pope had dispensed the ex-Bishop of Autun from excommunication and other penalties, the latter chose to interpret this step as a leave to marry, and he accordingly espoused Madame Grand. This step was formally condemned by the Vatican, while Bonaparte declined to receive her at court, considering her as virtually unmarried. It turned out that she was utterly unsuited as an intellectual companion, being what is called "stupid;" and she was destined to receive celebrity from the well-known capital anecdote, which her husband repeated of her : her complimenting Demon on his shipwreck as Robinson Crusoe, and her inquiries after "*ce cher Vendredi.*"

On the eve of the marriage, to make the adventurous character of her life continuous, who should appear in Paris but Mr. Francis, to whom, however, she made an appeal for discretion and silence as to the old Calcutta days ! Sir Elijah Impey, another of her Calcutta admirers, was also, strange to say, in Paris, and renewed his acquaintance ; and through the lady he became sufficiently intimate with her husband to be one of the Englishmen most frequently invited to his table. At one of these assemblies, this remarkable *rencontre* took place, of persons not likely ever to have met beneath the same roof under any circumstances less fortuitous. These persons were: Mr. and Mrs. Fox, Sir Elijah and Lady Impey, M. and Madame de Talleyrand, Sir Philip Francis, and M. le Grand.

Returning now to Mrs. Hastings, we find that she proved herself a valuable assistant and companion to the Governor; and when his enemies began to threaten the attacks that were afterwards formally made, he despatched her, in 1783, to London to prepare the way for his own return. Her appearance was one of the sensations of the court, from the barbaric splendours she displayed—proceedings more likely to excite the prejudice against him than to allay it. She was supported by the favour of the royal family.

"She was not deficient in those accomplishments which adorn society; for, though she had already passed the limits of youth, her person still preserved many attractions. Her conversation was interesting, and her deportment unexceptionable in private life. She was besides a stranger to England, by birth, by a long residence in Asia, and by her unacquaintance with our modes of life and our manners. Even her figure furnished matter for malevolent criticism; as, at a time when every fashionable female's head-dress was elevated twelve or eighteen inches high, and formed a barbarous assemblage of powder, pins, and other fantastic ornaments piled on each other, she had the courage to wear her hair without powder.

"When she was presented at the drawing-room in this astounding guise, the wits of the *noblesse* made merry over her appearance. Major Scott, another *avant-courier*, had been diligently preparing the public mind for the coming of his principal. Both were thus sung in these lively but disrespectful lines:

> Now shall the levee's ease thy soul unbend,
>   Fatigu'd with royalty's severer care!
> Oh! happy few! whom brighter stars befriend,
>   Who catch the chat—the witty whisper share!
>   Methinks I hear
>   In accents clear,
> Great Brunswick's voice still vibrate on my ear—
>   "What?—what?—what?
>   Scott!—Scott!—Scott!
>   Hot!—hot!—hot!
>   What?—what?—what?"
>   Oh! fancy quick! oh! judgment true!
>   Oh! sacred oracle of regal taste!
>   So hasty, and so generous too!
> Not one of all thy questions will an answer wait!
>   Vain, vain, oh Muse, thy feeble art,
> Monarch of mighty Albion check thy talk?
> Behold the squad approach, led on by Palk!
> Smith, Barwell, Call, Vansittart, form the band—
> Lord of Britannia!—let them kiss thy hand!—
> For sniff!—rich odours scent the sphere!
> 'Tis Mrs. Hastings' self brings up the rear!
>   Gods! how her diamonds flock
>   On each unpowdered lock!
>   On every membrane see a topaz clings!
>   Behold!—her joints are fewer than her rings!

> Illustrious dame ! on either ear,
> The Munny Begums' spoils appear !
> Oh ! Pitt with awe behold that precious throat,
> Whose necklace teems with many a future vote !
> Pregnant with Burgage gems each hand she rears ;
> And lo ! depending questions gleam upon her ears !
> Take her, great George, and shake her by the hand,
> 'Twill loose her jewels, and enrich thy land.
> But oh ! reserve one ring for an old stager ;
> The ring of future marriage for her Major.

"The present of the great diamond made a great noise at the time. It was thought improper that his Majesty should have accepted from a private person what, it was imputed, must have been gained by plunder."

Never was there such a fall. The magnate, at whose word and nod the Easterns had trembled, was brought to trial, and had to bend his knee submissively as he entered Westminster Hall. He left it an acquitted but ruined man, and dragged out the rest of his life in obscurity, subsisting on a pension of 4000*l.* a year, which was no doubt heavily mortgaged. A modest one-horse chaise was all he could afford to take him to church.

Miss Burney thus described him on his trial : " Poor Hastings sitting by and looking so meek, to hear himself called villain and cut-throat, etc ! The recapitulation of the dreadful cruelties in India was worked up to the highest pitch of eloquence and passion, so that the orator was seized with a spasm which made him incapable of speaking another word. I think I never felt such indignation as when Burke, with Sheridan standing on one side, and Fox on the other, said: ' Vice incapacitates a man from all public duty; it withers the powers of his understanding, and makes his mind paralytic.'"

Madame Talleyrand died on December 11th, 1835, aged seventy-four. She had been separated from her husband for thirty years, though he said he had chosen her, on account of her very stupidity, "*pour reposer l'esprit.*" A strange scene occurred at her deathbed:

"After the last religious ceremonies had been performed, an assemblage of friends surrounded the bed of the dying, who in a faint voice asked for a particular casket, which she delivered with much earnestness to the Archbishop of Paris, and requested that after her death he would make it over to Madame d'E——, as her valid gift and last testimonial of her affection. At the same time she called upon all present to be witnesses of this bequest. No sooner had the archbishop received in his hands this deposit than the *homme d'affaires* of Prince T——,. who had privately mixed with the group, stepped forward, and formally opposed the delivery of the casket, which he claimed on behalf of his constituent."

It was noted as curious that this man of business's

name was Demon. It would be curious to imagine an attorney in England with the name of Devil! The Prince gave directions that the inscription on her tombstone should indicate the fact of the marriage as slightly as possible. After stating her birth, etc., at Martinique, she is described as "*Veuve de M. G——, après civilement mariée à M. de T——.*" Here his dominant foible comes out; he hopes that by treating the ceremony as a civil contract, at that period of the Revolution, he may now palliate that stigma in the eyes of the clergy, which is irreparably attached to the position of a *prêtre marié*.

The dispute as to the casket was at last compromised by a payment of 8000*l*.

Francis, who had entered Parliament on his return to England, took part in the impeachment of his old enemy. During the course of the investigation his old quarrelsomeness broke out, and he related to his second wife—the wife of his old age—some amusing particulars:

"During Hastings' trial there was a Nottinghamshire baronet, Sir Richard Sutton, a warm, hearty man, who hated liberal politics from his heart, and was an intimate personal friend of both Hastings and Impey. This gentleman, in the warmth of his defence of the accused, not only repeated Chancellor Thurlow's wish that the vessel containing Francis, Monson, and Clavering had been lost at sea, but added some personal reflections on Francis. He had just inquired of his neighbour the name of his accuser, who was a stranger to him, and was deliberating in what way to notice the attack, when a strange incident happened in the House. A member had entered the House in that strange state of intoxication which some men are liable to, when wine causes a kind of insanity rather than common sottishness, like the famous Jack Fuller twenty years after. This hero directed all his spleen against the Speaker; he marched up to him while the House was engaged in watching the rising storm which seemed coming on between Sutton and Francis, and, without giving the right honourable gentleman any notice, tried to eject him from his chair in the most summary way, *vi et armis*. The Speaker resisted like Falstaff, on compulsion; but the Bacchanal pulled so hard that all the members near flew to the rescue, thinking assassination or some personal injury was intended. By this time all the members were on their legs, and the house in an uproar; all order was at an end; queries from one part, and peals of laughter from another, were all that was heard; all tried to get near the chair, where the crowd was the most dense, and where the new Speaker was defending himself with much gravity and logic. Sir Richard's speech had come to an abrupt conclusion, and Mr. Francis, finding there was no chance of any public satisfaction at that time, took the opportunity of all having quitted their seats to step across the house to the Treasury benches, where Sir Richard was standing, and asked him upon what footing he was to consider his personal attack upon himself? Sir Richard, who was a quiet and respectable man in private life, out of politics, though somewhat stern and fierce-looking when disturbed, answered him that he had not the least intention or thoughts of offending him; that it was merely on public grounds he spoke, and was sorry if he had offended him; and Sir Philip, though not believing him, took the apology, merely adding, 'Then I hope, sir, I shall not have to complain of you in future?' 'Certainly not, sir,' said the other; and so they parted. Francis went down the next day to East Sheen, and on Sunday, while happy in the company of his then young and promising family, particularly Elizabeth and Harriet, who were just rising into womanhood, and equally distinguished for beauty of person and mental endowments, a friend came in all haste from town, to give him the *pleasant* intelligence that Sir R.'s speech was in all the papers. Francis, after a few moment's consideration, took his line of conduct, and, begging his friend to remain with his family to guard them from any alarm, he returned alone to town. He proceeded to the club-houses, and at Brookes's the only person he met was Captain Macnamara of the Navy, afterwards so well known by the famous duel with Colonel Montgomery about their dogs, while quarrelling in the Park. Mr. Francis was at the time now in question very slightly acquainted with Macnamara; but, finding himself *tête-à-tête* with him, he mentioned his dilemma, when the naval hero immediately offered his services, for, he observed, not an hour should be lost in vindicating honour. Francis was at least sure that his new friend would not compromise him, to avoid coming to extremities; he therefore sat down and wrote the words that he wished to appear the next day in the papers which had reported Sutton's speech. This paragraph, which disavowed the offensive expressions, and all purpose of casting the slightest imputation on Mr. Francis, he wished to have with Sir Richard's signature, and sent it to him by Captain Macnamara for that purpose, at the same time informing him that it would appear in the papers that had contained the report complained of. This at first appeared rather unpalatable to the baronet, but Captain Macnamara was a very firm and gentlemanly man, and at length succeeded in convincing him that he had been deceived in the estimation he had formed of Mr. Francis's character, and that he really owed him reparation; on which he signed the paragraph which appeared in the newspapers; and Mr. Francis felt very well satisfied with the conduct of his ambassador, who had brought the affair to an amicable termination and yet enabled him to vindicate his honour. But the consequence of this little negotiation was, that not long after, Mr. Francis was drawn into an actual duel, though not as a principal. Harvey Aston had some *démêlé* with Captain Macnamara, and being a celebrated duellist, as was well known, called him out; the latter was not a man to decline such an invitation. Captain Macnamara, on receiving the challenge, remembering the service he had lately rendered Mr. Francis, immediately applied to him. On Sunday, one fine summer morning, the hostile parties met in a field near a village at some distance from town. They took possession, therefore, of the corner of a field protected by high quick hedges. The day was so far advanced that the bells from the village church near began chiming for the service of the morning, which perhaps hurried the gentlemen; for though both were dead shots, a brace of pistols was discharged on each side without effect. Both being still unsatisfied, they called to their seconds to reload, which they were unwillingly going to do, when a voice from behind the hedge called out, "Stop, gentlemen, I cannot allow this business to proceed any further." On looking to see from whom the voice proceeded, to their great surprise the clergyman of the parish, in his canonicals, attended by his congregation, appeared through every aperture in the hedge, which was in fact lined with faces, which had been stationary there during the whole proceeding, to see the upshot and probable downfall of at least one of the party. In vain the bells had been impatiently ringing for the last half hour; not one would move from the interesting spot, or spoil the sport.

"The vicar, after issuing his injunction to stay further proceedings, made his way into the field of battle, and very politely accosting the party, said: 'Gentlemen, I saw from the first what your intentions were, and, making allowances for the feelings of men of honour, I would not deprive you of the satisfaction you required; but now you have done enough. I know the laws of honour as well as any of you, and request you will give me your words that this affair shall end here.' The gentlemen, who could scarcely keep their countenances at meeting with so chivalric a parson, gave him the assurance he required, and Mr. Harvey Aston's second said to Mr. Francis, 'To tell you the truth, I am very glad it has finished as it has; for our gentlemen were very likely to have gone on till one fell, and it would not have been very pleasant to bring a man home dead to a widow and six children, which I might have had to do.' By this time Macnamara was looking at his watch, and expressing some anxiety at finding it so late. 'Why,' said Francis, 'we shall get back to town in very good time for the Park or Gardens.' 'Yes, but my dear friend, I have a carriage waiting for me at the inn here; for the fact is, that I have another little affair of the same nature a few miles farther off, and I am afraid that the other party will have to wait for me, which has always an awkward appearance in such cases.' 'Very true; but pray am I to accompany you?' 'I am sorry to say I have another friend, who would be affronted if I were to ask anyone else as second in this affair, and I am to call on him in my road, and if I disappoint him it will probably produce a third meeting, which for the pleasure of your company and assistance I shall not mind if you will be my friend; but it was a favour I could not previously ask, having been of so little service to you.' 'My dear sir, you could not have done better; but I assure you I have not the least wish to disappoint your friend, and therefore will take the carriage we came in immediately back to town, as you have another, in which I hope you will arrive in time to turn the practice of this morning to good account.'"

The rest of Francis's life was more or less turbulent. His singular reserve as to his writing of "Junius" is well known, and in his old age, when some unthinking guest, emboldened by encouragement, would begin, " Sir Philip, I want to ask you a question," the other with a stern, haughty look, would warn him off the subject, and hint that he would make it a personal matter. Innumerable volumes have been written on this favourite subject of speculation, including Mr. Twistleton's sumptuous quarto; but no completely convincing solution has been arrived at. It is impossible, however, for an unprejudiced person to read the controversy without arriving at the conclusion, first, that the authorship of Francis offers the least difficulties; secondly, that his natural character, career, and style, offer almost convincing evidence in his favour; and finally, that no other of the candidates named are gifted with the proper qualifications. He died on December 23rd, 1818, and his last moments are thus described by his wife :

"DEAR SIR,

"I received his last breath; I was alone with him in his last moments. On Saturday night, I sat up alone with him, and in the middle of the night read the newspapers and some letters to him, sitting upon his bed. On Sunday night, not being at all aware of his danger, as we were assured from his medical attendant that he would recover this attack, and being much fatigued, I left him for some hours, but returned on Monday morning at seven o'clock to his bedside, which I never quitted again for a minute till he was no more; and never was a death so worthy of such a life—his spirits composed, tranquil, and even cheerful; his mind apparently as strong as ever, and his perception as quick. Though he evidently feared disturbing himself by talking, he expressed his gratitude for all my little attentions and cares during that sad and solemn, yet, upon reflection, consolatory, night, in the most touching manner. I was not aware at the time, though I now am, that he knew how short his time was. He showed the greatest anxiety that I should not leave him a moment, no doubt anticipating my future regrets had I done so, which I often assured him I would not; but he never expressed the least fear or anxiety on any other subject. Towards the morning he was lulled into a sweet trance, from which he revived and spoke to me, and took some refreshment. About ten in the morning, he fell by degrees into a deep sleep; his breath was free, his cough gone, his pulse good. It had lasted four hours, and I was flattering myself with the hopes of his waking much restored; Mrs. Cholmondeley had just left me, when, on a sudden, the breathing I had been listening to so contentedly, being easier, stopped. I thought he had awoke, and undrew the curtain, hung over him, and met his last breath; not a sigh, not a motion, not a change of countenance. Heart, pulses, and breath stopped at once without an effort. How blessed! how merciful!"

EARLY LOVES OF GIBBON AND PITT.

VOL. I.

EARLY LOVES OF GIBBON AND PITT.

ONCE rummaging those pleasant boxes of old books which line the quais of Paris opposite the Academy, (and which certainly offer the best returns for such careless digging), down towards the Quai Conti, where Yorick bought his gloves from the famous grisette, the writer came on a little morocco-bound almanac interleaved. It had belonged to some royalist family, and was full of interesting addresses, such as that of Target the lawyer, and others. Among them, however, was one of special interest—that of Mademoiselle Curchod, then living *près de Genève*. The name of this young lady—an obscure Swiss parson's daughter—gave the little book all its interest; for she was to become celebrated, first, as the early love of Edward Gibbon, when he was merely a clever young man travelling, and pursuing diligently his studies for the great book which was to make him famous; later, as the wife of a real statesman, Necker, and on account of her own brilliancy, accomplishments, and sterling virtues, the faithful admiring wife and clever writer; and lastly, as the mother of a daughter far more famous—the restless, half-manly, brilliant observer, Madame de Staël. These are substantial claims to notice. Yet she belongs to a class of characters who are not at all conspicuous, and whose name, rather than life, is familiar to the popular mind. But by the reader and student they are considered with extraordinary respect, on the grounds of weight and of worth; and the eye that follows the strange chaos of the Revolution, and the frenzy which seemed to sweep away all honour and principle, settles with satisfaction on this image of a true woman—calm, firm, gentle, beloved by all who had the happiness of knowing her.

The face and figure of Gibbon are familiar to us from the profile usually found at the beginning of his collected works. The testimony of foreigners as well as of Englishmen, both sufficiently prove its accuracy. To corroborate it farther, there is the well-known story of the blind French old lady, and Charles Fox's coarse lines, neither of which testimonies could be well produced here. This great man was a lover—a lover when he was old as well as when he was young. The style of his letters was rather pedantic and like a page of his history, and the result proved that he was not what is called a successful lover. The story of his early life is well known; his conversion to the Catholic religion, and his expatriation by his father to Switzerland, to be placed under the care of a divine there, who was to reconvert him. Change of scene, and perhaps an absence of earnestness, made the task not difficult; and the tutor was soon able to report that grace and conviction had done their work. How successful that labour had been, a famous chapter in his history was presently to show.

He was established at Lausanne, read a great deal, saw not a few remarkable people, and being known as "an *Anglais* of fortune"—crow s of whom were then overrunning Europe under the charge of "bear-leaders," a subject which Sterne was to choose presently for a sermon—was taken much notice of. His extraordinary information and studiousness were another recommendation. Not very far away there was a little village up in the mountains that separated the Pays de Vaud from Burgundy, and there a humble clergyman looked after a more humble flock. The learned convert, who soon made his acquaintance, could praise his gifts in a phrase that reads very much like a note out of his "Roman History." "His profession did not extinguish the philosophy and moderation of his temper;" a strange sort of compliment, pleasantly in keeping with the satiric vein of this profound writer. The clergyman's wife was a French lady, to whom the young student was more gallant, saying that she had preferred her religion to her country—having, in short, been obliged to quit France through the severity of the penal laws.

But this pair had a daughter Susanne. She seems to have been a charming person; and her later career showed that the young man at that time was at least as well able to judge of human character in real life as he was when he had to decide on its old incomplete manifestation in books. She used occasionally to pay a short visit to her friends, and come across the mountains to Lausanne; and she left behind her every mouth filled with the praises of the wit, beauty, and erudition of the clergyman's daughter. Young Mr. Gibbon soon heard of this prodigy, and became curious to see her. He was presently introduced, and was quite captivated by her.

Not many years later, a Frenchman—Suard—met Mr. Gibbon, and described him in a rather malignant fashion. Leaving a margin for ill-nature, it must be accepted as tolerably accurate. "The root of Mr. Gibbon's nose seems to be sunk deeper into his forehead than ever Calmuck's was; and the shapeless trunk of his body, with its stomach of Silenus, rests on a pair of spindleshanks." His blemishes had not, of course, been developed at this time, but were *in posse*, as it were. But the young lady that attracted him had many charms. He himself gave a graceful and illustrative description of her attractions. He found her 'learned without pedantry, lively in conversation, pure in her sentiments, and elegant in her manners." The young *élève* was fascinated. "I saw her," he says, "and loved." His "first sudden emotion" was fortified by the habits and knowledge of a more familiar acquaintance. His advances were encouraged. From mere meetings at Lausanne, it came to formal visits at her father's modest little parsonage over the mountains. He looked back to these as very happy days. The father and mother honourably "encouraged the connection." "In a calm retirement," says Mr. Gibbon in his stately historic way, as though he were describing the Empress Helena, "the gay vanity of youth no longer fluttered in her bosom. She listened to the voice of truth and passion; and he might venture to hope that he had made some impression on a virtuous heart."

Mr. Gibbon pursued his studies for a year or two longer, still speaking "in the voice of truth," and was then summoned home to England by his father. In all this was Mr. Gibbon, with his "voice of truth and passion," and his "impression on a virtuous heart," his vows to a simple country girl, very much like a modern officer in a garrison town.

Like the latter, he is ordered away, or has to go and "see his family," and, as invariably, a third person steps upon the scene and forbids the banns.

Mr. Gibbon despatches the rest of the business very quietly: "On my return to England I found that my father *would not hear* of this strange alliance, and that without his support I was destitute and helpless. I sighed as a lover; I *obeyed as a son*." The reader will note the curious use of the word "strange" in the sense of "foreign" or "incompatible;" and the awkwardness of the confession that he only discovered his dependence on his father at so convenient a moment. The "voice of truth" and even of passion was hushed in presence of this unsentimental argument. We may think of the poor girl in the lonely mountains, waiting for the lagging English post, then having this news broken to her with all the ingenious and elegant diction of the author of the "Decline and Fall;" her mortification, too, before the Lausanne coterie, with nothing left to console her but the "erudition without pedantry," which had so charmed her faithless admirer.

When he said he had "obeyed as a son," it must be owned that Mr. Gibbon gives a rather unhandsome account of the short sequel of the affair; or it may be that his lofty "Decline and Fall" manner had made him view everything as having historical bearings of some kind. That strange irony, sometimes unintentional with him, had grown into a habit; and so he goes on: "My wound was insensibly healed by time, absence, and the habits of a new life. My cure was accelerated by a faithful report of the *tranquillity and cheerfulness of the lady* herself, and my love subsided into friendship and esteem."

Mr. Gibbon's tranquil version of the incident might have proved the authorised or accepted one, only that the other day her papers were published in a work called "The Salon of Madame Necker," and which supplies her version of the episode. Mr. Gibbon does not figure handsomely. It appears that he left her for four years in a state of uncertainty, whether or not he had completely broken off, or was seriously neglecting her; and that, instead of taking her desertion "with the cheerfulness and tranquillity" that he speaks of, she waited another year, making five in all, and then addressed him this piteous and affectionate remonstrance :

"Monsieur,"—she wrote, "I blush at the application I am now going to make. I would willingly hide it from you; I would also hide it from myself. Is it possible, good heavens ! that an innocent heart should so far demean itself? What a humiliation ! I have had greater troubles, but never one that I felt so keenly. I cannot help it, and in spite of myself I feel as if I had lost my head. My own peace of mind exacts that I should make this effort; and if I lose this present opportunity I shall never have another. Whenever I have had a moment's relaxation, my heart, ever ready to torment itself, has always imagined your signs of coldness to be proofs of your delicacy of feeling. For the last five years I have been indulging in this idle fancy in the most exceptional and unaccountable way; but at last, romantic as I may be, I am now convinced of my error. Upon my knees I beseech you to dissuade a maddened heart. Make a frank avowal of your complete indifference to me. I shall then be in a position to govern my own actions. Certainty will bring with it the repose for which I am anxiously longing. If you refuse me this mark of openness, you will be the most contemptible of men; for God, who sees my heart, and who loves me though He so sorely tries me—God, I say, will punish you in spite of my prayers, if there is the slightest prevarication in your answer, or if by your silence you treat carelessly my peace of mind as though it were a plaything."

His answer to this reasonable and tender appeal has not been found, but it would appear to have been cold, if not cruel. She thus again expostulated:

"A separation of five years did not do so much to alter my feelings as what has lately taken place. I could have wished that you had written to me sooner, or that your last letter but one had been couched in a different tone. Exalted ideas, when they are supported by an appearance of virtue, may lead one into great errors. You might well have spared me five or six that are now irreparable, and which will for ever determine my lot in this life. I know as well as you that what I am now saying may appear to be neither delicate nor kindhearted. For a long time past I have lost my self-control, but I am pleased to find that I still have enough left to me to feel the bitterness with which I now reproach you. I would, at the same time, ask your pardon, and beg that you do not distress yourself at the unhappiness of my condition. My father and mother are dead; what chance can hope offer to me? It was not to you that I sacrificed my hope, but to an imaginary creature who never existed but in a mind such as mine, crack-brained with romance. For as soon as your letter undeceived me you were then to me no more than any other man; and after having been the only one for whom I could feel attachment, you became one of those for whom I had the least inclination, because you are the most unlike my *beau-idéal* of a sentimental lover. And you are the only one who can recompense me.

Carry out your plans of which you have given me the outlines. Join your friendship to that which my other friends have professed for me. You will find me as open-hearted, as kind, and at the same time as indifferent to you as I am towards them. You may believe me when I say that it is not petulance that makes me speak in this way; if I make use of this last term (no matter how true it be), it is only to assure you that my heart in the end will save yours. My conduct and my sentiments have deserved your esteem and your friendship. Let me reckon upon the one and upon the other, so that henceforward there be no further question of our late intimacy." The future historian replied:

"MADEMOISELLE,—Must you still continue to offer me happiness which prudence compels me to refuse? I have lost your affection, though I still possess your friendship. In giving me that you do me so much honour that I have no room left for doubt. I accept it, mademoiselle, as a valuable exchange for mine, which is most perfectly yours, and as a treasure whose value I know so well that I can never part with it. But of our correspondence, mademoiselle, if I feel all its pleasures, I perceive also all the dangers. I feel this as regards myself, and I fear for both of us. Pray let my silence protect me. Excuse my fears, mademoiselle; I think they are not unfounded."

The lady accepted this cold and "author-like" production, and nothing more took place until they met one day at Ferney, when Gibbon's chilling manner and neglect stung her into writing a letter full of bitter reproaches, which effectually put an end to all intimacy.

But she had made a large circle of friends, among whom this desertion caused no little indignation. Rousseau did not care to conceal his opinion. Some one had written to him with a message or commission for Mademoiselle Curchod, and he wrote back to say that he was certain to acquit himself badly in it, on account of his esteem for her. "The cooling-off of Mr. Gibbon has made me think meanly of him. I have been going over his book, and he seems to me to be straining at *esprit*. He is not the man for me; nor can I think that he will be the one for Mademoiselle Curchod. Anyone who does not know her value is not worthy of her; but a man who has come to that knowledge and then withdraws himself, is only worthy of contempt. . . . I would sooner a thousand times that he left her poor and free among you than that he brought her rich and miserable away to England." This was plain-speaking, and later was duly published with the rest of the philosopher's letters, and read by Mr. Gibbon, who made a half-good-humoured, half-indignant protest against such treatment; but through the protest we almost see a secret consciousness of wrong.

Mr. Gibbon then went into the militia, and passed through the pleasant exercises of encampment. It is stated that it was this training that really made him give such graphic power to the military portions of his history; and some distinguished person lately, speaking of the volunteers, quoted this passage. It was received with good-humoured merriment—a good test of the value of so ridiculous a statement. The deserted young lady remained in her retirement until the death of her father left her almost penniless. She then went to Geneva, and was driven to the calling of a governess; and there, says Mr. Gibbon oddly, "She earned a *hard subsistence* for herself and her mother; but in *her lowest distress* she maintained a spotless reputation and a dignified behaviour." This mixture of compliment and awkward reminder was scarcely in his best taste.

But by-and-by was to come the reward. A rich Swiss banker, who did business in Paris, M. Necker, came that way, and, Gibbon says, "had the *good sense* to discover this inestimable treasure." Accident and labour, rather than good sense, generally guide discoveries. Her later career is well known, and the compensation for that early trial was destined to be brilliant. The banker became the minister; not only the minister, but a sort of "heaven-sent" one, called in to save France. The world now knows Madame Necker as one of its heroines—the clever, charming wife, the pleasant agreeable writer, the devoted partner, the good and pious woman, and the mother of the more famous "Corinne"—Madame de Staël. Mr. Gibbon found his way to Paris, where they were living, when the past was prudently forgotten; and in her *salons* was exhibited the distinguished Englishman, now very famous.

He, however, paid this homage to his early love— he never married. He was wealthy, and might have done so with advantage. The curious society at Lausanne and in Switzerland, where he saw Voltaire act, had a special charm for him. And so he pored over his Tillemont and his Baronius, collected books and wrote, and grew fat and gouty and almost absurdly out of shape; and it was precisely at that crisis, when he was just fifty years old, he chose to fall in love again. The dramatic finale of that attachment was so comic, and placed him in so ridiculous a light, that it almost seems a Nemesis in consequence of his old desertion. It took place in the same locality.

Lady Elizabeth Foster, who afterwards became Duchess of Devonshire,—a daughter of the eccentric Bishop of Bristol, and of whom we have a glimpse in the account of the beautiful duchess,— was on her travels over Europe. She was a true specimen of the dilettante English who were then found on the Continent, and who really did noble and liberal acts with their money in the service of art. Fancy a lady of title nowadays printing an *édition de luxe* of Horace at an Italian press, exquisitely illustrated, and costing a fortune!

Mr. Gibbon was at that really dramatic passage of his life, in the middle of the year 1787, when he was completing his History, and, on a certain night in June, had written the last line of the last page of the great work. Great as it is, it seems now to be regarded more with respect and awe than affection; a feeling that Mr. Dickens very happily expressed when he made Mr. Boffin choose it for the work with which he was to make his first acquaintance with literature. Very familiar is the description of the almost solemn act performed in a pavilion at the end of his garden. Laying down his pen, he took several turns in the "acacia alley," with a feeling of joy at getting back his liberty after this long and arduous servitude; but dashed with a certain melancholy, as he thought, however lasting might be the reputation of the book, the days of the writer might be numbered.

The lady arrived shortly after, and struck him, as she struck all, with the elegance of her form and manner, her *esprit*, cleverness, and, above all, the nice *à propos* of her compliments. She took a great interest in that dramatic completion of the great History, and was one morning asked to breakfast to inspect the very scene. In the meantime, Mr. Gibbon had interpreted her "sweetness" and elegance, and all the compliments, as so many proofs of the impression he was making upon her heart. And it seemed this occasion would do excellently well to bring on a *dénouement*. After breakfast was over, he brought her out to look at the famous acacia walk, and the view of lake and mountain which it commanded. She was enthusiastic in her delight, and expressed herself in all the raptures becoming admiration for scenery, when the historian suddenly affected to be jealous of the praise bestowed on such objects, and electrified her by an eloquent and passionate declaration, at the same time falling on his knees.

The astonished lady could hardly understand at first; then burst into a fit of laughter. The situation must have been ludicrous indeed; the unwieldy lover still pouring out his vows, and she remaining some paces off and trying to soothe him. At last he understood his mistake, and then she bade him get up. But this was impossible; gout, enormous fat, and rheumatism utterly incapacitated him. The brilliant lady, cruelly ignoring the romance of the situation, came to his aid, and tried to raise him; but it was in vain. Then both parties agreed to look at the matter in a prosaic light; and it was determined that she should go for assistance, and give out that Gibbon had fallen. She went, and two stout peasants of the place came up, raised him between them, and landed him in his familiar easy-chair. These honest creatures soundly rated him for his folly, and told him he should not stir without the help of servants. To her honour, the duchess never mentioned this ludicrous adventure during his lifetime; but she afterwards told it to the Chevalier A. de Montor, who relates it in the "Biographie Universelle." The late Dr. Russell, the learned and amiable President of Maynooth College, has called attention to this scene in his "Life of Mezzofanti," as well as to the curious blunder of Lord Brougham, who makes Mdlle. Curchod the heroine. Had the rejected Mdlle. Curchod ever heard of this ludicrous scene, which no doubt she did, a smile must have come to her lips; and she, perhaps, felt that her old wrong had been more than avenged.

With the name of Mr. Pitt, the great English minister, nothing like romance is associated. His face and figure, which, in murky bronze, presides at the top of George Street, Hanover Square—the ugly nose and thoroughly official figure, seemed to warn off all such associations. The grim prose of politics, reports, speeches, and despatches were what engrossed him. He died unmarried. All the comic papers of the time are exceedingly merry on the subject of his callous indifference to female charms; and in the "Rolliad" there was much jesting on "the immaculate boy," as he was styled. Mr. Pitt, however, had his "pleasant vice," viz., a fondness for port wine, resorted to for the purpose of stimulating his parliamentary exertions, great speeches, etc. He was also fond of soldiering, and conscientiously looked after the militia regiment of which he was colonel.

Yet he was not so unsusceptible to female charms as was supposed. Lady Hester Stanhope declared that no one could have a more just or critical eye in such matters, and that often, on returning together from a party, he pleasantly expatiated on the merits of the various dames and beauties, and noted in artistic defects in their dress. To one he showed such devotion that he is said to have drunk out of her shoe. The truth was that this self-denial was not a fresh proof of the heroism of his character; he felt that his talents and time were his country's. In the service of that country he had sunk himself in debt; under which load he might hope to struggle on, if he remained unencumbered by the burden and distractions of a family. Such a luxury as the *placens uxor* was only for statesmen in easy circumstances. In this condition of things he bore with good-humour and protest the unmeaning and even scandalous attacks that were made upon him by his enemies, who used this ordinary and not uncommon condition of celibacy as an engine of personal attack. And yet all the time, cold and unimpassioned as he was supposed to be, he was secretly burning with the gentle passion.

With the active official politician and officer, Mr. Eden—who became Lord Auckland—Mr. Pitt was on the most intimate and affectionate terms for many years. Lord Auckland had a favourite daughter, Eleanor, whom her fond father afterwards described as "a very beautiful and good creature, with every advantage of a strong mind and right principles." Mr. Pitt found his way often to Eden Farm, and was much attracted by this charming girl. The hopes of the family were much raised. To be the wife of so celebrated a man, and of the prime minister of England, might seem a brilliant conquest. The young lady was only twenty, Mr. Pitt eighteen years older. Already the affair was a matter of gossip, and Mr. Pitt's attentions to Miss Eden were subject of congratulation. It may be conceived with what pain and consternation it was found that her lover had abruptly broken off this intimacy; and the father soon received an explanation, in the shape of a sort of official *communiqué*, the tone of which is characteristic. He "found it totally impossible to return thither without having (as far as it might depend on himself) formed a decision on a point that had remained in suspense too long already." He added:

"It can hardly be necessary to say that the time I have passed among your family has led to my forming sentiments of very real attachment to them all, and of much more than attachment to one whom I need not name. Every hour of acquaintance with the person to whom you will easily conceive I refer, has served to augment and confirm that impression. In short, it has convinced me that whoever may have the good fortune to be united with her, is destined to more than his share of human happiness."

He then proceeded to "blame himself for not having sooner looked into his difficulties, which he now finds have become insurmountable; but feels it impossible not to avow his attachment, and leaves it to Lord Auckland's discretion to impart what he had written to the person most concerned."

Several letters passed between Lord Auckland and Mr. Pitt. The former suggested arrangements by which the marriage might in time take place without imprudence; but the stoical Mr. Pitt declared that, "though he was sacrificing his best hopes and dearest wishes to his conviction and judgment, further discussion would lead only to prolonged suspense and increased anxiety."

It is pretty plain to anyone who considers the matter impartially, that Pitt behaved honourably, though, perhaps, with coldness. He withdrew in time, and certainly before any formal proposals or expectations could have been reasonably made. A friend of the late Lord Stanhope, who had seen the letters, declares that the transaction began with Pitt's confession of poverty and embarrassment, and that Lord Auckland frankly confessed that the objection was reasonable, and that he was not inclined to expose his daughter to poverty and privation.

On the other hand, Lord Auckland's representative, who had the papers before him, did not accept this view, adding that "an erroneous account is given of the correspondence that took place respecting the interesting affair of 1797. If it were of the character described by Lord Stanhope, there could not possibly have been the slightest objection to publish it; but the fact is, a long and painful discussion took place on that occasion, which terminated honourably to all parties concerned. It is entirely incorrect to state that Lord Auckland was in the slightest degree averse to the marriage on account of Mr. Pitt's pecuniary difficulties; on the contrary, believing that his daughter was attached to Mr. Pitt, he was naturally anxious that it should take place."

On this painful explanation the intimacy between the parties was broken off. Friends of both felt that this was a pity, and that Lord Auckland's advice was useful to the minister and to the country. The Archbishop of Canterbury accordingly wrote to propose that the former should pass over his daughter's treatment and make due allowance. "I am persuaded that it will be a relief to both your minds to meet, though the first moment will be unpleasant. Subjects more than enough will present themselves for conversation, and as soon as it appears that the particular subject will not be introduced on either side, discussions will engross you both, and things will go on between you much more easily and naturally than they will ever do if the present separation continues for a time. You wait for him to begin. I think he can't do it. He does not know what he is to expect in the meeting." Lord Auckland took this advice, and his advances were gratefully received :

"My dear Lord,

"I cannot say how much I feel obliged to you for your kind and friendly note. It will be the greatest satisfaction and assistance to me to think and talk over with you the subjects you mention, as soon and as fully as possible. "W. Pitt."

Accordingly they were soon friends again.

Miss Eden was not long left single. A clever rising politician, Lord Hobart, afterwards Earl of Buckinghamshire, within two years offered his hand. When the news was communicated to his former admirers it is characteristic to note how he behaved in rather an awkward situation :

"My dear Lord,

"I have heard from the Speaker the circumstance which you desired him to mention, and give you many thanks for your very kind attention in making the communication, and in making him the channel of it. There could be no event interesting to any part of your family which would not be so to me; and, certainly, this is not the instance where I feel that sentiment the least. I congratulate you and all around you with the most cordial good wishes.

"Ever affectionately yours,

"W. Pitt."

Such was the end of Pitt's early love.

THE STORY OF L. E. L.

THE STORY OF L. E. L.

ONE of the most interesting and even romantic of literary figures is that of Letitia Landon—whose curious signature of three letters seems always to bring before persons quite unacquainted with her story, poetical associations of a special and interesting kind. There are but few now alive who know her sad history: there are two, however—persons of great age—who were intimately acquainted with her, and who know well the details of the last sad episode of her life. There was something in her history, and a genuine tone of romance in her poems, which fell into the "Book of Beauty" and "Annuals" category, attractive to the young and impulsive. Her portrait, too, which was published, invites the same interest.

This pleasing young creature, born at Chelsea in 1802, found herself at Brompton about the year 1814, the neighbour of one who was then an important literary personage, the director of the most

influential journal of the day, *The Literary Gazette.*
"My cottage," he says, "overlooked the mansion and grounds of Mr. Landon, the father of L. E. L.; a narrow lane only dividing our residences. My first recollection of the future poetess is that of a plump girl, grown enough to be almost mistaken for a woman, bowling a hoop round the walks, with the hoop-stick in one hand and a book in the other, reading as she ran, and, as well as she could, managing both exercise and instruction at the same time. The exercise was prescribed and insisted upon: the book was her own irrepressible choice." This presently led to the usual request, modestly made, in such cases, "would Mr. Jerdan just cast his eyes over some lines of poetry?" He did so, and encouraged the young girl. He became to her a sort of guide and friend and educator, and in a naïve passage the grave editor seems to more than hint that he was regarded as an "ideal":

> It is the very essence of the being I have so faintly portrayed, not to see things in their actual state, but to imagine, create, exaggerate, and form them into idealities; and then to view them in the light in which vivid fancy alone has made them appear. Thus it befell with my tuition of L. E. L. Her poetic emotions and aspirations were intense, usurping in fact almost every other function of the brain: and the assistance I could give her in the ardent pursuit produced an influence not readily to be conceived under other circumstances or upon a less imaginative nature. The result was a grateful and devoted attachment; all phases of which demonstrate and illume the origin of her productions. Critics and

biographers may guess, and speculate, and expatiate for ever; but without this master-key they will make nothing of their reveries. With it, all is intelligible and obvious; and I have only to call on the admirers of her delicious compositions to remember this one fact, to settle the question of their reality or romance—that they are the effusions of passionate inspiration, lighted from such unlikely sources. It was her spirit which clothed them according to her own unreal dreams.

Gradually her poems began to excite attention. She soon became a useful assistant on the *Gazette*, doing, besides her verses, reviews and essays; carrying that hod, as it were, which secured, at least, a satisfactory daily wage. She became known and sought. She received good prices for her books, though these were conceived in a spirit of romance that might be called "second hand;" the scenes she describes being laid in Italy, where she had never been. Her friend furnishes the following prosaic but satisfactory table of receipts—" Romance and Reality" it might be called :

For the " Improvisatrice " she received	£300
For the " Troubadour "	600
For the " Golden Violet "	200
For the " Venetian Bracelet "	150
For the " Easter Offering "	30
For the " Drawing-room Scrap Book "	105
For " Romance and Reality "	300
For " Francesca Carrara "	300
For " Heath's Book of Beauty "	300
And certainly from other Annuals, Magazines, and Periodicals, not less in ten or twelve years than	200
In all	£2,485

The fair L. E. L. became herself editress of one of those engravers' books which were then in high fashion, bound in blue or crimson silk, and printed on wove, hot-pressed paper, and for which elegant amateurs were glad to furnish verses and sketches; the names of persons of fashion being mingled with those of the professionals. But it took a great many years before she attained to this elevation. Lady Blessington was the successful conductor of another of these publications; and readers of the life of Dr. Madden will gather a good idea of the almost abject lengths to which the literary aspirant would go to secure a place in her venture.

One of the pleasantest views we have of her is a little "junketing"—evidently a great effort—she took to Paris, in 1834, by the somewhat homely conveyance of one of the General Steam Navigation Company's packets from St. Katherine's Wharf. She wrote regularly to her first friend Jerdan, who always seemed flattered by her attentions; but an attractive young woman, who was at the same time amusingly anxious about the "siller," insensibly begins to flatter the editor, whom she likes, and on whom at the same time so much depends. She writes from Boulogne:

"I began a letter to you yesterday, but on taking it up this morning I find it is, even to you, scarcely legible, so will begin it over again. I have also another reason: I wrote on English paper, which is heavier, and I have to pay the inland postage, and to-day my time *ne vaut pas mes sous*. You cannot think how I missed you. I really thought the morning never would pass. It did pass, however, and then I wished it back again. The wind blew directly in our teeth. It was impossible to read for three reasons: the sun, the wind, and the noise.

"And when I endeavoured to get into a pleasant train of thought it made me melancholy to think I was leaving my native country. I was fairly dying with a desire of talking. I am quite cured of my wish to die for some time to come, as I really think that now I quite understand what the sensation is. I was not sick —scarcely at all; but so faint! As to what Boulogne is like from the sea, I cannot tell. I scarcely recollect anything about my landing. Misfortune first recalled my scattered faculties. At the Custom House you are searched."

Again she wrote:

"We could not get places to go to Paris till Sunday. Miss Turin wanted to have taken the whole *coupé*, which would have been very comfortable; but a gentleman has already one place, and it is scarcely worth while waiting till Tuesday. Moreover, the *conducteur* says that '*c'est un monsieur si poli.*' How he has ascertained the fact I do not know. It has a very odd effect hearing a strange language spoken under our windows; and now I have told you everything that I can think of, which does not amount to much. However, I have taken two things for granted, first, that you would expect my first letter, and also that you would be glad to hear how I was. I fear I shall never make a traveller. I am already beginning to count the days for my return. Kind regards to all inquiring friends, and hoping that you are missing me very much."

In another letter:

"The first thing that I did was to write to you from Boulogne, and the first thing that I do is to write to you from Paris; but truly the pleasure of seeing my handwriting must be sufficient. Never was there a worse traveller. I arrived in Paris more dead than alive, and till this evening have not held up my head. The beginning of our journey was delightful; the road is like one avenue, and it was so pretty, having the children, every hill we ascended, throwing roses into the carriage, asking for sous. I was scarcely sensible when we arrived at Paris, and was just lifted out of the *diligence*. Since then the extent of my travels has been from the bed to the sofa. We have very pleasant apartments, looking on the boulevards—such a gay scene. It seems so odd to see the people walking about in caps, looking so neat, and, I must add, so clean. Mercy on the French carriages and horses; they make such a clatter; drive far more with their tongues than the reins. We have delicious dinners, if I could but eat, which at present is an impossibility. I am still a horrid figure with my sea and sunburning.

"Be sure wafer, and thin paper. I shall be very glad to see England again.

"I wish I could find any channel of writing by the ambassador's bag, for the postage which I have to pay is two francs, and, what is much worse, the post-office is at the other end of the town, and even when I have a messenger, whom I must pay, the chances are that he will not pay it. I long to see the *Gazette;* and now must end abruptly or lose my opportunity. Pray write to me. I wish I were at home without the journey. I shall write the moment I have anything to tell, and must watch my means of going to the post-office.

"Love and fear are the greatest principles of human existence. If you owed my letter of yesterday to the first of these, you owe that of to-day to the last. What, in the name of all that is dreadful in the way of postage, could induce you to put the *Gazette* in your letter? Welcome as it was, it has cost me dear—nearly six shillings. I was so glad to see your handwriting that the shock was lost in the pleasure; but truly, when I come to reflect and put it down in my pocket-book, I am 'in a state.' The *Gazette* alone would only have cost twopence, and the letter deux francs; but altogether it is ruinous. Please, when you next write, let it be on the thinnest paper, and put a wafer. Still, I was delighted to hear from you, and a most amusing letter it was. The *Gazette* is a real treat. It is such an excellent one as to make me quite jealous.

"My only approach to an adventure has been as follows: I was advised, as the best remedy against the excessive fatigue under which I was suffering, to take a bath, which I did early one morning. I found it quite delicious, and was reading 'La Dernière Journée', when I fell asleep, and was, in consequence, nearly drowned. I suppose the noise of the book falling aroused me, and I shall never forget the really dreadful feeling of suffocation, the ringing in my ears, like a great bell, with which I was awakened."

She then adroitly turns to "business":

"I think some very interesting papers might be written on the modern French authors. We know nothing of them. If I do write them I must buy some. At Galignani's they only allow two works at a time, and I can scarcely get any that I desire. I am thinking of subscribing to a French library. One feels the want of a gentleman here very much.

"I was so glad of your letter.

"I have been hitherto too ill to do anything; but I have quite arranged my plan to write in my own room four or five hours every morning; so I hope to get a great deal done. Adieu, *au revoir*."

"35, Rue le Grand, lundi,
"Which, being done into English, means Monday.

"I hope you will not think that I intend writing you to death; but I cannot let this opportunity pass. Miss Montgomery leaves Paris to-morrow, and so write I must. I am quite surprised that I should have so little to tell you; but really I have nothing, as ill-luck would have it. I went to call on Madame Tastu, from whom I received a charming note; and, while I was out, Monsieur Sainte-Beuve and Monsieur Odillon Barrot called. However, the latter wrote to me offering his services as cicerone, etc., and I expect him this morning. M. Heine called yesterday; a most pleasant person. I am afraid he did not think me a *personne bien spirituelle*, for you know it takes a long time with me to get over the shame of speaking to a stranger. By way of conversation he said: 'Mademoiselle donc a beaucoup couru les boutiques?' 'Mais non.' 'A-t-elle été au Jardin des Plantes ?' 'Mais non.' 'Avez-vous été à l'opéra, aux théâtres ?' 'Mais non.' 'Peut-être Mademoiselle aime la promenade ?' 'Mais non.' 'A-t-elle donc apporté beaucoup de livres, ou peut-être elle écrit ?' 'Mais non.' At last in seeming despair, he exclaimed : 'Mais Mademoiselle, qu'est-ce que c'est donc qu'elle a fait ?' 'Mais—mais—j'ai regardé par la fenêtre.' Was there ever anything *si bête?* but I really could think of nothing else. I am enchanted with Madame Tastu ; her manners are so kind, so encouraging. I did not feel much embarrassed after the first. She has fine features, though there was something about her face that put me in mind of Miss Roberts, but with a softened expression. If I had known as much of Paris as I do even now, I would not have come. In the first place, there is nobody here ; *à la campagne* is almost the universal answer. Secondly, it is of no use coming with only a lady ; I might almost as well have stayed in London. Thirdly, it is too short a time ; I shall not have made a little acquaintance before I must leave. Fourthly, one ought to be married, and fifthly, I wish myself at home again."

Once more to business :

"If I had the opportunity, the time, and could procure the books, I am sure a most delightful series of articles might be written on French literature. We know nothing of it ; and it would require an immense deal of softening and adaptation to suit it to English taste. How well you have done 'The Revolutionary Epick !' though with less vanity, Disraeli has all the elements of a great poet ; but there is something wanting in the putting together. Taste is his great deficiency.

"I quite dread—though impatient for it—my journey back again. I shall never make a traveller.

"My present address ought to be well known to you.[1] I write on purpose to scold you. Why have you not sent me the *Gazette?* it would have been such a treat. Also, you have not (like everybody else) written to me, and I quite pine for news

---

[1] "From my translation and publication of 'L'Hermite' of Jouy.'

from England. I would return to-morrow if I had the opportunity. I do not think that you have properly valued my letters; for things ought to be valued according to their difficulty, and really writing is no little trouble, to say nothing of putting my epistles in the post. I have been very unwell ever since my arrival, and for the last three days I have scarcely been off the sofa. The fatigue and the heat are equally overpowering. I feel so unequal to the exertion of hearing and seeing. I cannot tell you half the kindness and civility which I have received. Of all the persons I have met, or, rather, who have called upon me—for there is no meeting anybody now, all the *soirées* being over—I have been the most struck with M. Heine; his conversation is most original and amusing. Poor Miss Turin is still in the doctor's hands, and of course it is impossible for me to go out by myself, or accept the attendance of any gentleman alone, so that I am surrounded with all sorts of little difficulties and embarrassments. I never again would think of going anywhere with only a lady; one might almost as well stay at home. I had no idea till now how useful you gentlemen are—I might say, how indispensable. We are very comfortably situated; we have delightful bedrooms, a little antechamber, and the prettiest saloon, looking on a charming garden. The quiet is such a relief; for in Rue Louis-le-Grand we could not hear each other's voice for the noise; and above my head was a printer, and opposite my window a carpenter's. I do not know what it may be in the City, but at the West End there is nothing that can give an idea of the noise of Paris; the streets are all paved, the omnibuses innumerable, and carts and carriages all of the heaviest kind. If my money holds out, I shall buy several works and translate them at home, but I doubt being able to accomplish it; for though I have bought nothing but what was indispensable, such as gloves, shoes, paper, etc., I have little more left than will bring me home. The dust here is something not to be told; before you have walked a hundred yards your feet are of a whitish brown. A great deal of my time has hung heavily on my hands, I have been so languid and so feverish; still, I feel that I have quite a new stock of ideas, and much material for future use. One ridiculous misfortune is continually befalling me; I am always falling down; the *parquet*, *i.e.* the floor, is so slippery, and I am never very steady on my feet. I really thought I had broken my arm yesterday. I am very anxious about getting home. I like our new lodgings so much. They are, according to Sir William Curtis's orthography, three C's, namely, clean, cool, and quiet."

After all her many hints and allusions, she now came to a formal proposal :

"This is quite a business letter, so I beg you will read it with all due attention. I have read now a considerable portion of French new works, and find a great many which, translated with *judgment*, would, I think, sell. I underline judgment, for not a little would be required. What I propose, is to make an annual, consisting entirely of French translations—prose and verse. I could get it ready in about a month. To be called—what? We must think of a good title. 'The Laurel; or, Leaves from French Literature;' 'The Exchange; or, Selection of French Authors,' with a little vignette on the title-page, of the Bourse, or 'The Stranger,' etc. etc.

"I do not propose new prints; anyone who knew how to set about it might form here a collection of very pretty prints of all sorts of popular subjects. You must please see if any publisher will undertake this, and if they will, please write as soon as possible. I feel convinced I could make a very amusing book; shortening, softening down, omitting, altering in my translations, according to my own discretion. I could have my part of the volume ready in about six weeks."

These extracts from her letters will be found singularly sprightly, especially the naïve reference to "business," as her money was going rapidly.

This interesting woman, as may be imagined, was much sought for her own personal gifts—"a great warmth of feeling; a peculiar charm of manner and address; an affectionate, loving nature; a simplicity of mind wholly free from affectation; a guileless character, childlike in many of its traits, devoid of all suspicion of evil intentions and designs, and yet not free from impulsive tendencies and some degree of wilfulness, being her characteristics."

This confidence—and she went much about by herself—made her likely to be the victim of would-be sympathisers of an unsuitable sort; and when it is found that the well-known Grantley Berkeley, Dr. Maginn, and other gentlemen of the kind were interesting themselves in her and championing her cause, it shows she was not over-prudent. She had the tendency of all heroines—to trust in everybody she met. With this she had a painful, acute sensitiveness, which made her feel and exaggerate slights and injuries to an extravagant degree; and this had the unfortunate result of raising up hosts of enemies, who harassed the unprotected creature for years with anonymous attacks and rumours. "Her peace of mind," says her friend Dr. Madden, "was more than disturbed by those diabolical efforts to annoy her—it was destroyed by them; and when labouring under recent inflictions of outrages of this sort, all her energies, bodily and mental, were disordered and impaired by them; the first paroxysms of suffering were usually followed by syncopes, spasms, tremors, and convulsive attacks, approaching to epileptic seizures. And when the violence of this nervous agitation would cease, then would come intervals of the most profound dejection of spirits."

It may be conceived that there were many suitors for so interesting a prize; but these enemies, by a dreadful system of persecution, seemed always to interpose, and succeeded in breaking off the engagements. One of the most eminent sculptors of her day was eager to make her his wife, but their cruel interference broke off the match.

With this gaiety of nature before us — which seems almost childlike—we turn to a letter written by Lady Blessington, after her death, which outlines L. E. L.'s tragic history, and serves as a curious commentary on her life thus far:

"Poor dear L. E. L. lost her father, who was a captain in the army, while she was yet a child. He had married the widow of an army agent, a woman not of refined habits, and totally unsuited to him. On his death, his brother, the late Dean of Exeter, interested himself for his nephew and niece, the sole children left by Captain Landon; and deeming it necessary to remove them from their mother, placed the girl (poor L. E. L.) at school; and the boy at another. At an unusually early age she manifested the genius for which she afterwards became so deservedly popular. On leaving school her uncle placed her under the protection of her grandmother, whose *exigence* rendered the life of her gifted grandchild anything but a happy one. Her first poetical effusions were published many years ago, and the whole of the sum they produced was appropriated to her grandmother.

"Soon after, L. E. L. became acquainted with Mr. Jerdan, who, charmed with her talents, encouraged their exertion by inserting her poems in a literary journal, with all the encomiums they merited. This notice drew the attention of publishers on her, and, alas! drew also the calumny and hatred of the envious, which ceased not to persecute her through her troubled life; but absolutely drove her from her native land. There was no slander too vile, and no assertion too wicked, to heap on the fame of this injured creature. Mr. Jerdan was married, and the father of a large family, many of whom were older than L. E. L. Those who disbelieved the calumny refrained not from repeating it, until it became a general topic of conversation. Her own sex, fearful of censure, had not courage to defend her, and this highly gifted and sensitive creature, without having committed a single error, found herself a victim to slander. More than one advantageous proposal of marriage was made to her; but no sooner was this known, than anonymous letters were sent to the persons who wished to wed her, filled with charges against her honour. Some of her suitors, wholly discrediting these calumnies, but thinking it due to her to refute them, instigated inquiries to trace them to the original source whence they came; not a single proof could be had of even the semblance of guilt, though a thousand were furnished of perfect innocence. Wounded and humiliated, poor L. E. L. refused to wed those who could, however worthy the motive, seem to doubt her honour, or instigate inquiry into her conduct; and from year to year dragged on a life of mortification and sorrow. Pride led her to conceal what she suffered, but those who best knew her were aware that for many months sleep could only be obtained by the aid of narcotics, and that violent spasms and frequent attacks of the nerves left her seldom free from acute suffering. The effort to force a gaiety she was far from feeling, increased her sufferings even to the last. The first use she made of the money produced by her writings was to buy an annuity for her grandmother; that grandmother whose acerbity of temper and wearying *exigence* had embittered her home. She then went to reside in Hans Place, with some elderly ladies who kept a school, and here again calumny assailed her. Dr. Maginn, a married man, and father of grown daughters, was now named; though his habits, age, appearance, and attachment to his wife ought to have precluded the possibility of attaching credence to so absurd a piece of scandal, poor L. E. L. was again attacked in a manner that nearly sent her to the grave.

This last falsehood was invented a little more than four years ago, when some of those who disbelieved the other scandal affected to give credit to this, and stung the sensitive mind of poor L. E. L. almost to madness by their hypocritical conduct."

Driven to despair almost by this persecution, and panting for repose, an opportunity now presented itself of release. A gentleman called Maclean, who had an appointment at Cape Coast, was attracted by her, and after some months proposed for her. Lady Blessington relates the next portion of the episode :

"Wrung to the quick by the slanders heaped on her, she accepted his offer; but he deemed it necessary to return to Cape Coast Castle for a year, before the nuptials could be solemnized. He returned at the expiration of that term, renewed his offer, and she, poor dear soul! informed all her friends—and me amongst the number—of her acceptance of it, and of her intention of soon leaving England with him; soon after this Mr. Maclean went to Scotland, and remained there many months without writing a single line to his betrothed. Her feelings under this treatment you can well imagine. Beset by inquiries by all her friends as to where Mr. Maclean was? when she was to be married? etc., etc., all indicating a strong suspicion that he had heard the reports, and would appear no more, a serious illness assailed her, and reduced her to the brink of the grave. When her friend wrote and demanded an explanation from Mr. Maclean, he answered, that, fearing the climate of Africa might prove fatal to her, he had abandoned the intention of marrying, and felt embarrassed at writing to say so.

"She, poor soul! mistook his hesitation and silence for generosity, and wrote to him a letter fraught with affection; the ill-starred union was again proposed, but on condition that it should be kept a secret, even from the friends she was residing with. From the moment of his return from Scotland to that of their departure, he was moody, mysterious, and ill-humoured—continually sneering at literary ladies—speaking slightingly of her works—and, in short, showing every symptom of a desire to disgust her. Sir —— remonstrated with him on his extraordinary mode of proceeding; so did all her friends; but the die was cast. Her pride shrank from the notion of again having it said that another marriage was broken off; and she determined not to break with him. Mystery on mystery followed; no friend or relative of his—though an uncle and aunt were in London—sanctioned the marriage; nay, more, it is now known that two days previous to it, he, on being questioned by his uncle, denied positively the fact of his intention to be married.

"The marriage *was a secret one*, and not avowed until a very few days previous to their sailing for Africa; he refused to permit her own maid, who had long served her, to accompany her, and it was only at the eleventh hour that he could be induced to permit a strange servant to be her attendant. His conduct on board ship was cold and moody. This indifference continued at Cape Castle; and what was worse, discontent, ill-humour, and reproaches at her ignorance of housekeeping met her every day, until her nerves became so agitated that the sound of his voice made her tremble. She was required to do the work of a menial; her female servant was discharged, and was to sail the day that the hapless L. E. L. died."

To one so bright, and fond of society and sympathy, this expatriation must have been terrible. On arriving at the gloomy Cape Coast Castle, of which her husband was a sort of governor, she found that she was the only lady in the colony. Mr. or Captain Maclean assumed a severe mode of conduct, not to say discipline, and, as the poor indiscreet lady wrote home by way of complaint to her friends, he had said "that he will never cease correcting me till he has broken my spirit, and complains of my temper, which you know was never, even under heavy trials, bad." Too much importance should not be attached to such speeches. Her husband was in wretched health, dyspeptic, with an affection of the liver, and thus not likely to be what is called compatible. The place itself, at that time, was a gloomy, wretched one, containing only a few European traders, with a number of half-castes. The Castle was a dismal building, and the acting governor had no more than £500 a year. He delighted in mathematics, and was fond of expressing his contempt for literary matters. With such elements, things did not promise well. Still, it was but a short probation. The marriage took place on June 7, 1838, and by October 15 of the same year, within four months, the gifted L. E. L. had died by poison, accidentally taken. One Mr. Cruickshank, a local merchant, has given a very pleasing picture of the last days of this ill-fated lady.

He wrote, he said, "as one who enjoyed and keenly felt the fascinations of her society, who only ten hours before her death had sat and listened with a rapt attention to her brilliant sallies of wit and feeling."

"I sent in my name by the servant, and immediately afterwards Mrs. Maclean came to the hall and welcomed me. I was hurried away to his bedroom, Mrs. Maclean saying, as she tripped through the long gallery, "You are a privileged person, Mr. Cruickshank, for I can assure you it is not everyone that is admitted here.' I took a seat by the side of his bed, upon which Mrs. Maclean sat down, arranging the clothes about her husband in the most affectionate manner, and receiving ample compensation for her attention by a very sweet and expressive smile of thankfulness.

"As the day drew near for my departure, she occupied herself more and more in writing to her friends in England. I agreed to dine and spend the evening of the 15th with the Governor and his lady, the day before the vessel sailed. At eleven o'clock I rose to leave. It was a fine and clear night, and she strolled into the gallery, where we walked for half-an-hour. Mr. Maclean joined us for a few minutes, but not liking the night air, in his weak state, he returned to the parlour. She was much struck with the beauty of the heavens in those latitudes at night, and said it was when looking at the moon and the stars that her thoughts oftenest reverted to home. She pleased herself with thinking that the eyes of some beloved friend might be turned in the same direction, and that she had thus established a medium of communication for all that her heart wished to express. 'But you must not,' she said, 'think me a foolish moon-struck lady. I sometimes think of these things oftener than I should, and your departure for England has called up a world of delightful associations. You will tell Mr. F——, however, that I am not tired yet. He told me I should return by the vessel that brought me out; but I knew he would be mistaken.' We joined the Governor in the parlour. I bade them good night, promising to call in the morning, to bid them adieu. I never saw her in life again."

The following was written on the morning of her death, and quite disposes of all:

"My dearest Marie,

"Cape Coast Castle,
"October 15th.

"I cannot but write to you a brief account of how I enact the part of a feminine Robinson Crusoe. I must say in itself the place is infinitely superior to all I ever dreamed of. The castle is a fine building, the rooms excellent. I do not suffer from heat; insects there are few or none, and I am in excellent health. The solitude, except an occasional dinner, is absolute. From seven in the morning till seven, when we dine, I never see Mr. Maclean, and rarely anyone else. We even welcomed a series of dinners which I am glad are over, for it is very awkward to be the only lady; still the great kindness with which I am treated, the very pleasant manners of many of the gentlemen, made me feel it as little as possible. Last week we had a visit from Captain Castle of the *Pylades;* his story is very melancholy. We had also a visit from Colonel Rosch, the Dutch governor, a most gentleman-like man. But fancy how awkward the next morning! I cannot induce Mr. Maclean to rise, and I have to make breakfast and do the honours of adieu to him and his officers —white plumes, moustachios, and all. I think I never felt more embarrassed. I haven't yet felt the want of good society the least. I don't wish to form new friends, and never does a day pass without my thinking most affectionately of my old ones. On three sides we are surrounded by the sea. I like the perpetual dash on the rocks; one wave comes up after another, and is for ever dashed in pieces like human hopes that can only swell up to be disappointed. We advance: up springs the slimy froth of love or hope, 'a moment white and gone for ever.'

"The servants are tolerable, but they take so many to work. The prisoners do the scouring; and fancy three men cleaning a room that an old woman in

England would do in an hour, besides a soldier, who stands by, his bayonet drawn in his hand! All my troubles have been of a housekeeping kind; and no one could begin on a more plentiful stock of ignorance than myself. Like Sindbad, the sailor, in his cavern, I begin to see daylight. I have numbered and labelled my keys—their name is Legion—and every morning I take my way to the store, give out flour, sugar, butter, etc., and am learning to scold if I see any dust and miss the customary polish on the tables. I am actually getting the steward of the ship to teach me how to make pastry; I will report progress in my next. We live almost entirely on ducks and chickens; if a sheep be killed it must be eaten almost on the same day. You cannot think of the complete seclusion in which I live; but I have a great reason in writing, and I am well and happy, but I think even more than I expected, if that be possible, of my English friends.

"Dearest, do not forget me. Pray write to me: Mrs. George Maclean, Cape Coast Castle, care of, etc. Write about yourself. Nothing else half so much interests your affectionate

"L. E. MACLEAN."

Next day a hurried message came to Mr. Cruickshank to go to the castle. She was dead. He was brought into a room where the doctor was trying to see if life had not fled. "I seized her hand and gazed upon her face. The expression was calm and meaningless. Her eyes were open, fixed." Poor L. E. L.!

Her maid was, it seems, leaving for England by a packet that was sailing that day. This had affected and agitated her much, as the desolate creature felt she would be left still more alone and helpless. The maid had come to her door in the morning, but could not open it. On doing so she found her mistress dead on the floor, with a phial in her hand, containing extract of prussic acid, which she foolishly used, as nervous persons use choral now. There could be no doubt from the evidence that she had accidentally poisoned herself by an overdose, from the wish to allay her agitation. But so vehemently did her friends in England take up the case, that it was said she had destroyed herself in despair at her treatment. Nothing could be further from the truth. Mr. Maclean was an uncongenial man, but he was in no way concerned in this matter.

The night before her death she wrote some letters. In one she says: "The castle is a very noble building, and all the rooms large and cool, while some would be pretty even in England." The room in which she is writing "is painted a deep blue, with some splendid engravings," "Mr. Maclean's library is fitted up with book-cases of African mahogany, and portraits of distinguished authors."

And she adds—" But I, however, never approach it without due preparation and humility, so crowded is it with scientific instruments, telescopes, etc. etc., none of which may be touched by hands profane."

"Mr. Maclean," wrote Lady Blessington, "admits that indisposition and mental annoyance must have rendered him far from being a kind or agreeable companion to poor Letitia; but adds, that had she lived a little longer, she would have found him very different, as he was—when not ill and tormented by various circumstances, which he does not explain—easy and good-tempered to a fault. He says, that never was there so kind or so faultless a being on earth as that poor, poor girl, as he calls her, and that he never knew her value until he had lost her. In fact, his letter seemed an answer to charges preferred against him by the departed; and, what is strange, the packet that brought the fatal news, brought no letter of recent date for her ——, though she never missed an opportunity, and they occur rarely, of writing to him. Her letters, all of which have breathed the fondest affection for him, admit that she had little hope of happiness from her stern, cold, and morose husband."

By a most extraordinary coincidence, Dr. Madden, well known for his acquaintance with Lady Hester Stanhope, who was also second in the preliminaries of a duel between the late Charles Mathews and Count d'Orsay, a man of great knowledge, industry, and literary gifts, as his friends know, was despatched on a Government inquiry to Cape Coast. He had been much interested, like all her friends, in poor L. E. L., and determined to prosecute his inquiries on the spot; for the rancour of partisanship had gone so far as to insinuate that her husband was responsible for her death in more direct fashion than mere harshness. This visit was in 1841. Dr. Madden noted the gloomy desolation of the castle—the large courtyard where L. E. L. was, oddly enough, buried, over whose grave the soldiers were drilled, and in the wall of which a memorial tablet was inserted shortly after his arrival. He frankly told him that he would like to inquire into the matter fully, and was met in the same spirit. Dr. Madden was enabled to vindicate him completely. However, the Commissioner was not very *bien vu* by the natives, and being presently seized with the fever of the place, conceived they had attempted to poison him: on which he had himself hurriedly removed from the castle.

Such was the strange story of the heroine L. E. L. She was sung in verses by Landor and others: she was held to be a victim: her memory is still cherished by those who recall her. Captain Maclean died ten years later, in 1848, and was interred in the courtyard beside his wife. He was a poor man; but had he lived three months longer he would have inherited a large fortune from Sir John Maclean, who bequeathed it to him.

END OF VOL. I.

CHARLES DICKENS AND EVANS, CRYSTAL PALACE PRESS.

www.ingramcontent.com/pod-product-compliance
Lightning Source LLC
Chambersburg PA
CBHW031414230426
43668CB00007B/308